SEX LIVES OF THE
HOLLYWOOD IDOLS

In the same series by Nigel Cawthorne:

Sex Lives of the Popes
Sex Lives of the U.S. Presidents
Sex Lives of the Great Dictators
Sex Lives of the Hollywood Goddesses
Sex Lives of the Great Composers
Sex Lives of the Great Artists

All published by Prion

SEX LIVES OF THE HOLLYWOOD IDOLS

NIGEL CAWTHORNE

PRION

First published in Great Britain in 1997 by
Prion Books Limited,
Imperial Works, Perren Street,
London NW5 3ED
www.prionbooks.com

Reprinted 1998 and 2000

A catalogue record of this book can be obtained from
the British Library

ISBN 1-85375-249-5

All the star portraits used in the picture insert are
reproduced courtesy of the Vintage Magazine Company

Printed in Great Britain by
Creative Print and Design, Wales

CONTENTS

Introduction   *vi*

1 Tramp   1
2 The Great Lover   25
3 The Incomparable Barrymore   55
4 The Swordsmen   89
5 In like Flynn   117
6 Less-Than-Able Gable   145
7 Flying the Coop   177
8 Cary on Camping   201
9 Pillow Talk   221
10 Rebel without his Draws   239
11 In Bed with Madonna   251

Bibliography   *267*
Index   *271*

INTRODUCTION

We live in boring times. Where are the Flynns, the Fairbanks, the Barrymores, the Coopers and the Gables? These men were giants, who drank and womanized in epic proportions. In their day, they were great artists who kept the world enraptured. Now they would be condemned as politically incorrect. In *Sunset Boulevard*, Gloria Swanson said that she would always be a star 'only the pictures got smaller'. If there is no room in the modern world for the type of men who inhabit this book, then it is not just the pictures but the world that got smaller.

Back in the golden age of the Gables, Grants and Coopers, men deceived women and women cheated on men in the most sophisticated and charming way possible. There was no room for the sordid truth. The world of the movies is a world of illusion. The truth belongs on TV, on the Oprah Winfrey show.

Big-screen Hollywood was a world of fiction, demanding creative hypocrisy and a mastery of double standards. From the very beginning of the movies, sex was the subject matter. D.W. Griffith packed his early biblical epics with scantily clad young women. Producers and directors knew that was what the public was interested in. Indeed, that was what they themselves were interested in. Many of them had only got into the movie industry because of the availability of willing young actresses bent on building a career by any means necessary. Movie pioneers Mack Sennett, D.W. Griffith and Charlie Chaplin romped among the teenaged starlets who appeared in their movies in a way that would now bring charges of paedophilia.

The problem was that it was all a little too blatant. Cardinal Mundelein of Chicago spoke out against the immorality of the movies in the pamphlet *The Danger of Hollywood: A Warning to Young Girls*. Then came the Arbuckle scandal.

Roscoe 'Fatty' Arbuckle was a plumber's mate. He was discovered by the legendary Mack Sennett in 1913, when he came round to unblock the comedy producer's drains. Weighing 266 pounds, he was as round as a butter ball, but surprisingly agile at throwing, and dodging, custard pies in slapstick comedy fights.

By 1917, he was so popular that his salary had soared to $5,000 a week. To celebrate his latest pay rise, the studio laid on a party for 'the Prince of Whales' at Brownie Kennedy's Roadhouse in Boston. They knew the fat man's tastes and laid on twelve 'party girls'. A waiter peeking through a crack in the door to see how the party was going saw the girls on the table stripping and the fat man in a state of undress.

As he was not party to the fun, the waiter called the police. Public decency had, apparently, been outraged. The studio ended up paying $100,000 in bribes to the District Attorney and the Mayor of Boston to hush the whole thing up.

Four years later, on Labour Day weekend, Arbuckle was hosting a party in San Francisco to celebrate his new $3 million contract with Paramount. Carloads of movie people made the 450-mile dash up the coastal highway. Among them was raven-haired Virginia Rappe, an ambitious young actress who was already making her way in the movies. She also had something of a reputation after giving half of Mack Sennett's studio the crabs. Sennett had to have the place shut down and fumigated. Arbuckle had had his eye on Virginia for some time.

Fatty had taken three adjoining suites on the twelfth floor of the Hotel St Francis, filling the joint with bootleg liquor. The party began on Saturday and on Monday afternoon it was still in full swing. Girls were doing the shimmy. Some had lost their pyjama bottoms. Soon after three, Arbuckle appeared in his dressing-gown. He grabbed Virginia.

'This is the chance I have been waiting for for a long time,' he said and dragged her into the bedroom.

Screams were heard, then low moans. The revellers, growing concerned, beat on the door. Arbuckle opened up and strode out. He said to some of the other girls: 'Get her dressed and take her to the Palace. She makes too much noise.'

They found her practically naked. Her clothes had been ripped to shreds.

'He hurt me,' she said. 'I'm dying.'

She was whisked off to the Pine Street hospital where she told a nurse: 'Fatty Arbuckle did this to me. Don't let him get away with it.'

Five days later she died.

The cause of death was peritonitis. Her bladder had been ruptured, presumably during rough sex with Arbuckle. He was charged with rape and murder.

Newspaper speculation went wild. Was Arbuckle's weight simply too much for the petite Virginia? Could a bladder be ruptured during the normal sex act? Or had he indecently assaulted her with a champagne bottle or a jagged piece of ice?

The whole country was up in arms. Even Paramount did not have enough money to hush this one up. Arbuckle's films were withdrawn; his contract cancelled.

Arbuckle went to trial three times and was eventually acquitted. The jury in the last trial said that, not only was Arbuckle not guilty, there was not the slightest evidence to connect him to any crime. But the damage had been done. Arbuckle was a broken man. He never worked under his own name again.

Hard on the heels of the Arbuckle scandal came the murder of director William Desmond Taylor. He was shot through the heart with a .38. When the news broke, studio boss Adolph Zukor rushed to Taylor's home and managed to burn some evidence before the police turned up. But he had not had time to do a thorough job. The police found a collection of pornographic photographs featuring some of the prominent movie actresses of the day, including Mary Pickford. Nestling between the pages of *White Stains*, a book of erotica by Aleister Crowley, were love letters from Mabel Normand and Paramount's virginal star Mary Miles Minter. Both Mabel and Mary had visited Taylor on the night of his murder. It transpired that the ever-active Taylor was also having an affair with Mary's mother, Charlotte Shelby, who was surrendering her body in the hope of advancing her daughter's career, blissfully unaware that her daughter was doing the same thing.

Mabel Normand was the last person to see Taylor alive. As a parting gift, he had given her the latest volume of Freud. Ten minutes later a shot was heard and a figure was seen leaving the house. Whoever it was was dressed like a man, but walked like a woman. This has always been assumed to be Mrs Shelby in drag.

At the inquest, the contents of Mr Taylor's wardrobe were revealed – a vast collection of expensive ladies' lingerie, each item signed and dated. Apparently, Taylor liked to keep souvenirs of his sexual encounters. One item was of particular interest. It was a pale pink, sheer silk nightie. Delicately embroidered on it were the letters 'M.M.M.' – Mary Miles Minter. There went her virginal image and with it her career.

In the eyes of America, the Taylor scandal was further evidence that Hollywood was a cesspit of sexual depravity. Church groups, women's committees and purity leagues demanded a clean-up.

The studio bosses realized they had to act. They set up the Motion Picture Producers and Distributors of America as a watchdog and brought in William H. Hays to head it at a salary of $100,000. Hays was Postmaster General in the administration of Warren Harding, one of the most corrupt administrations in the history of Washington. Harding had a string of lovers, an illegitimate child and was the first president to be caught making love to his mistress in the Oval Office. His cabinet frequently met at a house on H Street for drunken orgies with chorus girls. Then there were the financial scams. Hays himself admitted accepting a sizeable bribe during the infamous Teapot Dome Scandal. He was also caught paying off the political bigwigs and other 'moral leaders' who were now calling for some modern-day Hercules to sweep out Hollywood's Augean stables. Hays seemed the perfect man for the job.

Then everything went badly wrong. Contrary to expectations, Hays took the job seriously. He set about purifying the movies and the movie makers. In 1930, he drew up the infamous Code. This banned lingering and lusty kisses and insisted that if two people went anywhere near a bed they had to keep one foot on the ground at all times.

The Hays Office also insisted that 'morality clauses' were written into actors' and actresses' contracts. If any scandal were to occur in their private lives, they were to be fired immediately. But movie stars could not be monks and nuns. A famous Hollywood director once defined being a star as 'knowing that everyone in the room wanted to go to bed with you'. What was the point of being a star if you could not take advantage of it? The male stars, the studs of the silver screen, certainly did. Many of them died young, but very, very happy.

Of course, there have been too many bad boys – and girls, as chronicled in the companion volume, *Sex Lives of the Hollywood Goddesses* – in Hollywood to fit into one book. This is merely a selection of some of the baddest boys seen on the silver screen.

It is interesting to note that these Hollywood screen idols did not just bed other Hollywood stars. They also bedded people who bedded *US Presidents, Great Dictators, Kings and Queens of England* and, who knows, *Popes*. This volume is another chronicle in the vast, interconnected world of the rich and famous that makes up the *Sex Lives* series. I have written many books before – both serious and trivial – but this sprawling *Sex Lives* series is my masterwork. It makes me feel like Balzac. Instead of the *Comédie Humaine*, I am giving you the *Sexualité Humaine*. Pretentious? *Moi*?

1

TRAMP

Charlie Chaplin was the first international film star. With his bowler hat, cane and funny walk, he was loved by millions all over world as an innocent little tramp. In his private life, Chaplin was also a tramp, but there the similarity ends. He was reputedly anything but little, and he was certainly not innocent, unless you consider him an innocent *savant*.

Born in the Elephant and Castle, London, in 1889, Charlie Chaplin learnt to sing and dance by watching his mother Hannah, who was a minor music hall star. One night, in Aldershot, her voice gave out and the five-year-old Charlie went on stage to finish the song for her. His debut was a triumph. The audience applauded vigorously and hurled money on to the stage.

When Charlie's father, an alcoholic, died and his mother was incarcerated in Cane Hill lunatic asylum, Charlie quit school and joined a troupe of clog dancers called the Eight Lancashire Lads. His brother Sydney, who was a comedian, introduced Charlie to the great British vaudevillian Fred Karno.

'Fred Karno didn't teach Charlie and me all we know about comedy,' said Stan Laurel. 'He just taught us most of it.'

He also taught the young Charlie most of what he knew about sex.

Karno had married a young dancer early in his career.

He kept her a virtual slave at home and flaunted his other sexual conquests in public. As an impresario he exercised a shameless *droit de seigneur* over the women he employed. Any girl who expected to work for him, first had to visit his casting couch. Once under contract to him, she belonged to him body and soul, but especially body.

When seventeen-year-old blonde Elsie Manners arrived at Karno's Kennington headquarters looking for a job, she was ushered into the great man's office. Karno told his secretary to go to lunch, then produced a large piece of paper and asked for her measurements. Next he told her to stand in front of him and began unbuttoning her blouse. She pushed his hands away, but he persisted.

'If I hire a thirty-six-inch bust I want to know I am getting what I paid for,' he said.

'I just stood there until he had unbuttoned my blouse completely,' Elsie recalled. 'Mr Karno looked at my breasts and grudgingly admitted that they could be the thirty-six inches I claimed.'

'Right,' he said. 'There are two jobs – one for two pounds a week, one for four. Which do you want?'

Elsie naturally said the one for four.

'Okay,' said Karno. 'Get the rest of your clothes off, get on the couch and we'll see if you're worth four quid.'

Elsie grabbed her coat and ran out of the door.

'Stupid cow,' Karno yelled after her. 'Think I'm going to chase after you? I get dozens like you coming in every day.'

Another who turned up at Karno's office was Phyllis Dixey, who later achieved fame with a rather coy strip act. Long before she began taking her clothes off in public, she went to Karno to audition as a singer for a show called *Laffs* at the London Palladium. Karno was not interested in her voice. The first thing he asked was whether she was a natural blonde.

'Collar and cuffs match, do they?' he enquired.

Next he began fondling her to see whether she was wearing a girdle.

'I came here to be auditioned as a singer,' she said, 'not to be pawed.'

'No need for an audition,' he said. 'You've got the part.'

He handed her a contract and a pen. When she leant over to sign it, he thrust his hand up her dress and pushed her over the desk. The quick-thinking Phyllis stabbed him in the hand with the pen.

'I failed my first audition,' Phyllis said. 'I couldn't sing in the horizontal position.'

Sometimes there were tragic consequences. A young dancer named Harriet Morrison sneaked off between performances at the Camberwell Palace to get married. Karno caught her showing off her wedding ring to the other chorus girls. He ordered her to report to his office in Kennington. There he upbraided her for 'betraying' him by getting married without his permission. He tore her clothes off, raped her and kicked her out on the street. Humiliated and bruised, Harriet could not face returning to her husband after what had happened. She was found floating in the Thames three days later. Among her effects, her new husband found explicit pictures of his young wife in pornographic poses with Karno.

Karno liked being photographed with his conquests. He would frequently send these pictures to his long-suffering wife with handwritten inscriptions saying things like: 'See, she'll do all those things you won't do.'

When the poor woman tried to divorce him, he got her drunk, had sex with her and announced the fact triumphantly in court the next morning. This left his wife, a modest woman, no option. She produced the collection of pornographic pictures her husband had sent her. The divorce was granted and she was awarded the princely sum of £10 a week.

Charlie was playing with the Karno Company at the Streatham Empire when he first fell in love. Ahead of them on the bill was a dance troupe called Bert Coutts' Yankee Doodle Girls. Charlie watched them from the wings. The second night, one of the girls slipped and the others began to giggle.

'One looked off and caught my eye to see if I was also

enjoying the joke,' he said. 'I was suddenly held by two large brown eyes sparkling mischievously, belonging to a slim gazelle with a shapely oval face, a bewitchingly full mouth, and beautiful teeth – the effect was electric.'

When she came off, she asked him to hold a small mirror so that she could do her hair. This gave him an opportunity to scrutinize her at close quarters. He liked what he saw. Her name was Hetty Kelly and he asked her out.

He took £3 from his savings to take Hetty up to the West End for a slap-up dinner at the Trocadero. When she turned up, she had already eaten but the table was booked so they went anyway.

Charlie was a natural showman. Although he was uncertain which cutlery to use to eat the elaborate meal he felt obliged to order, he put on the performance of a lifetime.

'I bluffed through the meal with a *dégagé* charm, even to my casualness with the finger-bowl,' he recalled.

After dinner, Hetty wanted to walk home to Camberwell. Charlie accompanied her in such a state of euphoria that he distributed the remainder of the £3 among the tramps on the Embankment.

For the next three days, he met her in the morning and walked her to the tube station. On the third morning, her feelings towards him seemed to have cooled. Sensing that he was losing her, he immediately asked her to marry him. She said she was just fifteen and too young to get married. He was only nineteen.

Charlie was heartbroken. In fact, he never really got over Hetty.

'Although I met her but five times, that brief encounter affected me for a long time,' he said. For the rest of his life, he pursued underaged women.

Eight years later, in 1916, when he was already a big star, Chaplin was in New York to sign a contract with the Mutual Film Corporation. He heard that Hetty was living with her sister on Fifth Avenue. Too shy to visit, he hung about on the street outside, hoping to bump into her but with no luck. Six months before she had married Lieutenant Alan Horne, son of the MP for Guildford, and was back in London living in Mayfair. In July 1918, he received a letter from her out of the blue, asking if he remembered 'a silly young girl...' He most certainly did. Indeed, he recognized her handwriting.

'When I caught sight of the envelope, my pulse quickened,' he said when he wrote back to her. 'I quickly tore open the envelope and – lo and behold! – it was from you. You, above all people, to hear from and after so many years! I was certainly thrilled.'

In his reply, Charlie pointed out that he was still a bachelor – 'but that is not my fault'. And he begged her to write to him again – 'I shall be anxiously counting the days until I hear from you'.

But he did not hear from her again. In 1921, he was in London and hoping to see her, when he discovered that she had died later in 1918 and had probably never received his letter.

At nineteen, though, after he lost her, he did not have to wait long for consolation. The Karno Company had just been booked by the Folies Bergère in Paris. One evening, during the interval at the Folies, he met a 'gracile creature with a swan-like neck and white skin that made my heart flutter'. She dropped her glove. He picked it up.

'*Merci,*' she said.

'I wish you would drop it again,' he said coyly.

'*Pardon?*' she said.

Thinking that she spoke no English – he spoke little French – he found an interpreter to intercede.

'There's a dame that arouses my concupiscence,' Charlie explained. 'But she looks very expensive.'

'Not more than a louis [twenty francs],' the interpreter warned. It was a lot, but Charlie's savings could just about run to that.

The interpreter fixed the price with the lady and explained that Charlie would have to pay the cab fare to her apartment and back too.

'Couldn't she walk?' said Charlie, exasperated.

'This is a first-class girl,' the interpreter explained. 'You must pay her fare.'

It would be no more than ten francs. Charlie reluctantly agreed.

After the show, Charlie hailed a cab. The interpreter had thoughtfully provided him with a card with useful phrases like '*Je vous adore*' and '*Je vous ai aimée la première fois que je vous ai vue*' written on it to use at propitious moments. He tried them out in the back of the cab. The girl praised him on his French, but explained, under the circumstances, he should be using the rather more intimate *tu* than the formal *vous*.

Then she asked him what time it was, explaining that she had an important appointment at twelve o'clock. Charlie protested that he was paying her 20 francs to spend the night with him.

'*Non*,' she explained. '*Pas toute la nuit!*'

'*Vingt francs pour le moment?*'

'*Oui, c'est ça.*'

It was too much. Charlie stopped the cab and paid the driver.

'I got out,' he said, 'a very sad and disillusioned man.'

But Charlie was not disillusioned for long. The Karno Company were soon touring America where he found the red-light districts better suited his pocket.

He was especially intrigued by a brothel in Chicago called the House of All Nations. It was run by two middle-aged spinsters, the Everly sisters, who boasted that they had girls in their house of every nationality. The rooms were decorated in the styles of different countries. There was a Turkish room, a Japanese room, a Louis XVI room, even an Arab tent. It was elaborate and, of course, expensive. Its clientele included millionaires, tycoons, senior politicians and judges. Conventions would take the place over for a week and one wealthy sybarite stayed there for three weeks without ever seeing daylight.

Further west, Charlie and five other members of Karno's army would put their money together to take over a local whorehouse for the night. Sometimes a girl would fall for one of the company and follow him to the next town.

Butte, Montana, Charlie insisted, had the prettiest women of any red-light district in the Midwest. The town, then, consisted of one long street. The side streets were filled with hundreds of cribs with a young girl of sixteen or so installed in each. They cost just $1. Charlie was in heaven.

In Hollywood, Karno's intensely visual slapstick comedy appealed to Mack Sennett and he signed up Charlie, his brother Sydney, Stan Laurel and other Karno creations. He also co-opted Karno's trademark 'K' for the Keystone Kops. (Karno was born Frederick Wescott, but stole the name Carno in 1888 when substituting for another act. He changed the spelling to make it more stylish and officially changed his name to Karno by deed poll in 1914.)

Sennett was a man after Karno's own heart. Aside from the Keystone Kops, he was famous for the Mack Sennett Bathing Beauties. Many of the legendary actresses of the era – Gloria Swanson, Mabel Normand, Norma and Constance Talmadge, Ruth Rich, Alma Rubens, Juanita Hansen and Barbara Lamarr – started their movie careers in swimsuits as Sennett Bathing Beauties, or rather out of them in Sennett's office. The comics on the lot kept 'race cards' on which they marked off the Beauties they had had. Sennett did not bother. No woman was allowed on the set unless she had graduated from the Sennett casting couch.

During his early days in Hollywood, Charlie did not have much time for the pleasures of love. But he had a fling with Peggy Pierce, a Mack Sennett ingenue, and Mabel Normand. Then, in the great tradition of the movies, he fell in love with his co-star, Edna Purviance.

Charlie met her in 1915 when he started his own studio. He had already built up a stock company of comedians, but needed a leading lady. A cowboy who had worked for 'Bronco Billy' Anderson, another Karno comedian, recommended a blonde who frequented Tate's Café on Hill Street, San Francisco. She was traced. Charlie was instantly captivated and she starred opposite him in thirty-five films.

At the time, Charlie was living at the Los Angeles Athletic

Club and she was seen dining there with him most nights of the week. His screen persona took on a distinctive romantic tenor. The little tramp is seen caressing flowers. In *The Champion*, he even got to kiss her passionately but the kiss was coyly hidden from the camera. On other occasions, when he kissed her with anything approaching desire, the picture faded out. But there was always something furtive about Chaplin's attitude to sex. In his autobiography, he resorts to phrases like 'upper regional domes immensely expansive' instead of saying 'large breasts'.

In three of his early films, Charlie appeared dressed up as a woman, which suited him surprisingly well. In fact, his last drag movie *A Woman* was banned in Sweden until the 1930s.

In private notes, Chaplin could express passion. He addressed Edna as 'my own darling' and called her 'the cause of my being the happiest person in the world'.

Replying to a love note she had sent him, he wrote: 'My heart throbbed this morning when I received your sweet letter. It could be nobody else in the world that could have given me so much joy. Your language, your sweet thoughts and the style of your love note only tends to make me crazy over you. I can picture your darling self sitting down and looking up wondering what to say, that pert little mouth and those bewitching eyes so thoughtful. If I only had the power to express my sentiment I would be afraid you'd get vain.'

Only months later, Charlie was mooning about on Fifth Avenue, hoping in vain to catch a glimpse of Hetty.

Edna had wanted to go to New York with Chaplin, but he said that he could not take her with him. So while he was away, Edna went to visit her parents in Lovelock, Nevada. He promised to write, but did not.

'I really don't know why you don't send me some word,' she wrote to her 'Boodie', chastising him. 'Just one little telegram is so unsatisfactory. Even a night letter would be better than nothing. You know, 'Boodie', you promised faithfully to write. Is your time so taken up that you can't even think of me? Every night before I go to bed I send out little love thoughts wishing you all the success in the world and counting the minutes until you return. How much longer do you expect to stay? Please, hon, don't forget your "Modie" and hurry back.'

Plainly, 'Modie' had an inkling that something was going on.

'Have you been true to me?' she went on. 'I'm afraid not. Oh well, do whatever you think is right. I really do trust you to that extent ... Lots of love and kisses.'

Edna was right to be suspicious. Although by his own account he had a quiet time in New York, Charlie set off home via Chicago. Now a wealthy man himself – thanks to the $670,000 contract with Mutual signed in Manhattan – he made a two-day stopover in the city of All Nations.

Charlie and Edna continued to be close, dining together almost every evening in the Los Angeles Athletic Club. Then he met actress Constance Collier who decided that he needed a broader social life. She introduced him to Sir Herbert Beerbohm Tree and Douglas Fairbanks who, though married, was wooing Mary Pickford. Towards the end of his life, Chaplin said that Fairbanks was perhaps the only close friend he had ever had, but at the time, Charlie did have another close friend, Julian Eltinge, a female impersonator.

By 1917, Charlie and Edna were thrust into the dizzy whirl of Hollywood's social life, attending perforce dinners and galas in aid of the Red Cross and other war charities. Unused to these formal gatherings, Edna would grow jealous of the other women who monopolized Charlie. To summon him to her side, she devised an irritating ruse. She would faint and, when she came round, she would ask for Charlie, who would then be stuck with her for the rest of the evening.

One night, at a party given by the beautiful actress Fanny Ward, Edna fainted as usual but instead of calling for Charlie, she asked for Thomas Meighan, Hollywood's latest heart-throb. Charlie was naturally suspicious and jealous. During a furious row, Edna suggested that, from now on, they would be just 'good friends'.

Later, Charlie discovered that Edna was seeing Meighan and broke off with her. Meighan was ten years older than Charlie, and married. The affair was brief but Charlie never took up with Edna again. They continued to work together and she remained devoted. She never married and to her dying day she kept every newspaper cutting about Charlie that she could lay her hands on.

Edna can hardly be blamed for having a fling with a handsome movie star. A graduate of both the Karno and Sennett school of seduction, as a studio boss, Chaplin now ran a casting couch of his own.

Brother Sydney, who did not have the weight of the studio on his shoulders, was even worse. Having laid waste to Mack Sennett's Bathing Beauties, he extended his activities to anyone under twenty who wore a skirt. Having four women Sydney considered an average day's work. He told his sidekick, the young Darryl Zanuck: 'Hollywood is a town full of pretty girls out there for the taking. They're aching for it. You would be an idiot not to take advantage. Give it to them and then get out before they get their hooks into you. There's plenty more where they came from.'

Sydney bragged that he could lay any woman in Hollywood. Zanuck thought this empty boasting and challenged Sydney to prove it. They drove to Hollywood High School when the children were leaving and picked out a teenaged girl at random. Sydney went over to her and chatted. Within minutes he was showing her into the back of Zanuck's open tourer. Then he asked Zanuck to drive them somewhere quiet. Zanuck had to sit there, red faced, while Sydney proved his point on the back seat. Next time, Sydney told Zanuck as they drove the girl home, he should try and come up with a more difficult challenge.

Zanuck thought he had done just that some weekends later when he and Sydney checked into the Coronada Hotel which was popular with honeymooners. Sydney was boasting about his prowess again, so Zanuck pointed out a fresh-faced bride who was checking in with her brand new husband.

'Now that is impossible,' said Zanuck.

After lunch, Zanuck could not find Sydney, then heard himself being paged. The front desk told him to go to Sydney's room immediately. When he opened the door, he saw Sydney with the young naked bride. Only years later did Zanuck discover that the whole thing had been set up. The 'bride' was an extra named Elizabeth McNeill, her 'husband' was from Central Casting, and Sydney, a skilled vaudevillian, had pushed Zanuck into picking her in the same way a magician makes a member of the audience pick a particular card.

Charlie had no time for such frivolity. He considered himself a workaholic. He said he would only take a girl for 'an hour when I am bored'. Between pictures, though, he would chase what he called 'the most beautiful form of human life – the very young girl just starting to bloom'. His liking for young girls could cause problems, though.

In 1916, he met child actress Mildred Harris at a party given by Sam Goldwyn. She was just fourteen, but she had been a movie actress from the age of ten and had appeared practically nude in the notorious Babylonian scene in D.W. Griffith's *Intolerance*. Chaplin was immediately infatuated. The affair was actively encouraged by Mildred's mother, who was a wardrobe mistress at the studio and knew of Chaplin's tastes.

When Mildred was sixteen, her mother informed Chaplin that the child was pregnant. Fearing prosecution for statutory rape, Charlie had no choice but to marry Mildred, even though, as he confided to Douglas Fairbanks, she was 'no mental heavyweight'. No sooner were they wed than Mildred discovered that she was not pregnant after all.

Louis B. Mayer was quick to cash in. He put Mildred under contract and started making a film about domestic strife called *The Inferior Sex*, starring 'Mrs Charlie Chaplin'. Charlie was more than a little annoyed about this blatant exploitation of his name. He made his feelings known when he bumped into Mayer in the foyer of the fashionable Alexander Hotel. Mayer responded to Charlie's accusations by calling Chaplin a 'filthy pervert'. Charlie asked him to step outside. Mayer, a former scrap-metal dealer from New Brunswick, whipped off his glasses and punched the little tramp in the face there and then.

In 1920, Mildred really did get pregnant, but gave birth to a hideously deformed child who died after three days. The marriage broke up amid charges of cruelty and infidelity. Mildred had belatedly noticed the herds of young starlets passing through Charlie's dressing-room and had quit the conjugal bed for that of the notorious lesbian Alla Nazimova. They divorced.

Charlie claimed that Mildred's mind had been 'full of pink-ribboned foolishness'. So he temporarily changed his habits and took up with an experienced woman rather than a little girl.

Ex-Ziegfeld Follies girl Peggy Hopkins Joyce had five marriages behind her and $3 million in the bank, earned in the conjugal bed and the divorce courts. The term 'gold digger' had originally been coined in her honour. She was a simple girl at heart who wanted, she said, a home and babies. The truth was she was a heartbreaker. A young man in Paris had committed suicide after she left him for richer prey in the form of the wealthy French publisher Henri Leteiller.

When she met Chaplin, the first thing she said was: 'Is it true what the girls say about you?'

Chaplin was proud of being well endowed. He called his penis the 'Eighth Wonder of the World' and considered himself a human sex machine. He stimulated himself by reading passages from *Fanny Hill* and boasted that he could have sex five or six times with only a few minutes rest between each bout.

Charlie and Peggy took off to the island of Catalina. They found a secluded bay where they could go nude bathing unobserved – or so they thought. In fact, news that Chaplin – who was by then the most famous man in the world – was frolicking naked with a woman soon got around. Local people assembled on a nearby hilltop to watch the couple through powerful binoculars. Before long, the randy goats that inhabited the islands were nicknamed 'Charlies' by the locals.

Peggy soon moved on to richer pickings, in the shape of Irving Thalberg. It was Charlie who profited from their brief affair by using her colourful reminiscences of gold-digging exploits in *A Woman of Paris*.

The Hollywood gossip columnists linked Chaplin's name with Thelma Moran Converse, Lila Lee, Anna Q. Nilsson and the artist and writer Clare Sheridan, who was Winston Churchill's cousin. Clare Sheridan sculpted his bust. Chaplin's press representative, Carlyle Robinson, denied that they were having an affair by pointing out that 'Mrs Sheridan is old enough to be Mr Chaplin's mother' – not Charlie's cup of tea at all.

Rumours of an engagement to New York actress May Collins were admitted, then denied. The beautiful actress Claire Windsor was also described as Charlie's fiancée when she staged a dramatic disappearance. Charlie joined in the search and posted a reward, but later he discovered that the whole thing had simply been a ruse to get his attention.

Chaplin met the ravishing Polish actress Pola Negri in Berlin in 1921. She had wonderful colouring – jet black hair, white even teeth, and a very pretty mouth. Charlie was particularly impressed with her voice, though the only words she could say in English were: 'Jazz boy Charlie.'

'I fell in love with Pola the instant I met her,' he recalled. 'The only reason I didn't tell her so was because I was too bashful to confess it. I did tell her she was the loveliest lady I had ever met and I'm sure she must have guessed the secret of my heart.'

He managed to convey this in the three words he spoke of German and they spent four days together in Berlin. Then, for nearly a year, the Atlantic separated them.

'An ocean is an awful bar to a successful love affair,' Charlie said.

When Pola turned up in Hollywood, Charlie deliberately avoided her, because he knew how an affair between them would pan out.

'Isn't it sad how we instinctively feel the fate that is about to overtake us?' he said.

But he could not avoid meeting her at the Actors' Fund Pageant at the Hollywood Ball in October 1922. Pola was playing Cleopatra on stage and Chaplin was conducting the orchestra.

'Strangely enough we missed each other at rehearsals,' Pola recalled. 'It was not until the actual performance that I saw him wielding his baton. And as I walked towards him I looked into his face. It was then that I realized I had been in love with him for more than a year, without being aware of it.'

Charlie was overwhelmed too.

'When I saw Pola in all her glorious beauty as she swept towards me that fateful day of the pageant, I could not resist her any longer,' he said. 'Something I can't describe surged all over inside me. I felt like a drowning man – yet excited as I have never been before.'

They met after the performance and the following day he called at her home.

'It was not long before I confessed my love and, to my happiness and surprise, I learned that Pola felt the same way about me.'

After that they were inseparable. The King of Comedy beds the Queen of Tragedy was the way the press saw it. Jesse Lasky at Paramount said that there was nothing in Pola's contract that prevented her from marrying and the Pope dissolved Pola's previous marriage to the Polish Count Domaska. Pola arranged to announce their engagement at a press conference. Charlie blushed and squirmed. She snuggled on his shoulder and spelt out their marriage plans.

There were rumours that they had actually married the year before in Europe. Then, five weeks after the press conference, it was all over. Charlie announced that he was 'too poor to marry'. Pola was devastated.

'Now I will live only for my work,' she told the press through much-photographed tears. 'As for the rest, the happy days are dead for me.'

Six hours later, it was on again. Pola told another press conference that Chaplin had told her 'he loved me and he could not live without me'.

Charlie said that he had always wanted a wife, a home, children and waxed lyrical about his ideal woman.

'Until I met Pola this woman remained a dream. Today she is a reality,' he said. 'She is everything I have ever dreamed of. But why she should love me is something I will never understand. I lack the physique, the physical strength that a beautiful woman admires. Perhaps it is best that I do not question the gift of the gods.'

Soon after, Chaplin's valet found a young Mexican girl named Marina Varga in Chaplin's pyjamas in Chaplin's bed, while Charlie himself was downstairs dining with Pola. The girl had run away from her husband in Vera Cruz and crossed the border disguised as a man in the hope of bedding her idol.

The next day, she was found lying in a flower bed in Chaplin's garden, claiming to have swallowed poison. Pola turned up and the ensuing altercation became so heated that Charlie had to cool the two of them off with a bucket of cold water.

Later, at a party, Pola swooned with emotion over the incident. While others rushed for water, Chaplin pretended to swoon too and lay down beside her. The Queen of Tragedy was not amused. A few days later, they were seen at the reopening of the Ambassador's Coconut Grove at separate tables. Pola told the press: 'I realize now I could never have married him. He is too temperamental, as changing as the wind. He dramatizes everything. He experiments in love.'

Pola Negri never married. At the end of her career, she retired to San Antonio with a Texan heiress. When her friend married, she caused a stink and threatened to sue. The woman divorced and returned to San Antonio and her Pola.

The problem was, at thirty, Pola was much too old for Charlie. For his 'experiments in love', he liked them young. He had met the second Mrs Chaplin, Lillita McMurray, when she was just six years old and 'the sweetest little thing you ever saw'. He took her under his wing and for nine long years he groomed her for a starring role in his life.

She played the 'Angel of Temptation' in *The Kid* and by 1923 she had 'filled out enough' to be the leading lady in *The Gold Rush*. Although the studio announced that she was nineteen, she was in fact just fifteen.

There can be little doubt that her mother, Nana McMurray, knew what was going on. She had worked at Chaplin's studio during his marriage to Mildred Harris. Like the true Hollywood mother she was, Mrs McMurray coached her daughter in the role she would have to play if she wanted to secure a movie contract. After extensive tests, Lillita was signed under the name Lita Grey, at $75 a week.

At first, little Lillita had trouble in getting to grips with the part. In his hotel room, 'he kissed my mouth and neck and his fingers darted all over my alarmed body,' she wrote in her auto-biography. 'His body writhed furiously against mine, and suddenly some of my fright gave way to revulsion.'

Eventually, after a naked romp around his house, Charlie took her virginity on the tiled floor of the steam bath. Lillita was both surprised and flattered. He could have had any one of a hundred girls, she said.

'No, a thousand,' he said, correcting her. 'But I wanted to be naughty with you, not them.'

Lillita not only tolerated sex with Chaplin, who was twenty years her senior, she got to enjoy it. Charlie enjoyed it too. He hated using condoms which he described as 'aesthetically hideous'. Since in all his hundreds of sexual encounters he had made only one of his lovers, Mildred Harris, pregnant, he fig-ured that he must be nearly sterile. It was thus a surprise when Mrs McMurray announced to the cast of *The Gold Rush* that her precious daughter was pregnant. Chaplin suggested that Lillita have an abortion. She refused. Her grandfather turned up toting a shotgun. Chaplin offered Lillita $20,000 to marry someone else but she said it was her Charlie she wanted.

Then Lillita's kindly old Uncle Edwin stepped in. He was a lawyer. There was talk of a paternity suit which would bring with it, under Californian law, the small matter of statutory rape which carried a penalty of up to thirty years in jail. Chaplin quickly agreed that marriage to his beloved Lillita was the best option.

Marrying a child bride had been controversial enough when he was twenty-six. Now he was thirty-six, he decided that a quiet wedding was probably wise, somewhere south of the border perhaps.

Charlie had other troubles at the time. He was at a party on board William Randolph Hearst's yacht, the *Onedia,* along with Hearst's mistress, the actress Marion Davis, producer Thomas Ince, and a then little-known journalist, Louella Parsons, among others. When Hearst found Marion with a man, half undressed making love, he went to get his gun. Marion began to scream and her companion beat a hasty retreat. Hearing the screams, Ince came running. He put his arms around Marion, trying to calm her down. Hearst returned with a pistol and, mistaking the situation, shot him dead. The unidentified lover was rumoured to be Chaplin.

Everyone agreed that there was no point in crying over spilt milk. They cooked up a story between them. Ince had never been on board. He had felt ill on the way to Hearst's yacht, turned back and had died after an acute bout of indigestion. The Hearst press trumpeted the story. A compliant coroner confirmed it. Ince was quickly cremated and no questions were asked. Ince's widow ended up $5 million richer, while Louella Parsons became a syndicated Hollywood gossip columnist on Hearst's newspapers.

Chaplin headed for Mexico with Lillita. On the way, he half jokingly suggested that his wife to be end it all by throwing herself from the train. Not surprisingly she didn't take him seriously and he had to go through with the marriage.

Charlie had planned a quiet wedding but the couple were pursued by a posse of Hearst's reporters. In the small, dusty town of Empalme in the state of Sonora, where they eventually tied the knot, the newlyweds were besieged by newsmen. Chaplin tried his best to smile. As he headed back to LA, Charlie was heard to say: 'Well, boys, it's better than the penitentiary but it won't last.'

He was wrong. It lasted for two harrowing years.

Lillita gave up her movie career to give birth to Charlie Chaplin Jnr just seven months after the nuptials. Her mother said that she was 'too young and inexperienced' to run a household and moved in. Plainly, this did not cramp Charlie's style too much because, exactly nine months after the birth of Charlie Jnr, a second son, Sydney, came along.

By this time the whole of the McMurray clan had settled in Chaplin's house. They held loud, drunken parties after he had had a long, tiring day at the studio. There were rows and fights. Eventually, it was all too much for Charlie and he threw them out. Divorce papers were filed. It was going to be messy, but Lillita – and her mother – said they would settle amicably for a cool $1 million.

He broke off filming *The Circus* and fled to New York, where he found refuge with his attorney, Nathan Burkan – only to find that good old Uncle Ed had sequestered his assets in California. Charlie issued a statement saying that he still loved his wife and wanted to stay married. Uncle Ed countered by publishing the transcript of Lillita's Bill of Divorcement as a fifty-page pamphlet selling for 25 cents a copy. Tens of thousands were sold.

It was only when Chaplin got hold of a copy that he discovered his wife was a talented diarist. Each morning she had made copious notes of the goings on of the night before. She claimed that during their twenty-five month marriage, Chaplin had maintained at least five long-term mistresses. He had often suggested that they liven up the marriage bed by introducing another young girl into it. He said that he wanted to film them having sex, or do it in front of an audience. He also suggested that she indulge in an 'abnormal, against nature, perverted, degenerate and indecent act' – which turned out to be fellatio. When she seemed less than keen, he said: 'Relax, my dear, all married people do it.'

However, oral sex was illegal under Californian law. Worse than this, however, was the fact that he had read her a page from the then banned *Lady Chatterley's Lover*, he had made light of the institution of marriage and the laws of California, suggested employing a well-known prostitute to perform the acts little Lillita shied away from and made persistent efforts to 'undermine and corrupt her moral impulses and demoralize her rule of decency' – all in the name of 'having some fun together'.

The pamphlet was an inspiration to fellow film-makers. Numerous stag films circulated, showing Chaplin lookalikes doing some of the things suggested.

In court, Chaplin found himself in deeper trouble. The complainant threatened to name five prominent motion picture actresses with whom Chaplin had had sex during their marriage. One of them promised to be Marion Davis, whose beach-house had often been his refuge on nights when the marriage had run into difficulties.

Chaplin's hair turned white almost overnight – and he settled for $625,000. For the time being, he had learned his lesson and again turned to older women.

He met twenty-one-year-old Louise Brooks when she first came to Hollywood. Their affair lasted two months. A former chorus girl and nude model, she was considered rather 'advanced'.

Chaplin took his lovemaking seriously. He erected a high-powered telescope to study the goings on in John Barrymore's bedroom.

'No art can be learned at once,' Chaplin explained. 'And lovemaking is a sublime art that needs practice if it's to be true and significant.'

Charlie certainly practised, or tried to. When the great Spanish surrealist director Luis Buñuel turned up in Hollywood, Chaplin obligingly arranged an orgy for him. Sadly, Buñuel recalled: 'When the three ravishing young women arrived from Pasadena, they immediately got into a tremendous argument over which one was going with Chaplin, and in the end all three left in a huff.'

His orgies with Louise Brooks were more successful. They often spent the weekend in an erotic foursome with Louise's best friend and well-known lesbian Peggy Fears and film financier A.C. Blumenthal. At the time, Chaplin was convinced that iodine prevented VD. One night at the Ambassador Hotel, he painted his entire genitalia and came charging at Louise and Peggy with a bright red erection.

But he had not entirely quashed his paedophile tendencies.

'He was a sophisticated lover,' Louise recalled. 'But his passion for young girls, his Lolita obsession, left him deeply convinced that he could seduce a girl only with his position as a director and star-maker.'

One such was May Reeves. Charlie groomed her to be his next leading lady during a long layover in Algiers but dropped her when he discovered that his brother Sydney had been grooming her too.

Paulette Goddard was another wannabe on the make. At fourteen she was a graduate of the Flo Ziegfeld casting couch. At sixteen, she married a millionaire. At nineteen, she divorced, walking away from the marriage with half a million dollars for three years' effort.

Determined to be a movie star, she headed for Hollywood. At a party on board producer Joe Schenck's yacht, she met the forty-six-year-old Charlie Chaplin, who described her as 'hot stuff'. He groomed her to star in *Modern Times*. Mystery surrounds their marriage. He said they were married in 1936. Others claimed they married in April 1934 on board his yacht, the *Panacea,* but he paid the captain to tear the entry out of his log. Some claim they were never married at all. There is no record of a licence.

She was a good stepmother to Charlie Jnr and Sydney but Charlie grew jealous of her youth and beauty. He made strenuous efforts to get her the part of Scarlett O'Hara in *Gone with the Wind*. When he failed, she decided that he was more of a hindrance than a help. They divorced in 1942. Cecil B. de Mille cast her in a number of movies, but her career took a knock when stories of a public sexual indiscretion got around – it was too much, apparently, for American audiences.

Chaplin dated twenty-two-year-old Carole Landis and the great Austrian raver Hedy Lamarr. He was also seen out with Greta Garbo. Then in 1941, the fifty-two-year-old Chaplin met twenty-two-year-old Joan Barry, a young woman who performed 'party girl' services. She and a bunch of other aspiring young actresses went down to Mexico for a party given by J. Paul Getty. There she was introduced to Chaplin who, as always, was looking for a new leading lady. She looked a little like Paulette Goddard and Chaplin liked her. He announced that he was grooming a new star.

He put her under contract at $100 a week, plus expenses, but she kept getting pregnant and abortions were expensive, so he cut her salary to $25. Joan took exception to this and to draw attention to her plight, she danced naked on Chaplin's front lawn under the sprinklers. The police recommended that he pay her fare back to New York, which he gladly did, but she turned up back at the house brandishing a gun. Apparently, Chaplin found this a turn on. He had sex with her on a bear-skin rug in front of his fireplace three times without stopping.

Pleasurable though this plainly was, there was a problem here. Chaplin had already met Oona O'Neill, the seventeen-year-old daughter of playwright Eugene O'Neill, who he intended to marry. He had already fought off the rivalry of his two sons who also fancied Oona. He was not going to let Joan queer the pitch now.

But Joan was not going to accept rejection without a fight. She broke into Chaplin's house, ripped her clothes off and jumped naked into his bed. This was not quite so much of a turn on. Chaplin called the cops and Joan was given thirty days in jail.

It was during her stay as a guest of the State of California that Joan discovered she was pregnant. While Joan was inside, Chaplin married his beloved Oona but, on her release, Joan slapped a paternity suit on him. Then the FBI stepped in. Although it was on the advice of the LAPD that Charlie had given Joan money to travel back to New York, he was indicted under the Mann Act, which is designed to stop interstate prostitution. The charge read that Chaplin 'did willingly, unlawfully, and feloniously transport and cause to be transported Joan Barry from Los Angeles to the city of New York with the intent and purpose of having her engage in illicit sexual relations with him'.

Chaplin was arrested, photographed and fingerprinted, and now faced up to twenty-three years in jail. His lawyer protested that it was ludicrous to suggest that Chaplin would transport a woman 3,000 miles just to have sex with her when she 'would have given her body to him at any time or place'. Chaplin was found not guilty, but he still had the paternity suit to face.

Chaplin denied that he was the father of Joan Barry's child, but he agreed to pay her $2,500 in medical expenses and $75 a week maintenance until it was born. Then he was confident blood tests would prove that the child was not his.

He was right. The blood tests proved that Chaplin could not have been the father of Joan Barry's child. He denied ever having sexual intercourse with her. By this time, the Hearst press had whipped up such a furore that Chaplin was condemned in court as 'a pestiferous, lecherous hound' and 'a little runt of a Svengali' who behaved like 'a cheap Cockney cad'. He was a 'reptile who looked upon Joan Barry as so much carrion', and when they were alone together he had 'read her a script about Bluebeard'! Indeed, Chaplin was working on a film about the modern-day Bluebeard, the French sex killer Henri Landru, called *Monsieur Verdoux*. It fell foul of the Hays Office who complained of the 'distasteful flavour of illicit sex' because the script suggested that Verdoux had actually slept with one of the women he murdered!

Barry's lawyer told the jury: 'There has been no one to stop Chaplin in his lecherous conduct all these years – except you. Wives and mothers all over the country are watching to see you stop him dead in his tracks.'

They did. Chaplin was ordered to pay $100 a week child support and Barry's child took the name Chaplin.

This was not the dream honeymoon that seventeen-year-old Oona had hoped for. But it did convince the world that they were not as mismatched as they may have appeared. On the stand fifty-five-year-old Chaplin was cross-examined about his virility and was forced to admit to still being sexually potent. He went on to prove it. Charlie and Oona went to live in Switzerland where they produced eight children. The last one was born when Charlie was in his early seventies.

'If I had known Oona or a girl like her long ago, I would never have had any problems with women,' he said. 'All my life I have been waiting for her without even realizing it.'

Stan Laurel said that from the days of Hetty Kelly, Charlie had been looking for a 'fairytale princess'. Mildred Harris, Paulette Goddard, Lillita McMurray had all looked like fairytale princesses.

'Notice that he always steered away, at least in marriage, from mature women like Edna who could really help him and be "good" for him.' But in Oona O'Neill, Laurel said, 'at last he got his fairy princess and they sure as hell lived happily ever after. I think it's one of the greatest love stories of history.'

2

THE GREAT LOVER

While Charlie Chaplin was a great star, Ruldoph Valentino was the great lover. Films such as *The Sheik, Camille, Passion's Playground*, and *Uncharted Seas* established him as the world's first Hollywood heart-throb. In his private life, he had a similar reputation. He seduced Pola Negri by strewing her bed with rose petals. It was 'a perfect act of love,' she said. But then, there were those who claimed he was homosexual. After all, his two marriages were to well-known lesbians and, as he was forced to avow in court, unconsummated.

Born Rodolfo Guglielmi di Valentina d'Antonguolla in the small town of Castellaneta, Italy, Valentino was a wayward boy, but widely admired for his beauty.

'He should have been a girl,' said many of the locals in Castellaneta.

At the age of eleven, he was sent away to agricultural college in Taranto and boarded at the Manzoni Institute, a convent that took both boys and girls. Soon he was boasting of his sexual exploits to his friends. Neither beatings by the fathers of girls he seduced nor the threat of hellfire from the local priest dampened the ardour of the young Casanova. On his first trip home, he turned up in Castellaneta with a ravishing young folk singer with whom he paraded around town.

He was thrown out of school after seducing the daughter of

25

one of the domestic staff. Each night he would climb out of the dormitory window and inch along a narrow ledge to her window. He was found out after repeatedly nodding off to sleep in class.

His mother let him go to Paris where he said he would seek work. Instead he hung around in bars and cafés, watching the apache dancers. He was approached by an old pederast named Claude Rambeau. The young Rodolpho resisted his advances, largely because he was too naive to realize what the old lecher was up to. Besides, his interests lay elsewhere. He particularly enjoyed the nudes of the follies.

'Nudity is the most beautiful thing in the world,' he wrote and he enjoyed it in a very earthly way. 'Just because a woman is a woman, I do not acclaim her with beating heart as a masterpiece from God, a divine acolyte of Venus, a lotus of love. When a woman is beautiful, she is a miracle. When she is not beautiful – she is a woman I pity and respect.'

But at the time Rodolfo's adoration of women was purely intellectual. Jean Martin and his lover Coco, who were teaching him to dance apache, told him that he must make love if he was going to master the virile dance.

'It is time for you to decide,' said Jean. 'You must decide whether you are going to make love with men or with women, you cannot be an adequate performer if you do not make love at all.'

When Jean sang the praises of making love to a woman and how it made you feel truly a man, Rodolpho blushed.

'See Coco there, standing waiting for me,' said Jean. 'Isn't she a magnificent creature? Listen to me. You go with her to our apartment. I will stop off for a drink. Once you have made love to one such as Coco, you will spit in the eye of Claude or any other queer.'

Rodolfo was shocked.

'You are telling me to go home with Coco, your woman, and make love to her!'

'Yes of course,' said Jean.

'But she belongs to you. She loves you and you are my

friend,' spluttered Rodolfo.

'That is what friends are for.'

Rodolfo could not deny that Coco was attractive. He had frequently sung her praises as the most beautiful woman in Paris.

Back at the apartment, Rodolfo emerged from the bathroom to find Coco naked on the bed.

'Come,' she said. 'Don't be ashamed.'

'Need I undress completely?' asked Rodolfo, weakly.

'You have a fine young body,' said Coco. 'Don't be ashamed of it.'

But Rodolfo was nervous and whatever she did she could not get him aroused.

'I'm sorry,' said Rodolfo. 'I know you want to be kind, but I can't.'

She cursed him as a 'goddamn queer'.

That night, he went to a homosexual café where Claude Rambeau hung out. He got drunk and they went home together. The whole experience left Rodolfo with an empty feeling. The next evening he left Paris for good and returned home to Castellaneta.

His early experiences in Paris left him with a hankering, not for sex, but for 'pure love'.

'I like the Madonna in women,' he said. 'The most beautiful women in Italy are the Madonna type ... serene faces, calm, soft eyes, overlying something deeper and stronger.'

His youthful ambition was to go to America to seek his fortune, but he had no money.

'If the father of every girl you've pestered gave a handful of lire,' a friend said, 'you'd have enough money to send you halfway around the world – and set up in business when you got there.'

Eventually, tired of the trouble his womanizing was causing with the local families, his mother gave him the fare and he set sail on the *Cleveland*. In New York, the new immigrant's life was tough. He took a few menial jobs while he learnt English. He got a job as a gardener, but was sacked after smashing up his employer's motorcycle while showing off to girls. He found himself homeless, destitute and near to suicide. After a period of living on the street, he found a job as a busboy in a popular Italian restaurant.

As a penniless immigrant, for eighteen months, he could only look at women. Then the other busboys and waiters introduced him to the world of dance halls, where single and married women alike came to meet lovers. But Valentino could only dance apache-style which was hardly appropriate. Any American girl would slap his face if he grabbed her in the rough way of the apache.

'I was one of the best wallflowers in the city of New York,' he would say. 'I supported more ballroom walls than any other man I've heard of.'

Soon a waiter taught him the rudiments of the waltz and the tango. His foreign looks, his deep, heavily accented voice and his hypnotic eyes quickly made him the most popular dance partner on the circuit. A cabaret owner kitted him out with an evening suit. Women would pay him to dance, or to sit with them. As a gigolo, he was soon making $6 a day, more than a week's pay as a busboy.

Women would fight over him on the dance floor, and to take him home. They had to pay for that privilege too, and ply him with expensive gifts. He would take a 'love break' between the afternoon tea dance and the evening session, then another one after he had finished for the night. By the time he was twenty, he had a smart, two-bedroomed apartment on East 61st Street and a wardrobe of expensive, hand-tailored suits.

Rudy was discerning and discreet. Those he turned down thought him celibate.

'Nothing ever happened to Rudy,' said a Ziegfeld Follies girl who knew him then. 'He might as well be a priest.'

'All the girls were hot to crawl into bed with Rudy,' said another. 'But I never heard of him trying to get into anyone's pants. I would have been damned envious if I had.'

He was a master of his trade, practising for hours in front of the mirror to perfect his smouldering-eyed look. The waist and hips of his evening trousers were taken in an inch. An inch was clipped off his own waist and hips by a tightly laced corset. He shaved off his moustache and brilliantined his hair flat against his scalp. He choreographed his low bow and his handkissing. His looks and manners struck others as effeminate, he knew, but they were the tools of his new-found trade and they earned him the nickname of 'Rudy the Peacock'.

'Better a peacock,' he would say, 'than a sparrow.'

Women saw him differently. One described him as 'a sensuous animal stalking the jazz jungle'.

Soon his dancing had progressed to the point where a dance hall paid him extra for demonstrating the tango with a professional dance partner. His performance drew applause. He still had one problem, though – no one could pronounce, or remember, his name, Rodolfo Guglielmi. So he became Rodolfo di Valentina, then later, Rudolph Valentino.

Valentino was hired by Maxim's as an exhibition dancer and was immediately a sensational success. After his number, he was supposed to dance with the clientele or sit at a table with wealthy society women.

One night, the headwaiter directed him to the table of Bianca de Saulles, the Chilean wife of one-time Yale quarterback Jack de Saulles. De Saulles was well known for his infidelity with actresses and chorus girls. His wife, a wealthy heiress in her own right, was determined to pay him back in kind.

She wore a daringly cut gown that attracted the attention of every gigolo in the cabaret but it was Valentino she wanted; and he wanted her, too.

'She's sensational,' he told the headwaiter. 'Tell the orchestra to play a tango.'

The two of them glided across the floor as if welded at the hip. Around them Maxim's clients cheered and roared.

'You have stolen my heart completely,' whispered Valentino, as his lips brushed her ear.

'You are everything I have been searching for,' she replied, trembling.

At the end of the number, he escorted her back to her table and they arranged an assignation. Later, when the other gigolos teased him about his new conquest, he snarled: 'How dare you comment on her. She is the woman to whom I have given my love.'

The following day, she came to his apartment. It was the beginning of a long and illicit affair.

'I was dazzled by the radiance of her beauty,' he said. 'She was the princess I'd rescued so often in my boyish imagination. When we danced, she was very happy. But afterwards her tears told me of the weight of her heart – loneliness for her homeland and bitter sorrow at the break-up of her marriage.'

He would weep too, and promise her undying love. He really did try to rescue her. When he discovered that de Saulles was dating a chorus girl, he followed them back to the girl's apartment one night, aiming to call a private detective and a photographer to get evidence for a divorce. But he made the mistake of pressing his ear to the door once they were inside. He heard the renting of clothes as de Saulles tore the woman's dress off. De Saulles mumbled something about buying her a new one, then Rudy heard the sounds of them violently making love. Sweat burst out on his forehead. He could all too easily imagine de Saulles taking his wife, Rudy's beloved, in that same brutal fashion. He turned from the door and ran.

Determined to stay faithful to his new amour, Valentino had to turn down the other women who pestered him nightly. The New York Vice Squad was beginning to take an interest in the cabaret scene. Several gigolos had been charged with prostitution and wealthy women were staying away, to avoid a scandal.

To escape the sex-starved socialites, Valentino quit Maxim's and became the professional dance partner of Bonnie Glass who was performing at the Winter Garden. At first, she paid him $50 a week – half of what he had been getting at Maxim's – but quickly upped it to $100.

They went on a tour of the eastern seaboard, culminating in a performance before the President, Woodrow Wilson, in Washington. But Bonnie Glass found herself a millionaire to marry and Valentino became the partner of Joan Sawyer, a star on the exhibition circuit who held him in ill-concealed contempt.

During their afternoon sessions, Valentino would complain about Sawyer while Bianca moaned about her husband. Bianca suggested that both their problems could be solved if Valentino inveigled his partner into bed with her husband. That way, she could divorce him on the grounds of adultery and they could be married.

Valentino introduced Sawyer to de Saulles at a social event. After de Saulles had taken his wife home, he returned and made a beeline for Sawyer. A few days later, de Saulles was served with divorce papers naming Sawyer as co-respondent. At the hearing in July 1916, Valentino told the court how he had accompanied Joan Sawyer to de Saulles' 'bachelor' flat and how he had seen them, again, at a hotel. The facts were corroborated by Sawyer's cook and de Saulles' valet. The divorce was granted and Valentino was out of a job.

De Saulles wanted revenge. He reported Valentino to the police and Rudy was arrested, along with a Mrs Georgia Thym, as part of a vice and white slavery investigation.

'Many persons of means, principally "social climbers", have been blackmailed after discreet visits to Mrs Thym's house,' reported the *New York Times*. Valentino was held as a material witness for several days.

Then Bianca shot and killed her ex-husband in a row over custody of their children. She was arrested and sent for trial. Valentino realized that any connection with him would do her no good, so he decided to get out of town. He took a job at $75 a week as a chorus boy in a musical comedy, *The Masked Model*, which was going out on tour. The show closed in the Midwest and the cast were paid off with just enough money to get to one or other of the coasts. Everyone, except for Rudolph, headed back to New York. He waited on the other platform and took a train west.

In Hollywood, he got a few jobs as an extra when swarthy heavies were required. More than once he took dancing jobs at some of Los Angeles' more dubious cafés to survive. When he got no more film work, he set up as a dancing instructor and, to make ends meet, he had to accommodate some of his female customers in the small room over the café in Santa Monica that he used as his studio.

'Downstairs they pay to jump on me,' he complained. 'Upstairs they pay me to jump on them.'

He charged $10 a time and spent the money watching himself, over and over again, on-screen for a brief few seconds in a film called *Alimony*, produced by Emmett Flynn, his last film before the parts dried up.

'Your type works against you,' said Hayden Talbot, author of *Alimony*. 'You're just too damned pretty.'

Valentino's eyes narrowed.

'Don't worry,' said Talbot. 'I'm not propositioning you. But you sure did react when I said you were pretty. Have the fairies been fluttering around you?'

'I have received a few proposals,' said Valentino.

'And you don't like that sort of thing?'

'No.'

'No offence intended,' said Talbot, 'but you look the type, you know. In fact, I'm a bit surprised to learn that you're no queer.'

However, Valentino had accepted an invitation to 'boys' night' at the Torch Club. The Torch was notorious in Hollywood. There were four pools where, on mixed nights, the sexes mixed freely. There were rooms to which couples – or threesomes, or foursomes depending on taste – could retire; and there was the infamous room 23, where newcomers ended up. The ceiling was a one-way mirror through which people could watch the action from the room above.

Rudy went along with a husky young extra named Bob who took him to one of the pools and stripped off.

'You have a lovely body, Rudy,' Bob told him. 'Would you like me to give you a rub down.'

Rudy recognized this as a proposition but, despite the disaster with Claude, he thought he ought to give it a try. Bob led him down to one of the locker rooms where, he promised, there was a big table Rudy could stretch out on. But there was already someone inside. It was a famous movie director, fat, balding, naked and chewing on a fat cigar.

'Well, well, well,' he said. 'So Bob, you delivered my pretty boy to me just as you promised.'

'Enjoy yourself, dear,' Bob said to Valentino as he left, locking the door behind him.

Rudy was sweating. He only had a small towel to cover his nakedness.

'Get yourself down on your knees, pretty boy,' said the director.

Valentino threw himself at the door, hammering on it and screaming in Italian until someone came and let him out.

Figuring that his career in the movies was over, Valentino began looking around for a job. He declined to do nude modelling for life classes at the J. Francis Smith college of art and design on Los Angeles' Main Street along with Beatrice Joy and Ramon Navarro. He did not want other men looking at him naked. If he was going to take his clothes off, he would rather do it for a smaller audience – one lady at a time. So he went back to work as a gigolo. He was dancing in the Watts Tavern when Emmett Flynn came across him again. He offered him a part as a villainous Italian count in *A Married Virgin*, but the film fell foul of a cameramen's dispute and was put on hold.

One night, movie star Mae Murray and her husband director Bob Leonard walked into the Vernon Club, a Bohemian dive in downtown LA where Rudy was then working. A large, heavily painted lady was groping him on the dance floor. Valentino grabbed her hand and pulled it above the waist.

'You paid to dance, so dance,' he hissed.

When he spotted Murray, he span his overweight partner around the floor, showing off his best moves and flashing his most smouldering looks.

Murray and Leonard asked who he was and were told: 'He's an Italian gigolo. Charges two bucks an hour to be pawed by dames and puts out to some of them back in his room.'

Nevertheless, they were impressed by his dancing; and Mae was smitten. Afraid of her husband's fiery temper, she knew that she could not risk having an affair with Valentino but that did not mean that she could not have any fun with him. She got her husband to phone him and offer him the role of leading man in her new picture, *The Big Little Person*.

It was clear to everyone on the set that Mae and Valentino put everything they had into the love scenes. When they were kissing, the crew hardly dared to look at Leonard. In one scene, where his hands ran all over her body, Valentino got completely carried away.

The genuine passion between the two actors showed on the screen and *The Big Little Person* was an instant success. Valentino was a success with Mae, too. She insisted that he star alongside her in her next picture, *The Delicious Little Devil*. Valentino was given $100 a week and got star billing along with Mae Murray herself. The love scenes in the second film were, if anything, more steamy than in the first. It was another hit. Then Leonard put his foot down. There would not be a third.

Magnanimously, Leonard recommended Valentino to Paul Powell to star alongside fifteen-year-old Carmel Meyers in *A Society Sensation*. The twenty-three-year-old Valentino was an instant sensation with Carmel.

'He is wonderful,' she said. 'What style he has – and what personality. There is something about him I can't explain. I guess it's sex. His voice is beautiful and deep, without accent. When he said I reminded him of his people, everything fluttered inside.'

Love blossomed between them after they did an intimate bathing scene together, but Carmel's mother stood in their way.

'Madam Meyers,' said Rudy, clicking his heels, one day in Carmel's dressing-room. 'May I have the honour of taking your daughter out to dinner?'

'I am very sorry, Mr Valentino,' she said. 'Carmel is much too young for that sort of thing.'

'Madam Meyers,' he continued. 'When I want something I don't usually let anything stand in my way.'

'Even when what is standing in your way weighs two hundred pounds?' replied her formidable mother.

'Touché, Madam,' Rudy concluded.

Valentino invested the money he earned in movies in improving his image. At the weekends, denizens of the movie colony would see him striding along the beaches of Santa Monica in a brief white bathing costume with two Russian Wolfhounds. Motorists would pull over as he came tearing down the highway in his huge Mercer convertible with some beautiful woman by his side.

Desperate for recognition, Valentino accepted any invitation that might bring him into contact with those who had power and influence in the movie business. One day, the actress Dagmar Godowsky invited him to a dinner party at a Santa Monica restaurant and introduced him to the great Russian star of the silent era, Alla Nazimova.

'How dare you bring this gigolo to my table?' spat Nazimova. 'How dare you introduce that pimp to Nazimova?'

Then, to complete Valentino's humiliation, Nazimova recounted the scandal surrounding his affair with Bianca de Saulles in New York. Even though Bianca had been acquitted, Valentino's reputation had been savaged.

Valentino left the restaurant in tears, convinced that his career would be ruined once news of Nazimova's insults got about. Instead, many people sympathized with him, including one of Nazimova's inner circle of lesbian friends, Metro starlet Jean Acker.

At a party given by actress Pauline Frederick, Valentino met Acker. Her hair was short, bobbed in a masculine style. She wore a suit with a white blouse and tie. They got on like a house on fire. Valentino enjoyed talking to her man to man, with none of the coquettish eyelash fluttering that he got from other actresses.

Acker was one of the attractive young women that Nazimova kept around her for her personal amusement and pleasure, and most of her intimate friends were women of distinctly sapphist inclinations. People who saw Valentino and Acker deep in conversation were greatly amused. Could Valentino, a man who jealously guarded his reputation for being virile and masculine, seriously be setting his sights on such an improbable target?

Acker refused his invitation to come home with him; nor would she meet him anywhere in private, but she agreed to have dinner at the restaurant of the Hollywood Hotel, where she had an apartment.

'I was already falling in love,' said Valentino, who had never come across women playing hard to get before. 'Even before I met her the next day, I knew that I wanted her for my wife.'

He did not hide his feelings. He took her for a horse-back ride in the moonlight through Beverly Hills.

'Isn't this romantic?' she said.

'Yes,' he said, 'but wouldn't it be more romantic if we rode to Santa Ana and got married?'

The next day they married by special licence and used a party given for Metro boss Richard Rowland at the Hollywood Hotel as their reception. The guests toasted the happy couple. Then Rudy took his wife by the hand and led her away.

By the time they reached the hotel lobby, he was practically dragging her.

'Slow down,' she cried. 'Give a girl time to think.'

'This is no time for thinking,' said Valentino, sweeping her up in his arms. 'This is a time for action.'

Some of the other guests had scurried around the back of the hotel, hoping to interrupt the couple's nuptials. Instead, they heard a furious row. Jean was screaming that the marriage had all been a horrible mistake. She could not bear to have him touch her. The thought of his body on hers nauseated her. He pleaded for her to give it a try, but in the face of her furious onslaught, he was forced to retreat. Valentino separated from his wife after just six hours. The marriage, everyone in Hollywood soon knew, had not been consummated. The Great Lover was a laughing stock.

In an attempt to salvage his reputation, Valentino took the advice of a friend: 'Get along to as many parties as possible, and go to town on the girls. You may be married, but there's no way they can accuse you of being unfaithful. You haven't had the chance to be faithful yet.'

Acker's friends shunned him. Others sniggered behind his back. But there was one place that he could never make a fool of himself – on the dance floor. He soon found a new dance partner, the big Metro star Viola Dana. Her interest helped Rudy get over his image as the rejected gigolo and he got parts in *Passion's Playground*, *The Adventuress* and *The Cheater*.

Through Viola, he met studio boss Lewis Selznick, who took a shine to Rudy. He upped his wages to $300 a week and assigned him to several movies that were shooting in New York.

'When I was here last,' he told his colleagues, 'I found friends among the showgirls and performers who were completely out with decent families. They would have nothing to do with me, and would not allow their daughters to have anything to do with me. But their daughters were anxious for romance and didn't pay any attention.'

Valentino was soon renewing his acquaintance with many 'delightful young girls from both sides of the social fence'. It was a triumphant return.

Rudy returned to Hollywood on the crest of a wave. He had been offered the lead in *The Four Horsemen of the Apocalypse*. Now that he was on his way up again, women flocked around him. He would sneak them into his hotel suite by the back entrance.

Actress Gertrude Astor would act as a scout for him.

'He would come to my place. I would have a girlfriend there and he would pair off with her,' she said. 'I would play the piano and we would sing a bit. He liked quiet parties, but he certainly knew what to do with a woman.'

Even Jean Acker, who had refused to answer his letters earlier, was complaining that her husband was refusing to support her. On 17 January 1921, she sued him for maintenance, claiming that he had deserted her. She wanted $300 a month, plus over $1,000 in lawyer's fees. Valentino was distraught. He broke every item of crockery on a luncheon trolley that a nervous waiter had trundled into his suite. But he vowed not to be brought down by fate again. He countersued for divorce, petitioning for the hearing to be put back six months. In the meantime, *The Four Horsemen of the Apocalypse* opened simultaneously in New York, Boston and Chicago to a rapturous reception. A star was born and the women of the world had a new heart-throb.

Even Nazimova was forced to eat crow. She stopped by one afternoon to watch Valentino rehearsing on the set. With her was another of her friends who immediately caught Valentino's attention.

'I saw before me no ordinary woman, but rather the reincarnation of some mighty goddess of the past,' he said.

He stared at her transfixed. Then she and Nazimova walked out of sight.

Valentino asked one of the crew who she was and was told that she was Natasha Rambova, a 'friend' of Nazimova's, her set and costume designer. Around the studio, she was known as 'The Icicle' for her cold and aloof manner.

Her real name was Winifred Hudnut and she was the stepdaughter of an American cosmetics millionaire. She had studied dancing with the Russian Ballet's Theodore Kosloff, who had given her her Russian name when they toured America together. The name Winifred Hudnut would have looked incongruous alongside those of two exotic Russian dancers.

Valentino was desperate to meet her, but it seemed impossible. He was still smarting from Nazimova's remarks and he was being shunned by her set after his bust up with Jean Acker.

It was Nazimova herself who effected the introduction. She may not have liked Valentino, but she was no fool. He was now Hollywood's hottest property and she wanted him to play Armand opposite her Marguerite in *Camille*. Valentino leapt at the chance.

Nazimova was also producing the film and, during preliminary discussions, she introduced him to her constant companion, Rambova.

'Natasha Rambova is my art director and costumier,' explained Nazimova. 'She is a young woman of great genius. I could not accept you if she did not approve of you.'

Valentino bowed low and kissed her hand, giving her one of

his smouldering looks directly in the eye. She was not impressed.

'Delighted to meet you, Mr Valentino,' she said, coldly.

She walked around him surveying him intently.

'Quiet now,' said Nazimova. 'She's thinking.'

Rambova's intense gaze unnerved Rudy.

'Perhaps it would help if I took off my coat,' he whispered.

'Only if you're becoming uncomfortable,' Nazimova snapped.

Valentino was beginning to wonder if Rambova has lost the power of speech.

'Well, what do you think,' said Nazimova at last. 'Does he know how to make love?'

'How should I know?' said Rambova. Valentino stiffened at this slur on his manhood. 'But why not give him a try? He looks as if he might do just fine.'

However, on the set, the Icicle began to thaw. Though, technically, she was only a designer, she paid a great deal of attention to the actors' hair and costumes – especially Valentino's. One afternoon, the hang of his trousers seemed to bother her particularly and she accompanied him back to his dressing-room. Within minutes, their clothes were tossed off and left lying where they fell.

Nazimova was waiting on the set.

'Where is that damned gigolo?' she demanded.

Even the director, Ray Smallwood, was getting angry.

'Who the hell does he think he is?' Smallwood bellowed. 'One movie and he thinks he's made it.'

He sent Harry Grieve, a young technical assistant, to find Valentino. Gingerly, Grieve knocked on the door of Valentino's dressing-room. There was no reply so he opened the door. Inside, on the day bed, he saw Natasha Rambova, a moan of pleasure escaping from her lips, her long, white ballerina's legs wrapped around Valentino's swarthy body, her long, meticulously manicured nails digging into his back.

Realizing that the coitus had been interrupted, Valentino swirled Rambova's black satin cape around them. Five minutes later, immaculately dressed in his tails and dress shirt, Valentino strode back on to the set. Behind him trotted Rambova looking flustered. The Icicle, it seemed, had melted and Valentino's reputation as a Latin lover soared to new heights.

Rambova was not to be his exclusive property, though. Soon, a new and even juicier piece of gossip was circulating. Three members of the studio's art department had been looking out of the window of their office which overlooked the whole lot. In a disused section of the studio, they saw eighteen girls in their late teens and early twenties lining up, all stripped to the waist. Nazimova and Rambova moved slowly along the line, talking, smiling and caressing the girls' bodies. They picked five and told them to report to Nazimova's house that night.

Valentino refused to believe this and other stories of Rambova's position in Nazimova's 'harem'. Rambova, he insisted, was the perfect woman, the woman he was destined for. She would be his wife.

Rudy and Natasha were soon deeply in love. They talked of marriage and children. But Rudy was still married to Jean Acker. Rambova knew how to deal with that. She got Valentino to hire a photographer to take some compromising shots of them and sent them to Acker. It was clear to Jean that the photographs were staged. Their two nude bodies were posed exquisitely, plainly by the famous art director herself. Nevertheless, she sent them to her lawyers.

Rambova also began to take an interest in Valentino's career. 'You've made the studio what it is,' she said. 'You merely debase yourself by working for $400 a week. Demand more.'

He did – and was refused.

'I can take any good-looking extra and make a star out of him, just like I did with Valentino,' said director Rex Ingram.

Under Rambova's influence Rudy became a prima donna. He turned up each morning behaving as though he had done everyone a favour by getting out of bed. Soon no one would work with him.

Rudy had been sharing a flat on the corner of Hollywood Boulevard and La Brea with French-born cameraman Paul Ivano.

To save money they moved into Rambova's tiny bungalow on Sunset. Ivano slept on the couch in the living-room.

For eight long months, Valentino was out of a job. Then along came *The Sheik*. The book had been condemned as trash by the critics. It told the tale of a young Englishwoman kidnapped by an Arab sheik who repeatedly forced her into sexual submission. It was a runaway best-seller and Jesse Lasky bought the film rights. The success of the film, he realized, would hinge on the erotic appeal of the villainous, yet tender, sheik. He remembered Valentino.

Rambova begged him not to do it. It would only confirm the public's impression of him as a gigolo rather than the artist he truly was. But he needed the money.

Condemned by the critics – again – the film was an instant hit. It broke all box-office records and some 125 million people saw it worldwide. Even hard-boiled New Yorkers who considered Valentino a fag went overboard. Damon Runyan said: 'He made me long for a fleet steed in the Sahara and the licence to capture any swell-looking Judys I found running around loose on the desert.'

But it was women, old and young, all over the world who were transfixed.

Valentino's international reputation as the ideal lover was about to take a dent, though. In the divorce courts, Jean Acker told how Valentino had burst into her bathroom and beaten her when she was naked. Asked why she had not let him visit her when she was filming on location, she explained that she had been sharing her room with a girlfriend. There were titters in court. It was also put to Acker that the only support she had lent her husband was to lend him rather too much of her perfume.

Then it came out that the marriage had never been consummated. A month after their wedding, they had even spent the night together in his apartment, but they had not made love. The divorce was granted. Valentino was to make a one-off payment to Acker. Lasky loaned him $5,000 as a down payment.

Rambova did not approve of Valentino's next movie either, *It* author Elinor Glyn's *Beyond the Rocks*. It was an 'insult to his talents'. He was to star opposite former Mack Sennett Bathing Beauty Gloria Swanson. Rambova insisted on full-time access to the set.

Natasha's almost hypnotic control over Valentino drove all those around him to distraction. There were tears, tantrums and walkouts. Nevertheless, his performance as the fearless bull-fighter in *Blood and Sand* established the newly created Paramount as one of the giants of the industry.

In the wake of the Fatty Arbuckle scandal, Will Hays arrived in Hollywood to clean up the movie industry. The first thing he did was call Lasky to point out that Paramount's major star, Rudolph Valentino, was a bigamist. On 13 May 1922, Valentino and Rambova had slipped over the border to Mexicali and tied the knot. Unfortunately, the divorce he had obtained from Jean Acker was only an interlocutory decree. The decree absolute would not be issued for another year.

Valentino was honeymooning in Palm Springs at the time. When he got Lasky's call, his first instinct was to flee but Lasky persuaded him that if he came back to Los Angeles to face the music, his public – and Hays – might forgive him. After all, he was the Great Lover and his passion for Rambova had blinded him to petty legal technicalities.

Rambova went into hiding in the Adirondacks, while Valentino gave himself up at Los Angeles' municipal offices. He entered a plea of guilty to the charge of bigamy before a Justice of the Peace, who granted bail on a surety of $20,000. But it was a Sunday and Valentino did not have that sort of money about his person. So Hollywood's biggest star was thrown in the slammer with drunks, derelicts and petty criminals.

Valentino cursed his jailers – and Lasky who he believed had engineered his Sunday surrender to teach him a lesson. By the time friends had rustled up the bail money, every reporter in Los Angeles was outside the jailhouse. Valentino played his release like a scene from one of his movies. He had erred, he admitted, but only because of his great love for Natasha.

Then irony cascaded from the heavens. The studio's attor-neys told Valentino that his only defence against the bigamy charge was non-consummation. He could not be guilty of bigamy if he had not consummated his marriage to Rambova. This was only months after the non-consummation of his first marriage had made front-page news around the world. Everyone would be asking was the Great Lover a flop in bed?

Valentino could not stand this humiliation. But his lawyers advised him that any other course would result in between one and five years in jail, possible deportation and a certain end to his movie career.

In the courtroom, Valentino hung his head when he told the judge that he had never occupied the single bed in his wife's hotel room in Palm Springs. On his wedding night, he said, he had slept in another room with two other men. On the next night, he had slept on a couch on a porch. Seven other witnesses swore that, since their marriage in Mexicali, Valentino and Rambova had not been alone together for a single second.

Valentino was cleared, but the District Attorney still had the option of convening a Grand Jury. This meant that Rambova would have to stay away from Valentino until his divorce from Jean Acker was final.

Lasky was delighted with the outcome. No amount of cash could have bought the publicity that the bigamy case had brought his turbulent star. When he had sworn that he had never made love to his wife, he had pleased every moralist in the country. As for the rest? His fans? No one believed him.

But he may well have been telling the truth. Despite the fun and games she had with Nazimova and with Rudy in his dressing-room, Rambova had strict views on marriage. A sincere union, she told Valentino, was a spiritual one. A mating of the flesh was, at best, fleeting and temporal. True love was spiritual love, unsullied by the demands of the flesh and the desires of the body. In place of sex, she had given him spiritualism.

'It was a good thing for them that they had spiritual intercourse,' said Nita Naldi, a close friend of Rambova and Rudy's co-star in *Blood and Sand*. 'I doubt if they ever had any other kind. Neither one of them liked that sort of thing – at least in a normal way.'

Naldi did admit that Valentino was hot-blooded, though.

'Rudy was a funny guy,' she said. 'Whenever I did a close-up with him, he liked to feel me up. He'd rub my breasts like crazy and chew at my ear, but that's as far as it ever went. Nothing off camera.'

Not that Nita would have minded. She often invited inter-viewers to feel her breasts to attest to their firmness and prove that they had not begun to sag.

'Fred Niblo, our director in *Blood and Sand*, caught him at it once and gave him hell,' she went on. 'He asked Rudy how he expected our love scenes to get by the censors with him touching me like that.'

Rudy would apologize, but claimed that the bright studio lights made it difficult to see his co-star, so he had to grope around to find her. Nita concluded that Rudy was frustrated and felt sorry for him.

'I always figured that the minute Rudy died and got to the spirit world himself, he would ask the head spook to leave him alone with some pretty little ghost for a good normal lay,' said Nita.

Natasha was in upstate New York, but she could still make trouble from there. A daily phonecall, briefing him for the shoot, made him impossible to work with. On *The Young Rajah*, she designed an outlandish costume, bedecked with baubles and beads, totally different from the macho image created by *The Sheik* and *Blood and Sand*. *The Young Rajah* bombed.

At Rambova's behest, Valentino demanded total artistic con-trol of his pictures. When Paramount refused, he quit. Paramount got an injunction preventing him from working for any other film company.

Short of money, Valentino and Rambova went on a dance tour of the US, sponsored by the Mineralava Beauty Clay Company. Valentino's divorce became final and they tried to wed in Chicago; but they were frustrated again. The law in Illinois demands a one-year waiting period after a divorce is finalized before a new marriage licence can be issued. So on 14

March 1923, they were secretly married in Indiana. They honeymooned on board the luxurious private railroad car – complete with gilt mirrors, Turkish rugs and oil paintings – provided by Mineralava.

With Valentino in gaucho garb and Rambova decked out flamenco-style, the tour was a sell-out. *Photoplay* serialized his biography, his movies were reshown around the country, and Valentino published a book of love poetry called *Day Dreams*, said to have been written during the year when marriage to Rambova was denied him. It sold in hundreds of thousands.

The poems were clearly not just written for his beloved Natasha, but also for his fans themselves. In 'You', he wrote:

YOU

You are the History of Love and its Justification.
The Symbol of Devotion.
The Blessedness of Womanhood.
The Incentive of Chivalry. The Reality of Ideals.
The Verity of Joy. Idolatry's Defense.
The Proof of Goodness.The Power of Gentleness.
Beauty's Acknowledgment. Vanity's Excuse.
The Promise of Truth. The Melody of Life.
The Caress of Romance. The Dream of Desire.
The Sympathy of Understanding. My Heart's Home.
The Proof of Faith. Sanctuary of my Soul.
My Belief in Heaven. Eternity of All Happiness.
My Prayers.
You.

Rambova told his adoring public that the poems came from Walt Whitman, Elizabeth and Robert Browning and other dead poets 'on the other side'. After all, English was not Rudy's first language.

Wherever they came from, Valentino was a star the like of whom had never been seen before. He hired George Ullman, the PR man who had arranged the Mineralava tour, to renegotiate his contract. Ullman was delighted to work for Rudy. He recalled their first meeting.

'To say that I was enveloped by his personality with the first clasp of his sinewy hand and my first glance into his inscrutable eyes is to state it mildly. I was literally engulfed, swept off my feet, which is unusual between two men. Had he been a beautiful woman and I a bachelor, it would not have been so surprising. I am not an emotional man, but I found myself moved by the most powerful personality I had ever encountered in man or woman.'

Paramount immediately caved in. They would give him $7,500 a week. He could choose the scripts, writers, directors, actors and actresses. The company's Long Island studio would be set aside for him. Rambova would be hired as technical advisor.

'Now, at last, we can begin our honeymoon,' said Valentino.

In July 1923, they fought their way through crowds of women to board the *Cunard* and set sail for England. They travelled on to France and Italy, where they visited his birthplace, Castellaneta.

Back in America, Valentino found he was as popular as ever. There had been a rush on the properties around Paramount's Long Island studio. There was not a room to be had for twenty miles. The studio was inundated with calls of an extremely intimate nature. Hundreds of letters turned up every day. Women sent pictures of themselves nude and underwear which they wanted him to kiss and return. Others simply detailed, graphically, exactly what they would like him to do to them. Some even had their wishes come true, the papers hinted. The Great Lover, it seemed, had a constant need to prove his masculinity.

He had a short fling with Maureen Englin, whom he had first known in his Parisian days.

'No one will believe this,' she said. 'The Great Lover of the screen is making love to me. What would Natasha think?'

'I'm afraid Natasha wouldn't really care,' he said. 'She is much more interested in my career than she is in me.'

But he was wrong. A young prostitute named Adele had found it easy enough to use her charms on the cast and crew to get Valentino's private phone number. She called and invited him to her apartment for a freebie. Although he hated the tawdry scene, once he saw her naked, he could not resist her.

'Don't be gentle with me,' she begged.

'Let's not rush it,' he said. 'I want to savour the magnificence of your body.'

But her passion became too much for him and it was all over in the blink of an eye.

Afterwards she sighed: 'That was wonderful, Rudy.'

He knew that she was lying.

It did not take long for this story to get round the studio. Rambova fumed. She took her revenge on any attractive young woman who worked there. Any woman who might take Rudy's fancy was summarily fired.

Jean Acker was causing problems too. She began appearing on stage as 'Mrs Rudolph Valentino'. Rambova was beside herself. She filed a suit, though she knew there was nothing she could do about it.

Valentino played the Great Lover, bewigged and powdered *ancien régime*-style, for his comeback picture *Monsieur Beauclaire*. To help him perfect his performance, he hired a director of etiquette, a dance master, a fencing teacher and a private violinist and poetry reader.

Monsieur Beauclaire was another resounding success – with the public that is. None of the people who worked on the picture would work with him again as long as the 'She Devil' – as they called Rambova – was around. This suited Rambova just fine. She had written the script for *The Hooded Falcon* which she would direct herself, as well as design the sets and costumes.

Up to this time, Valentino had simply been a henpecked husband who refused to stand up to his overbearing wife. Now he became her slave and, in recognition of his new status, she bought him a platinum slave bracelet for Christmas. She solemnly placed it on his wrist. Realizing its symbolism, he took her in his arms and kissed her passionately. He was a slave to her beauty, he said, and swore that he would never take that bracelet off.

But in his unquestioning devotion to Natasha he forged a rod for his own back. While at the studio he perfected his prizefighting skills for his role in *Cobra* under the tutelage of world heavyweight champion Jack Dempsey, at home he put up no resistance to his wife's increasingly vicious tirades. She derided his talents as an actor, as an artist and as a lover. Friends found these outbursts embarrassing and refused to come to the house. Many thought she had a hold over him, that there was some sexual secret in their marriage that she was using to blackmail him into staying with her.

'Natasha has threatened to tell the world that I am not a great lover,' he confided to Mae Murray. 'She has said that she will tell people what I am really in the bedroom. She will tell them that I am a freak, not a sheik.'

Inevitably, her admonitions turned up in the gossip columns. The papers branded him a wimp, but Rudy suffered his wife's slurs manfully. There was only one way to soften her heart and blunt her tongue – and that was for her to have a baby.

'How can we have children when you are living the kind of life you do?' she said. 'I will start having babies when you stop being an actor. Not until.'

She almost found herself in the family way sooner than she anticipated. Her meddling ruined his next few films. Her outrageous demands and her reckless overspending ruined one film company. Valentino found himself out of a job without a contract. He had, briefly, stopped being an actor as Rambova demanded.

All was not lost. United Artists offered him a contract that would bring him $1 million a year – provided that Natasha never darkened the studio gates. A special clause stated explicitly that she would have no say in the choice of scripts, the selection of directors, the casting of actors, the design of the costumes or the sets, or the hiring and firing of technical assistants. She was not even allowed to make the tea.

'Rudy will never sign a contract like that,' said Rambova. 'He knows he is totally unable to perform unless I am there to advise him.'

Valentino demurred. Like the hero from one of his own movies, he leapt to his feet, grabbed his wife by the shoulders and pushed her down in her seat.

'You have cost me my friends and you have humiliated me in public,' he yelled. 'You have mocked my work and abused my talent. But this time I will do things my way. Your job is to have babies. Mine is to make films.'

And he signed.

Natasha was not going to take this lying down. She badgered Rudy into giving her $50,000 to go into film production with her old chum Nazimova, and headed east to find a distributor. Press photographers captured the last farewell kiss at the station.

Rumours reached the newspapers that this separation would end in divorce. Rudy stoutly defended his marriage, issuing a statement saying 'this marital vacation will be a good thing for both of us'. In private, the story was different.

'Am I really incapable of love?' he would ask friends. While he could inspire sexual ecstasy in millions of female fans 'both my marriages have failed. Dear little Jean was my bride for only a month. And Natasha, she was never a wife at all.'

He rued the fact that he could never be the Great Lover everyone wanted him to be.

'I am no longer Rodolfo. They have made me Valentino – and there is no real Valentino,' Rudy sighed.

In truth, the distinction between what happened on-screen and what happened off-screen remained blurred. With Natasha away, Nita Naldi decided to let Rudy take his on-set groping a little further. Valentino's make-up artist, Mont Westmore, would crew the cabin cruiser Valentino had bought for Natasha while the Great Lover and Nita disappeared below. Mont's brother Frank recounted the scene.

'Often, while Mont stood on the bridge with his eyes peeled for the treacherous reefs off Catalina, he could hear Nita's melodious voice extolling Rudy's capabilities. Mont was always especially amused when she would comment on his soft, sweet-smelling hair.'

Nita savaged Rambova's reputation, putting it about that Natasha had had three abortions during her years with Rudy.

Valentino was also dating other eager young actresses.

He was seen publicly with Vilma Banky, the Budapest bomb-shell who was co-starring in his latest film *The Eagle*. Rumours that they were having a passionate affair were, of course, stren-uously denied. He was a married man, Valentino insisted, and his marriage would continue provided Rambova gave up her crazy notion of being in pictures.

The reaction of Vilma Banky's fiancé, a Hungarian baron, was more direct. He said he would kill the Great Lover if ever they came face to face.

Without Rambova's interference, *The Eagle* was a great suc-cess. By the time Rudy travelled to New York for the première, Natasha had moved on to Europe. In Paris, she filed for divorce, expecting Rudy to rush to her side, but he announced that he would not contest the action.

'It is no longer a question of love,' he said, 'but of pride.'

Although he was sad and lonely, Valentino consoled himself with the fact that he was back at the top at the box office. Everywhere he went women mobbed him and tried to tear off his clothes.

'What's your secret?' one reporter asked. 'How do you do this to women?'

'I don't know,' said Rudy. 'This is a matter-of-fact age, and everyone is starving for romance. I suppose they like me because I bring that romance into their lives for a few moments.'

In Paris, Valentino ran into Baron Imre Lukatz, Vilma Banky's aggrieved fiancé. He screamed abuse and launched a two-fisted assault on the Great Lover. Valentino floored the man with a single punch, taught to him by Jack Dempsey. Honour was still to be satisfied and Valentino suggested a duel. The Baron chose swords – bad move. Valentino had been taught fencing by experts for his screen duels.

The next morning, Valentino turned up in the Bois de Boulogne with his seconds. The Baron turned up twenty min-utes late, unaccompanied and without a sword. It had all been a terrible mistake, he said. He now understood that Valentino's lovemaking with Miss Banky had been confined to the screen and he offered his most humble apologies. The two shook hands. Valentino declared that honour had been satisfied.

A few days later, Valentino's divorce was granted. Rambova declared that she was getting on with her career. If Valentino wanted a housewife, he had better look elsewhere.

If a housewife was what he wanted, it was certainly not what he got. Another assertive woman had set her sights on him – the greatest movie actress of her day, Pola Negri. She made no secret of the fact.

'Once Rudy has experienced my love,' declared the hot-blooded Polish star, 'he will forget about all other women. I am ready when he is.'

At the time, she was wearing Chaplin's engagement ring, but she declared her intention of getting Valentino up the aisle.

Valentino was amused by her presumption and he was teased further when Pola repeatedly got Marion Davis to arrange for the two great stars to meet then, at the last moment, to phone up and cancel. When they finally did meet, Valentino could not take his eyes off her. He bent low to kiss her hand.

'Now you have got your wish,' she said haughtily, 'maybe you will stop hounding me.'

At that moment, the orchestra struck up a tango.

'Call it fatalism,' Pola said afterwards, 'but from our very first meeting I knew this man either had to destroy my life or so irrevocably alter its course that it would never be the same again. I knew it, and I waved it away. I had met a man acknowledged to be the world's most desirable man, and I desired him. That was all. The rest was no more than romantic gibberish.'

They next met at a party at the Biltmore restaurant, which she was hosting for Michael Arlen. Valentino was entertaining another party of guests at a nearby table and pointedly ignored her. Then she felt a hand on her shoulder. It was Rudy.

'I would like to dance with you,' he said.

As they glided across the dance floor he whispered in her ear: 'I must see you alone. Get rid of your guests and I will take you home.'

She simply nodded.

That night, naked among the rose petals, he conclusively crushed the rumours that two marriages to prominent lesbians had left him impotent. Later she told friends that the seduction had been wordless – as it should be for the two great stars of the silent screen. Only afterwards did they talk of all the things others said before. Soon they were constant companions.

Alberto, Rudy's brother, who was staying with him at the time, disapproved of Rudy's behaviour, chastising him for flaunting his immorality so publicly. Valentino laughed and said that he was simply living up to his reputation as the Great Lover.

One thing that was worrying the Great Lover, however, was his hair. He feared that he was going bald and was taking a patent remedy which, he thought, was responsible for the stomach cramps he was suffering. His reputation was also taking another public hammering. Eighteen hundred miles away in Chicago, a powder puff dispenser had been installed in the men's room of a dance hall and some witty editorial writer on the *Chicago Tribune* wrote a leader condemning the effeminization of the American male and blaming it all on Rudolph Valentino.

Valentino was in Chicago at the time and was beside himself with rage. He wrote to the *Tribune* , challenging the anonymous leader writer to a boxing match. When there was no response from the *Tribune,* he moved on to New York, where a burly journalist, the *New York Evening Journal*'s boxing correspondent Frank O'Neill, offered to defend the honour of the profession. The offer was accepted and in a makeshift ring on the roof of the Ambassador Hotel, Rudy knocked the big man to the ground.

'That boy has a punch like the kick of a mule,' said O'Neill. 'I'd sure hate to have him sore at me.' Afterwards Valentino was seen celebrating in a Prohibition strip joint that served ginger ale that was a hundred per cent proof with his ex-wife Jean Acker. Asked if they were considering getting married again, they said they were just good friends.

Acker turned up at New York's Polyclinic Hospital, where

Rudy was rushed when it was discovered that his stomach cramps were not caused by his patent baldness remedy but by peritonitis and gastric ulcers. She was not allowed to see him as his condition was grave. He lapsed into a coma and at 12.10 p.m. on Monday, 26 August 1926, with a priest's crucifix pressed to his lips, he died.

All over the world, women broke down at the news. Pola Negri began wailing his name over and over again. In London, an actress name Peggy Scott killed herself in her bedroom surrounded by pictures of Valentino. She had never even met him. A crowd of more than 12,000 people, mainly women, blocked the roads around the funeral parlour in New York where Valentino lay in state. In all more than 100,000 people filed passed the coffin.

Pola Negri arrived by train wearing a mourning outfit which cost $3,000, her press agent said. After viewing the body, she told waiting reporters: 'My love for Valentino was the greatest love of my life. I shall never forget him. I loved him not as one artist loves another, but as a woman loves a man.'

At the funeral Pola Negri looked near to collapse, but she was upstaged by Jean Acker who fainted.

Rudolph Valentino was gone but not forgotten. For years, a woman in black laid red roses on his grave on the anniversary of his death. It was not discovered until 1945 that she was Marion Benda, a former Ziegfeld beauty whom Valentino had met at a party shortly before he died. She later claimed to have been married to him.

3

THE INCOMPARABLE

BARRYMORE

After the death of Valentino, John Barrymore took over the role of Great Lover and was not nearly so self-conscious about it. He lived a life of total dissolution and self-destruction. A legendary sot and womanizer, he did just as he pleased from the beginning of his life to the very end.

'It is a slander to say my troubles come from chasing women,' he once said. 'They begin when I catch them.'

There is, he concluded, only one way to fight a woman: '... with your hat. Grab it and run'. It was advice he took himself, often.

John Barrymore had a lot to live up to. His father, the actor and playwright Maurice Barrymore, was a notorious drinker and womanizer who died of syphilis in 1905. At thirteen, John, already a wayward child, was packed off to a Jesuit school in Washington D.C. When the fathers went through their new pupil's pockets, they found a pair of brass knuckles, a packet of cigarettes and a half-pint flask of whiskey.

At fourteen, he was a chronic drunkard and at fifteen he was inculcated into the mysteries of love by his young stepmother, Mamie Floyd, whom Maurice had married within months of the death of his long-suffering first wife, Georgie. By all accounts Mamie was both passionate and sexually versatile, initiating John into varieties of lovemaking not normally experienced by boys of his age.

One evening in May 1898, one of the schoolmasters spotted a number of boys sneaking out of the dormitory. He followed them to a well-known whore house. The next day Barrymore's father was summoned.

'What were you doing in a place like that, son?' his father asked.

'Nothing,' said John.

'Then what the devil's the matter with you?' he said. 'You're a Barrymore, aren't you?'

At sixteen, he was sent to school in England to stay with his sister Ethel who, at nineteen, had wowed the British stage. At various stages in her life when Ethel was in London, she was rumoured to be engaged to Anthony Hope, Prince Kumar Shri Ranjitsinhji, a famous cricketer, the Duke of Manchester, Winston Churchill and Canatabrigian, future Maharajah of Nawanager. Margot Asquith was moved to say, 'No one has ever done anything like Ethel's done in London.'

Ethel rented a summer cottage for them in the village of Cookham. John enjoyed swimming in the Thames and would sometimes hire a punt. One day, the punt drifted off with John's clothes in it and he had to walk home naked through Cookham past clusters of gaping villagers.

Back in New York, John and Ethel took rooms at Mrs Wilson's, a theatrical boarding house on West 36th Street. Barrymore tried to seduce the other boarders – first Maude Williams, who was ten years older than him and took little interest in men of any age, then Ida Conquest, who was twelve years older than him and treated him like a schoolboy.

He made more progress with Margaret Bird, who was small but perfectly proportioned. He called her his 'pocket Venus', but she left to marry a prominent businessman.

John was nineteen when his father lapsed into idiocy, the final phase of the syphilis that caused his death. From then on, John adopted his father's lifestyle wholesale. He took to the stage as a way of making a living involving the least possible effort. He drank compulsively and displayed a voracious sexual appetite.

He came to blows with the young W.C. Fields over vaude-villian Nora Bayes.

'I fell in love with Mr Fields,' Barrymore recalled, 'and cared no more for Miss Bayes.'

Barrymore was befriended by the architect Stanford White, who was in his fifties at the time. Stanford White's mistress, Evelyn Nesbit, was a sixteen-year-old chorus girl from the hit Broadway show *Florodora*. In her memoirs, she described her own youthful face as oval, her curls copper and her mouth 'very red – a bit full, the lips pouting'. Barrymore first saw her one night when dining at White's apartment – which was famed for its red velvet swing where White persuaded young girls to sit without underwear so he could look up their billowing skirts as they swung back and forth. John could not take his eyes off her. When White was called away to the phone, Barrymore leant forward and whispered: 'Quick! Your address and phone number.'

He scribbled them down on his cuff.

When White left town on a two-week fishing trip, Barrymore turned up at the stage door every night to meet her. One night at dinner, he plucked a rose petal from the table decoration and floated it on the milk she had ordered.

'That is your mouth,' he said.

Later, he recalled: 'She was the most maddening woman, the most utterly distracting woman I have ever known. She was the first woman I ever loved.'

They got drunk and spent the night together. When Evelyn's mother found out, she cried: 'How could you forget your mother, your name, your future? Your reputation is ruined' – conveniently forgetting about her well-publicized affair with White.

Evelyn's mother immediately told White, who locked up his young mistress, depriving her of food and relentlessly cross-questioning her about the affair. Barrymore was cross-examined too. He claimed, as any gentleman would, that their relationship was platonic – but spoilt it all by turning to Evelyn and asking her to marry him.

'What would you live on?' demanded White.

'Love,' said Barrymore.

When White told Evelyn's mother that the young lovers planned to elope, she whisked her daughter off to New Jersey. There Evelyn became the mistress, then the wife, of the psychotic millionaire Harry K. Thaw. When Thaw heard about White's swing, he grew paranoically jealous, took a gun and publicly shot Stanford White dead. Discretion being the better part of valour, Barrymore got out of town until Thaw was safely behind bars.

Eventually, Barrymore was called to testify. The scandal reached new heights when, for a payment of $200,000, Evelyn took the stand and revealed the intimate details of how Stanford White had debauched her in her childhood. Thaw was found not guilty on the grounds of insanity and sent to a State Asylum. Seven years later, after a bizarre escape attempt, he was found to be sane and released.

Meanwhile, Barrymore went on the road with his sister, but he was drinking so heavily that she often had to cover for him on stage when he missed his cue. One night the stage manager found him in his dressing-room, dead drunk and stark naked, and had to go on in his place. When Barrymore awoke, he appeared in the wings, still naked, holding a pair of shoes, demanding to know who would polish them for him and distracting those on stage.

They were in San Francisco in 1906 when the earthquake hit. Barrymore was so drunk that he slept right through it. He emerged from the rubble of his hotel wearing an immaculate, flowered dressing-gown and was pressed into helping clear up the debris by soldiers.

'It took a calamity of nature to get him out of bed and the US Army to make him work,' his uncle said.

John was no slouch when it came to bedding showgirls. He had a fling with Irene Frizzel, the sixteen-year-old ingenue of *Peggy from Paris*, who was married to multimillionaire realtor Felix Isman. Barrymore and others were named as co-respondents in Isman's divorce suit. Isman went on to marry Ziegfeld girl Hazel Allen from the review *Midnight Frolic*, only to discover that she was one of Barrymore's lovers too.

Singer Elsie Janis called Barrymore 'my first love, I hasten to add that he will probably be my last – for once you start loving any of the Barrymores you find that, like jungle fever or lumbago, it comes back on you every now and then'. But Elsie's eagle-eyed mother seems to have prevented the affair from progressing beyond the two of them reading aloud from a deluxe edition of *The Ancient Mariner* that Barrymore had bought for her, while her mother sat in an adjoining room with the door ajar.

A more fulfilling lover was Lotta Faust. A former cashier from the Brooklyn department store Abraham & Straus, she scandalized theatre audiences by dancing naked under a diaphanous veil. Off-stage she was famous for her backless dresses.

Then came Bonnie Maginn, the blonde showgirl famed for her curves at the Weber and Fields Music Hall. She went on to marry money, while Barrymore turned his attention to the showgirl and model Vivien Blackburn who, as a fencing ace, became queen of the cigarette cards.

At a coming-out party, the twenty-seven-year-old Barrymore met seventeen-year-old heiress Katherine Harris. She was lithe, doe-like, with honey-coloured hair and a slight lisp. Barrymore was captivated.

Katherine's estranged father was aghast. A corporate lawyer, he did not want his daughter running around with a penniless actor – much less one who had been involved in the scandal surrounding Evelyn Nesbit. Under threat of withholding her alimony, he forced his ex-wife to take Katherine to Paris and enrol her in a convent.

Mrs Harris was not happy about this. She had been stage-struck since her youth and rather liked the handsome young actor. So did her mother, the widow of a New York State Supreme Court judge, who wrote to Katherine, saying: 'Jack looks as if he wants a woman's care. I saw him in the street. He is so handsome. If I were a young woman, I would be crazy about him myself.'

With the support of her family, Katherine returned from

Paris to the arms of the amorous Barrymore. She was now of age, so her father could not prevent their marriage, which took place at St Xavier's in New York on 1 September 1910. Her father did not attend and her mother had to sue to recover her alimony.

There was no honeymoon. Within a few days of their wedding breakfast at Delmonico's, Barrymore went off on tour with *The Fortune Hunter*. The play was so successful that he was away, except for flying visits, for almost a year. Katherine was determined this would not happen again and insisted on being given a part in subsequent productions.

In 1913, Adolph Zukor of Famous Players persuaded John Barrymore to follow brother Lionel and sister Ethel into the movies with a four-reeler called *An American Citizen*. Zukor and the critics quickly realized that John was a natural screen actor. That suited Barrymore, too. The money was good and there was a lot less work involved in a movie than in a long Broadway run. He made ten films for Famous Players. Zukor found him easy to work with, except for his propensity to go off on a drinking spree in the middle of the picture. On one occasion, while filming *The Lost Bridegroom*, director James Kirkwood ran him to earth in the bar of the Biltmoor Hotel. Barrymore promised to return to the set when they'd had one for the road. He ordered absinthes – doubles. They got back to the studio three days later.

Barrymore's drinking and his unconventional lifestyle made married life turbulent. His rows with Katherine were so tempestuous that residents of their apartment block in Gramercy Park got up a petition. It was never sent because the Barrymores suddenly turned over a new leaf and plunged into a period of connubial bliss. It did not last long. One night, Katherine escaped from their apartment in her night clothes after he threatened her with a sword. Discovering she had gone, he beat on the door of every other apartment in the building, demanding the return of his wife. The policeman who turned up to protect her began making amorous advances to her and she sought sanctuary with James Flagg, an artist friend of Barrymore's who frequently used her as a model.

Barrymore, who was incredibly jealous of any man who even looked at Katherine, had suspected for some time that something was going on between his wife and Flagg. He confronted the artist.

'You've been living with my wife,' said Barrymore.

'No, you've been living with her,' Flagg replied. 'I've been sleeping with her.'

Knowledge of his wife's infidelity made him drink more. At the time he was appearing in a melodrama called *The Yellow Ticket*, set in Tsarist Russia. Barrymore staggered on to the stage one night, drunkenly commiserated with the heroine about the difficulties of travelling around Imperial Russia and handed her a bunch of New York subway tickets. The curtain fell. When it rose again, an understudy had taken his place.

Barrymore's habit of staying out drinking until five in the morning caused more rows. Katherine divorced him in 1917 and won $350 a month maintenance. Alimony, said Barrymore, was 'the most exorbitant of stud fees, and the worst feature of it is that you pay it retroactively'.

The couple remained friends throughout her two subsequent marriages and Barrymore was at her bedside when Katherine died of pneumonia at the age of thirty-six.

In 1917, Barrymore met Blanche Thomas, who wrote poetry under the name of Michael Strange. They worked together on Tolstoy's gloomy tragedy *The Living Corpse*. World War I was in full swing and Blanche's husband was away at the front so they had to be discreet.

When Lieutenant Thomas returned in 1918, his wife told him of her feelings for Barrymore. Thomas assumed it was a passing affair and forgave her. In return, Blanche promised not to see Barrymore for six months while her husband took her off to Europe for a second honeymoon. If her feelings remained the same after that, Thomas said, he would stand aside.

While Blanche was away, Barrymore played in *The Jest* with his brother Lionel. John wore green tights copied from a portrait of a twelfth-century falconer in the Metropolitan

Museum, which 'left no faint fragment of his anatomy to the imagination'. His entrance was greeted with gasps and sighs. Hedda Hopper, later a Hollywood gossip columnist, was impressed.

'I am able to understand those fans who worship film stars,' she wrote. 'To the day he died, I was that way about John Barrymore.'

Barrymore's press agent Ruth Hale, wife of Heywood Broun and a founder of the feminist Lucy Stone League, was less impressed. One hot June afternoon, Barrymore refused to get dressed and sat around in his dressing-room naked. She marched in and said: 'Now listen, Jack, I see big Heywood and little Heywood like that everyday. It's no treat for me. You stop being foolish and get into your costume.'

While Blanche was away, Barrymore did play. He met Margaret Case, the daughter of the owner of the Algonquin, outside the hotel waiting for a taxi.

'You're in love, aren't you?' he said.

When she admitted she was, he became grandiloquent.

'I knew it,' he said. 'That lovely lost look, that exquisite, forlorn look, that roseleaf cheek that is not quite a blush, that brightness in the eyes that is not yet a tear. Who is the man?'

She told him that it was the English movie actor Percy Marmont.

'That ham! We must talk this over,' said Barrymore, helping her into a cab. 'Driver, take us to Tottenham Court Road, Tibet.'

Instead they drove around Central Park, while Barrymore begged her to put the Englishman out of her mind. Margaret did not have the heart to tell him that she had a schoolgirl crush on the actor, whom she had never even met.

Barrymore was delighted to discover that the teenaged Tallulah Bankhead had a crush on him and invited her to his dressing-room with the object of taking her virginity.

'He started making animal noises,' she said. 'Freely translated these indicated his desire to shred the seventh commandment. He rose and took my hands in his and started to lead me to a convenient couch. With such dignity as I could simulate under these fiery circumstances, I declined.'

Nevertheless, she turned up for thirteen be-tighted performances of *The Jest*.

'For the good part of a season I wore myself out trying to impress Tallulah,' he said. 'I felt like a bullfighter who makes his kill and is then publicly given the boot. But in all truth, I must report that our relationship was loathsomely platonic.'

He never knew that she kept his picture beside her bed.

Meanwhile, Barrymore was exchanging cloyingly poetic love letters with Blanche – they addressed each other as 'tiny' and 'fig'. For the sake of her two sons, her family begged her not to divorce – especially not for the likes of a drunken reprobate like John Barrymore. He swore to give up drinking, but was regularly seen staggering about the streets of New York. When she challenged him about it, he cabled:

OH MY BABY WHAT IN THE NAME OF GOD COULD MAKE YOU SO COLD TO ME I HAVE BEEN SO WRETCHED I HAVE WRITTEN YOU LETTERS THAT WERE LIKE THE LAST WAIL OF THE DAMNED IN THE VALLEY OF THE DEAD AND TORN THEM UP OH MY BELOVED MY DEAREST BELOVED I HAVE WAITED AND LONGED AND PRAYED AND CURSED FOR YOU ALL MY LIFE LIKE A MAROONED SOUL ON A DESERTED COAST PLEASE FOR THE LOVE OF HEAVEN BELIEVE THAT YOUR FUTURE IS STREWN WITH LITTLE PIECES OF MY HEART FOR YOUR FEET TO WALK ON SO THEY NEED NOT TOUCH THE EARTH I LOVE YOU I LOVE YOU I LOVE YOU

She divorced her husband and when she told her friend, the lesbian socialite Mercedes de Acosta about her plans to marry Barrymore, de Acosta said: 'I wonder who will kill the other first. You are both such egomaniacs that you will some day start a fight to the finish and one of you will do the other in.'

Michael Strange published a book of love poems which rather gave away the sex of the author.

O the fragrant breathing of this night
Savouring my breast –
And becoming the caress of my bridegroom's
Ivory and scented fingers

There was lots of 'pressing upon your evasive – flippant – tragic mouth', 'strange illicit dialogues', 'words like the hiss of approaching flood, across a droughted place' and that sort of thing. The frontispiece of these collected works shows a nude woman soaring heavenward above a gaggle of earthbound grotesques.

Barrymore, it seems, could not resist this 'eternal union,' as Michael Strange put it, and married Blanche in a private suite at the Ritz-Carlton. Lionel was best man; Ethel a witness. The bride was seven months pregnant.

For the first year of marriage, Barrymore eschewed the stage to devote himself to his wife and their daughter, while Blanche took the opportunity to crank out more poetry. Then she got an idea for a play, or rather, she stole the idea for a play from Victor Hugo. Despite Barrymore's efforts to deliver such lines as 'I am kissing your little white feet; it is like brushing sprays of silken flowers' with the appropriate passion, the production was savaged by the critics.

The couple began to fall out, largely over his drinking. Once she smashed a case of his champagne, so he downed a bottle of her perfume. Their rows were described as 'a tennis game in hell where nobody misses the ball'. One night after a blazing row he stormed from the house, or so she thought. She phoned Mercedes de Acosta and invited her over. Hours later, investigating a scuffling sound they heard coming from the basement, they found Barrymore barely conscious, surrounded by empty gin bottles.

Another cause of rows was sexual jealousy. Women threw themselves at Barrymore; men at Blanche. On holiday in Italy, Blanche deliberately encouraged a young man to stir up Barrymore's jealousy. As Mercedes de Acosta predicted, they began to fight. On one occasion, he tried to stab her with a knife. When Mercedes interposed, Barrymore flung a kerosene lamp at her.

There were suicide attempts, mock and real, but, occasionally there was blissful harmony between them and they would be seen out in matching unisex outfits of black velvet.

Despite his phenomenal drinking, Barrymore had a triumph on the screen with *Sherlock Holmes* and wowed Broadway with his *Hamlet*, who he managed to make sexy.

'I want him to be so male that when I come out on the stage they can hear my balls clank,' Barrymore said. In his closet scene with Gertrude, he openly caressed her cheeks, lay his head in her lap and touched her breasts and thighs. The critics acclaimed him as the greatest Hamlet of his generation. Later, he gave the actress who played Gertrude – Bohemian blonde Blanche Yurka who was seven years younger than her stage son – a portrait, inscribed: 'To my mother from her wildly incestuous son.'

Blanche missed the performance. She was no longer interested in his career. She went to Paris during his run on Broadway and cabled him, urging him to join her. Barrymore cabled back accusing her of numerous infidelities. Blanche protested her innocence but realized that, if it was impossible for her husband to trust her, their marriage was over. Nevertheless, they stayed together for a while yet.

Brother Lionel's marriage was also over. He had met up with John's old paramour Irene Frizzel, who now, after a couple of intervening marriages, was Irene Fenwick. Lionel's wife Doris caught them together.

'I have been married to Lionel Barrymore for seventeen years,' said Doris, 'but I would have given several years of my life if I could truthfully say that in all those seventeen years he looked at me just once in the same manner as I saw him look at that woman.'

A divorce was in the air and Lionel planned to marry Irene.

'Don't do it,' begged John. 'She's nothing but a whore.'

But Lionel did not listen. The divorce went through. He married Irene and, for years, the brothers barely spoke to one another.

John Barrymore headed for Hollywood, where Warner Bros were already billing him as 'the world's greatest actor'. On the set of *Beau Brummel,* he met seventeen-year-old Mary Astor.

'My awe for the great man made me confused and awkward,' she recalled. 'Mr Barrymore broke through my shyness by talking about everything under the sun but the picture.'

During a test shot, he whispered in her ear: 'You're so goddamned beautiful, you make me feel faint.'

This made her laugh.

'Gradually, skilfully, he made me feel that I was his contemporary as an actor and as a person.'

Then she told him her age.

'It seems so long since I was seventeen,' he said wistfully. 'I'm forty now.'

Actually, he was forty-one.

'Forty's not so old,' she said. And he fell in love with her there and then.

The romance had to flourish under the eyes of her parents, who were on the lot as her chaperones. Fortunately, there were plenty of intense love scenes in the movie where they could get to grips with each other. Between scenes, a prop man would put their chairs side by side so they could sit and exchange intimacies.

He turned all his charm on her parents, befriending her father and flirting with her mother. They were flattered by the attention the great Barrymore bestowed on their daughter. He took time to read Shakespeare with her and school her in acting. But still they chaperoned her everywhere.

He tried to drive them off the set by spicing the dialogue with four-letter words. This did not matter as the film was silent, but when it came out a number of deaf people who could lip read were offended. However, her parents weathered this barrage of bad language so they were on hand to cover their innocent child's ears.

Eventually Barrymore told her parents that, if she was really to benefit from his tuition, they had to be alone.

'She's too self-conscious,' he said. 'She's afraid of what you are thinking, instead of listening to me.'

When her parents gave each other a sideways look, he read their thoughts.

'Don't be ridiculous,' he said. 'She's just a child.'

But she was hardly that and more than eager for the amorous attention of a famous actor.

'He gave me love, affection, humour and, above all, beauty,' she said. 'Not for a moment was I concerned with the violation of moral laws or the breaking of commandments.'

At the end of filming, Barrymore had to return to New York, where his *Hamlet* was reopening. Mary had to go to New York, too, for her next film. While she waited for the studio to call, her parents would drop her at Barrymore's hotel at noon and collect her at six, every afternoon except matinées. The idea was that they spend the time rehearsing Shakespeare together. If they did, she rehearsed in a pair of burgundy satin lounge pyjamas with the monograph M.A.B. on the breast pocket that he had made for her.

The longer this arrangement continued, the more Mary was puzzled. Could her parents really believe that they were inno-cently rehearsing all that time? Nevertheless, they seemed sat-isfied with what she reported back to them.

'I think they're satisfied with what you don't report back to them,' said Barrymore.

Mary protested that her parents were much too straitlaced to imagine what they were really up to, but Barrymore had checked them out. Through shrewd cross-questioning, he had ascertained that, like many stage parents before them, they turned a blind eye to what was going on to stay in control of the situation.

'It's their way of letting you out on a rope, but keeping you feeling guilty, so they've got you,' he said.

'I just don't believe it,' said Mary. 'They're very straitlaced, truly.'

'My ass.'

Barrymore soon realized the danger of his position. When he went on tour with *Hamlet*, he wept, begging Mary to be faithful to him.

'You have become wise at deception,' he said. 'Don't use it against me. I need your fidelity. I need to know that there is someone in the world who can be faithful.'

That one person, of course, could not be Barrymore.

When the tour arrived in London, Barrymore caught up with Blanche once more. Even though they were married in name only, he was still consumed with jealousy. He fumed if he saw her dancing with another man and demanded to know who her lovers were. She taunted him with the 'fast' set she moved in, which included Oswald Mosley, William Randolph Hearst's wife Millicent, Vita Sackville-West and author George Moore, whose sexual attitudes, Blanche said, were 'very Latin, extremely un-English ... he asked me if I would mind undressing'.

Barrymore and Blanche decided on a formal separation and came up with an amicable 'no-blame' agreement under which Barrymore gave Blanche their house in White Plains and paid $18,000 a year for the support of her and their daughter Diana.

Barrymore returned to California and his love Mary Astor. They had been separated for five months. Jack Warner wanted Barrymore to play Captain Ahab in a splendidly mangled version of *Moby Dick* called *The Sea Beast*. For the movie, love interest had to be written in. Barrymore repeatedly rejected the women Warner picked to play the female lead. He wanted Mary Astor in the part. One morning he was in Warner's office pleading with him to postpone the production until Mary had completed her commitment on another movie shooting in New York, when he saw the nineteen-year-old blonde Dolores Costello coming in the studio gates. She and her sister Helene had been spotted by a Warner Bros scout touring in George White's *Scandals of 1924*.

'I fell in love with her instantly,' Barrymore said. 'This time I knew it was right.'

Dolores was, he said, 'the most preposterously wonderful creature in all the world'. He insisted that she play the female lead opposite his Ahab, and forgot all about Mary Astor.

Dolores mother, May, who acted as her chaperone, was delighted by Barrymore's attentions to her daughter – Shrimp,

Winkie or Small Egg as he called her. Her father Maurice Costello, a hard-drinking actor in the Barrymore mould, was not.

'John Barrymore is no man for Dolores,' he said. 'In the first place, he is old enough to be her father. He's of my generation.'

Mrs Costello pointed out that at forty-three, Barrymore was a mere stripling, the same age as herself.

'In the second place, he's a married man,' complained Maurice.

Barrymore had an answer for that.

'It is ridiculous to be prejudiced against a man because he is married,' he said in his own defence. 'The divorce courts were made to take care of trivialities like that. As for the difference in our ages – an actor is no older than he admits.'

Maurice Costello's third objection was more telling.

'I am something like Barrymore myself,' he said. 'That is why I don't want him for the husband of my baby.'

The confrontation came in the Costello home. Maurice called Barrymore a blackguard to his face. May slapped her husband across the face and he marched out of the house. The dispute ended in the divorce courts.

Barrymore's love for Dolores quickly paid dividends. *The Sea Beast* was a huge success, largely because of the intense love scene he played with his young leading lady. The director, Millard Webb, had been unable to decide between the numerous takes he had shot of the scene and simply spliced them all together. Blanche spotted it immediately.

'That's not acting,' she said. 'He's in love with the girl.'

Mary Astor grew suspicious, too.

'I hear Miss Costello is really lovely,' she said one day on the phone.

'She's divine,' said Barrymore, catching himself. 'But don't worry, my Goopher, she's just a chicken.'

When Mary returned to the coast, they took up where they had left off, but she soon found that Barrymore was breaking their dates because 'something had come up' or he had been mysteriously 'detained'.

Fortunately, Blanche was having some money problems, which Barrymore was helping her with, and was in no hurry to get a divorce. If he had been free to marry Dolores, the whole house of cards would have come tumbling down.

In his next role, Barrymore was type cast – he played *Don Juan*. According to the press handout, he planted 191 kisses on the likes of Myrna Loy, June Marlowe, Estelle Taylor and Phyllis Haver. Mary Astor played Adriana della Varnese, with whom Barrymore rides off into the sunset. He wanted Dolores for the part, but the studio already had Mary under contract. Even so, he managed to put a lot of conviction into his on-screen lovemaking.

However, during the filming of *Don Juan*, Mary said, 'all my hopes and dreams died, and I wanted to die with them'. She caught Barrymore and Dolores sitting together, just like he had sat with her during the filming of *Beau Brummel*.

'Dear Goopher, I'm just a son of a bitch,' wrote Barrymore, by way of explanation.

At first, Mary blamed her parents for not giving her freedom. Then she blamed his drinking. Then she decided he was probably right – he was a son of a bitch.

After *Don Juan*, Barrymore planned a three-week sailing trip with Dolores, but the thought of the two of them together in a cramped cabin, heaving on the Pacific swell, was too much even for Mrs Costello. Barrymore went alone, but filled the log with thoughts of love.

When he returned to play the lead in *When a Man Loves*, he insisted that Dolores play opposite him. They moved into an apartment together, ostensibly to be near to the set.

Despite Barrymore's heavy drinking, his pub crawls and his legendary drinking contests, Dolores stuck by him and began insisting on marriage. He bowed to the inevitable, divorced Blanche and did the decent thing. She accepted his proposal – provided he went on the wagon for six months first. He broke his pledge only once. After five months of abstention, he broke open a bottle of champagne with Blanche to celebrate her engagement to Harrison Tweed, a prominent society attorney.

Barrymore married Dolores Costello on 14 November 1928. When the priest said: 'For richer, for poorer,' Barrymore said: 'For richer, for richer.' The bride's father did not attend. Even though Barrymore supported him when he found himself in penury, Maurice Costello harboured murderous thoughts about his son-in-law. But he decided that Barrymore was not worth killing; besides, the house Barrymore had bought him on Tower Road was so much nicer than San Quentin.

Rumours that the marriage was bigamous surfaced in the papers. There was talk of a 'mysterious woman, heavily veiled and expensively dressed' stalking the marriage-licence bureau in Los Angeles. The mystery was cleared up when Blanche returned from vacation. Under New York law, the only grounds for divorce are adultery, so she had quietly filed for divorce upstate under another name. The documents detailing Barrymore's trespasses were sealed.

Shooting schedules meant that the newlyweds had to delay their honeymoon until the following January when they took off for three lazy months cruising the Pacific. They were very much in love.

Back in Hollywood, the usual machinations went into operation. The studio let it slip that Barrymore was having an affair with his leading lady in *The Tempest*, German actress Camilla Horn, even though she was, in fact, the mistress of studio boss Joe Schenck.

By July 1929, Dolores was pregnant with their first child. Barrymore grew jealous. One evening he snatched her away from a party when he saw her dancing with David O. Selznick, took her home and lectured her till dawn. A week before the baby was due, Barrymore threw the obstetrician, Dr John Vruwink, out of the house.

'If I ever find you in this house again, I'll break your jaw, you son of a bitch,' Barrymore yelled after him.

By way of explanation, he told Dolores: 'I don't want him around here because he's stuck on you and I don't want anybody stuck on you touching you, especially the way that guy has to touch you.'

Meanwhile, Barrymore was playing searing love scenes with Garbo in *Grand Hotel*. During the filming of *Bill of Divorcement*, Katharine Hepburn's first film, he invited the young actress to his dressing-room. According to one account, he threw off his dressing-gown and approached her stark naked. When she shied away, he said: 'What's the matter?'

'My father doesn't want me to have any babies,' said the virginal Kate.

But the veteran actor was insistent.

'Any young girl should be thrilled to make love to the great John Barrymore,' he said.

Errol Flynn's version was that, on the first day of shooting when Hepburn turned up at his dressing-room, Barrymore said: 'A pleasure to meet you, my dear, I trust we are going to have a very pleasant association. Now, would you like to get undressed.'

'What!' said Katharine, shocked.

'Very well, my dear, quite all right,' said the pliant Barrymore. 'Let's sit down and just talk over the part.'

Slowly his alcoholism and his pathological jealousy ate away at his marriage. For months on end, he would neither see nor speak to his wife. A single look or a smile would convince him that she was secretly encouraging another man. He had iron bars put on the windows of their home, so that she could not sneak anybody in. There would be drunken rages and, sometimes, he would hit her.

In a last ditch attempt to save their marriage, Dolores took him on another cruise, first scouring the yacht for any hint of alcohol. Again Barrymore drank his wife's perfume. He downed mouthwash, spirits of ammonia and, eventually, resorted to siphoning alcohol out of the boat's cooling system.

By the time they got back to shore, Barrymore had convinced himself that his wife aimed to have him committed. He packed secretly and phoned Dolores from the airport, telling her that he had received an irresistible offer from a radio network in New York. Instead, he travelled to England. There he signed a $60,000 contract with Alexander Korda at London Films to film *Hamlet*. By now, he was well into middle age and bulged out of his tights in all the wrong places; and his alcoholism made it impossible for him to remember the soliloquies.

So he headed on to India, where he sought healing and spiritual enlightenment with a guru – and found nirvana of a more earthly kind.

He arrived in Calcutta, where he intended to seek spiritual communion with a young saint and learn the true secrets of Heaven. Instead, on his first morning there, he was picked up by a pimp and taken to an amazing whore house. He called it a pelvic palace and went on to describe it in detail at Hollywood gatherings, so that no one would think he was stupid for missing his chance of spiritual enlightenment.

The brothel had a huge central room with a white and pink marble floor, covered with oceans of pillows. 'You have never seen such pillows,' Barrymore would say. 'They cooed at your buttocks.' The roof was supported by silver pillars, and clouds of coloured silk hung down from the ceiling, looking, Barrymore said, like a heaven of udders.

Incense pots belched aromas 'capable of reviving the most dormant of occidental phalluses.' And gentle music wafted through the room that 'went directly to the scrotum and cuddled there.'

Then a gong sounded and beautiful women appeared in twos and threes. Barrymore said that they moved slowly and their bellies undulated like snakes. On their fingers and toes hung little bells, so they made beautiful music when they moved and when they made love. The girls sang and danced for him, and draped themselves around him 'in artistic clutters until I felt like a public chandelier.'

There were numerous girls, mainly Eurasian, with a madam who, Barrymore said, looked like Moll Flanders. He gave her $1,200 to close the doors of the baglio so that he could continue his search for nirvana undisturbed.

Barrymore stayed there there for four exhausting weeks. He never left the pillows except to use a small commode which was within staggering distance. The girls even brought him his food there.

'I would be happy to describe the dainties that were supplied to me,' he would tell his audience, 'but there are ladies present.'

So Barrymore never got to meet his saint. He only met dancing girls, all of whom were devout students of the *Kama Sutra*, he said.

He returned to America, fully restored.

He went to visit Diana, his daughter from his second marriage who was then at school in Maryland. She turned up at the Baltimore restaurant where he was to meet her with a schoolfriend called Pamela Gardiner. After dinner, they went to the movies.

'Daddy sat with his arm around Pamela,' recalled Diana, 'and, as I watched, kissed her. I thought, horrified: "Why, they're smooching! How disgraceful of Pamela, even if she is nearly eighteen!"'

After his sojourn in India, it was quite clear to Dolores that their marriage was over. As part of a formal separation, Barrymore made a generous settlement on the children of the marriage.

In New York, a doctor told Barrymore that he would have to give up wine, women and song.

'Do I have to do it all at once?' Barrymore asked.

No, he was told, he could taper off.

'In that case,' said Barrymore. 'I shall quit singing.'

In March 1935, Barrymore's excessive boozing put him in hospital. A nineteen-year-old sophomore at Hunter College, called Elaine Jacobs, wrote to him. She was stage-struck and, since as a fourteen-year-old she had seen him in *Svengali*, Barrymore had been her idol.

Her letter said that, as part of her journalism course, she had been assigned to write a piece about him for the college newspaper. This was untrue, but Barrymore invited her to come and interview him in his hospital bed.

The nurse said she could stay for only three minutes. Barrymore kept her there for three hours. When finally she was forced to leave, he kissed her on the cheek and promised to phone her at nine o'clock that evening.

When she got home, her mother was almost as excited as she was.

She had seen Barrymore in his famous tights in *The Jest*.

'He was a god,' she said.

'He still is,' said Elaine.

Barrymore called at nine o'clock on the dot. Elaine's mother answered the phone.

'What an enchanting daughter you have,' he said. And he told her how much he looked forward to meeting her in person.

The next day, Elaine visited the hospital again. This time he kissed her on the mouth. The following day, she brought her mother and Barrymore told her that he was in love with her daughter.

Elaine Jacobs began calling herself Elaine Barrie, to get 'as near to Barrymore as I dare'. Her mother took the surname Barrie, too. It is not recorded what her father thought of this.

Elaine visited Barrymore every day for the rest of his convalescence. He wooed her with sweet words and drama lessons. When he was fit, he had arranged to go on a cruise with his daughter Diana and her stepfather Harry Tweed, of whom Barrymore had become fond.

Romantic telegrams flew back and forth between Miami and New York. Elaine signed herself Ariel; he Caliban. The Shakespearean metaphors flowed so thick that Elaine was prompted to say: 'I grew sick of hearing that name. I wish Shakespeare had never written that damn play.'

After two weeks, Barrymore returned to New York and began showering mother and daughter with gifts. He squandered $60,000 on entertaining them and they were seen in all the best places.

'Elaine was a nice girl who would go nowhere without her mother,' he said. 'But her mother would go anywhere.'

He even invited Elaine's journalism teacher for lunch at Tavern-on-the-Green in Central Park.

'I can't tell you how much I have enjoyed your work,' she said.

'Please tell me,' he said.

Then, suddenly, Barrymore disappeared. Elaine and her mother were frantic.

Two days later, late at night, Barrymore turned up at the Jacobs' tiny one-bedroomed apartment on Riverside Drive and 86th Street. He was drunk.

'Until then,' said Elaine, 'I hadn't the slightest suspicion that John had a drinking problem.'

He also had the flu. Elaine gave up her daybed in the living-room for him and slept on a cot in the kitchen; and she dropped out of college to look after him.

Barrymore's presence in the Jacobs' flat was the talk of the neighbourhood and Barrymore tried to live up to his reputation. He appeared one Sunday morning in a local Jewish delicatessen on Amsterdam Avenue, monstrously hungover, demanding to know if you had to be circumcised before you could buy pickled herring. When one of Elaine's schoolfriends, Iris Segal, stared at Barrymore in disbelief, he unzipped his fly ... and she fled.

Elaine was ambitious and told a journalist from the New York *Daily Mirror* that Barrymore was staying in the family's apartment. When the story took off, her mother kept the papers fed with juicy titbits.

When Barrymore was asked to perform a scene from *Twentieth Century* on the radio, he agreed, provided Elaine could read the Carole Lombard part. Then the two lovebirds went on a cruise to Havana and, naturally, mother came along. The trip was little short of a disaster.

Shortly before they sailed out of Miami harbour, Barrymore received a cable telling him that Dolores was filing for divorce 'charging habitual intemperance and extreme cruelty'.

In Havana, Barrymore became pathologically jealous over the attentions the Cuban menfolk who flocked to their yacht paid to Elaine. When he suspected that a Cuban nobleman was about to ask her out, he tried to heave the man overboard and cursed Elaine as a 'common little tart'. Once he slapped her but was so contrite that he asked her to marry him, and when she said yes he bought her an $1,800 diamond engagement ring. She neglected to declare this on their return to the US, explaining that, as Barrymore was not yet divorced, it would not have looked good. It cost him another $3,200 in import duties.

In an attempt to deny Dolores any fresh grounds for divorce, Elaine signed an affidavit saying that their relationship was strictly platonic based on mutual 'professional and artistic' interests. But according to her autobiography, *All My Sins Remembered*, Barrymore had sex with her in their flat while her parents were out. Not that this was a sordid seduction: 'John was covering me with kisses ... Trembling in my awareness of sin, I was utterly incapable of sweet abandon, his tenderness was extraordinary and my fears melted. I might have been a shivering bird, captive in his hand, warmed, safe – still eager for release.'

She called him 'the gentlest man ever to love a woman'. He called her 'my dove, my undefiled one' and 'O daughter of Jerusalem'. She said: 'His lips and hands were like the sun and breeze; his voice was an echo of a dream, the collective dream of maidenhood.'

Her parents must have been out for quite some time.

For his part, Barrymore seems to have been inordinately fond of her feet.

'I felt his sweet breath at my ankle ..."How beautiful are thy feet without shoes, O Prince's daughter, the work of the hands of a cunning workman ..."' she wrote. Otherwise, she was 'as fair as the moon, clear as the sun and as terrible as an army with banners ...'

On the other hand, she was quite complimentary about him.

'There were those who thought of John as a tired, jaded old man,' she wrote. "But with me, he was one and twenty.'

So maybe her parents needn't have been that long.

'I can still hear him whispering, "My Rose ... my Rose of Sharon,"' she recalled thirty years later.

After some months of living in her parents' apartment, they decided it was time to get a place of their own. Shopping for furniture at W & J Sloane on 5th Avenue, they went, naturally, to choose a bed. Elaine suggested he try it for comfort. When he lay down on it, she lay down beside him. At that moment, press photographers appeared from all over the store. Barrymore cursed them, and cursed at her. The next day, the cosy little bedroom scene was all over the newspapers.

Barrymore began to suspect that Elaine was using him. After a violent row, he stormed out of the Jacobs' apartment, taking Elaine's diamond ring with him. Elaine immediately employed a lawyer to demand its return. She was, after all, his fiancée. Barrymore went into hiding in Connecticut in the house of one of his business advisors, Frank Aranow.

Aranow was amazed by the Barrymore lifestyle: 'He would sleep rather late, but when he got up in the morning he had to have a glass of gin. He said he couldn't possibly open his eyes until he had that gin.'

Detectives were searching for Barrymore, so they could not go out. But one evening, the Aranows made the mistake of taking Barrymore to a party given by a very respectable New York stockbroker. Among the guests were the local minister and his attractive young daughter. Barrymore, naturally, got stuck into the drinks.

'The conversation ultimately led to love and the making of love,' Aranow recalled. 'After John had had several drinks, he went into a very minute and detailed description of how he made love; how he first undressed the female; then how he prepared her for the act of love by exposing her genitals and using his hands in order to make the female sensuous and anxious. By that time, most of the guests were running out of the room with screams of laughter and apprehension as to how far he would go. But John did not stop at anything ... Ultimately, the host brought out a bottle of champagne and thus we were able to inveigle John away from the minister and his pretty daughter.'

The Aranows left the stockbroker's house wiser and more humiliated than they had come. They did not take Barrymore out again.

Tiring of his houseguest, Aranow managed to cook up a deal with Elaine's lawyer – $5,000 would be put in trust for Elaine, provided that she left Barrymore alone and did not talk to the newspapers. He would also return the ring, provided she acknowledged that it was a simple gift not a symbol of their betrothal, and he would pay her lawyer's bill. She accepted graciously.

The newspapers were reluctant to leave the story at that. The New York *Daily News* got wind of the fact that Barrymore was on his way back to Hollywood and would be changing trains in Chicago. They hired a plane and flew Elaine there. With a reporter from the Chicago *Herald Examiner*, she boarded the westbound train. The reporter found out the number of Barrymore's stateroom and Elaine knocked gingerly on the door.

'John, this is your Ariel,' she said. 'I love you, John.'

The door was opened by a large porter.

'I love you too, Honey,' he said. 'But I am not the John you want.'

Barrymore had given her the slip. It made headlines across the nation.

Elaine got off the train at Kansas City and made a tearful appeal on the radio for John to return to her. She said she knew he needed her, more than ever. She would nurse him back to health and save him from those who would destroy him.

'Dear John, don't think I have deserted you,' she told the ether. 'I am here in Kansas City, awaiting your call. We have each other. That is all that matters.'

The phone stayed silent.

Nevertheless, when Elaine Barrie got back to New York she was a star. Pretty soon she was appearing in a farce aptly named *Katy Did, So What?* to rapturous reviews.

On 9 October 1935, Barrymore's divorce from Dolores became final. She went on to marry her obstetrician, Dr Vruwink, so maybe Barrymore was not so paranoid after all.

Barrymore immediately wired Elaine: 'DEAR DEAR LOVELY ROSE OF SHARON HOLD ON TO YOUR END OF THE RAINBOW GOOD-NIGHT MY LOVE CALIBAN.'

Elaine quit *Katy Did, So What?* and headed west with her mother, but when she arrived in Hollywood, Barrymore would not see her. He was going to a party that night. Elaine tried to crash it. The door was slammed in her face. Hollywood closed ranks against her.

The divorce from Dolores had left Barrymore penniless and he had not made a movie for eighteen months. Irving Thalberg cast him as Mercutio in MGM's *Romeo and Juliet*, with Leslie Howard and Norma Shearer in the title roles. For the duration of the shoot, Barrymore was housed in an institution for alcoholics called Kelley's Rest Home and guarded by Thalberg's men. Friends still managed to smuggle booze into him by tying bottles of gin to the end of a bedsheet that he lowered down from his window.

Elaine managed to get to him, too. She persuaded him that his penury was caused, not by his own mismanagement, but by his financial advisors who were stealing from him. Taken in, he gave her power of attorney over his affairs. With his wallet in her pocket, Elaine began working on him to use his influence to further her career and he got her bit parts.

Soon he was hooked again and paranoically jealous. When the studio sent her to dance classes, he insisted that she was taught by a gay man. Prop men were not allowed to adjust her costume, Barrymore had to do it. When she was wearing a low-cut dress in a restaurant one night, and the waiter bent over to take her order, Barrymore grabbed the menu and waved the man away. She could not even watch the entertainer in a night-club without Barrymore throwing a tantrum. Up to a point, Elaine was sympathetic.

'When packs of women were ready to fall on their backs for him, many of them married to important directors,' she said, 'how could he believe in such a thing as fidelity.'

But Barrymore outdid himself at Elaine's twentieth birthday party. He turned up monumentally drunk, slapped her face and ripped her dress. Then, over dinner, delivered the following memorable speech: 'The world has certainly changed. Tarts were never countenanced at a gentleman's table. Amongst such a lofty congregation, can you imagine anything more disgusting? These whores who are never seen in public without their lady mothers.'

Elaine and her mother fled. They had barely reached home in New York when the phone rang. It was Barrymore begging forgiveness. Elaine would not even speak to him. He kept on calling but she was resolute.

A few days later, Thalberg called. Elaine was delighted to speak to him. *Romeo and Juliet* was in trouble. Barrymore would not work. She had to come and help.

This was Elaine's big break. She pointed out that her help was worth, at the very least, an MGM contract. Thalberg promised to draw one up and, before they had even unpacked, Elaine and her mother were heading back to California.

They found Barrymore locked in a tiny cell in Kelley's Rest Home. He immediately leapt on her and tried to have sex with her. She found the surroundings less than conducive and, once again, fled.

Despite her MGM contract, she got no work out of the studio so she went back to New York. The newspapers avidly followed these to-ings and fro-ings. A minor celebrity, she got a spot on the radio reading poetry and walk-on parts in theatres in the outer reaches of Brooklyn and Queens.

But Barrymore was still hooked. He bombarded her with telegrams telling her: 'THE LOVE I FEEL DOESN'T COME OFTEN TO ANYONE' and 'I AM KISSING YOUR LOVELY EYES'. He lured her back to the coast with the promise of a part that never materialized; and he asked her again to marry him.

When friends asked him why he had done that, he said simply: 'It fits.'

He told reporters: 'That filly will make a racehorse out of me again.'

At his stag night, he announced: 'Gentlemen, you are talking to a man who is about to go over Niagara Falls in a barrel.'

His stag-night chums thought nothing of interrupting his wedding night with bawdy phonecalls. Elaine took it all in good part. Later she wrote: 'My feet were already wet when we dove into marriage. I had waded primly into sex. Inhibited, prudish, not in love, I was rather aloof. But now I gave myself freely to my husband and any diffidence disappeared in the wonder of our mutual love. He made me unashamed of the natural. He made me glory in my sensuality.'

Barrymore, for his part, wanted to know how she had suddenly got so good at sex. This set off another great display of jealousy. Next morning he was in a foul mood. On the set, he snapped at Jeanette MacDonald: 'If you wave that loathsome chiffon rag you call a handkerchief once more while I am speaking, I shall ram it down your gurgling throat.'

The thirty-four-year difference in their ages began to cause problems for the newlyweds. At first, Elaine said, Barrymore was 'a superbeing sexually'.

'In the beginning it was a nightly affair,' she wrote, 'but then the need to prove himself made him try too hard and there were failures.'

This was partially because Barrymore was always drunk. He hung out with a bunch of cronies that included W.C. Fields and the artist John Decker, who painted Barrymore as a nearly nude Christ on the cross flanked by, not two crucified thieves, but two women in a similar state of undress. The pals were known collectively as the Bundy Drive Boys, after Decker's studio on Bundy Drive where they used to hang out.

Other members of the group included screenwriters Ben Hecht and Charlie MacArthur, author Gene Fowler, and all-round intellectual Sadakichi Hartmann, of whom Gertrude Stein said: 'Sadakichi is singular, never plural.' The actor Anthony Quinn joined later.

They were largely a bunch of misogynists. Barrymore, who they called affectionately 'The Monster', spoke of women as 'the collecting sex' and 'twittering vaginas'. Fields said he loved the 'little nectarines' provided they were neither aggressive nor possessive. Barrymore said: 'Is there any other kind?'

They sent him a naked girl wrapped in cellophane and tied with a silver bow for his fifty-fifth birthday. Elaine and her mother did not approve. They thought the Bundy Drive Boys were a thoroughly bad influence. They were, they said, 'perennial undergraduates', 'a group of sodden children'.

Barrymore merely sighed and told them: 'I wish I had been

born a pansy. You women are poison.'

Most women thought much the same of them. When the US entered World War II, the Bundy Drive Boys went to sign up *en masse*. The young woman behind the recruiting desk took one look at this group of drunks, derelicts, womanizers, geriatrics and overgrown schoolboys and said: 'Who sent you? The enemy?'

One time, Fields lost the unlisted number to Barrymore's Tower Road home and begged the operator to put him through; it was an emergency.

'Please state the nature of the emergency,' he was told.

'Locked bowels,' Fields replied.

Barrymore's own one-liners were legendary. At silent movie star John Gilbert's funeral, he said to an old man at the graveside: 'Eighty-four? I guess its hardly worth going home.'

The Boys ripped it up in Hollywood restaurants and nightclubs. Barrymore would regularly get into fights for the ripe remarks he made to attractive young women. He did not care if they were not alone. One evening in Dave Chasen's place, he walked up to a young woman with an escort, bowed to her and said: 'If you will come to my place at midnight, I will give you the greatest lay you have ever had.'

His friends tried to hustle Barrymore away before her boyfriend hit him, but Barrymore looked down his nose at the man and asked in majestic tones: 'Who is this? A peasant with a petition? Let the peasant come forward.'

A riot ensued.

Elaine hung on, in the faint hope that her association with Barrymore would further her career. She was offered a role in a play called *The Return of Hannibal* which largely involved her dancing around the stage in a scanty toga. Barrymore went ballistic with sexual jealousy. Elaine stuck it out, but it did her no good. *Variety* said: 'She looks like Salome; acts like salami.'

It was the end of the line for their marriage. Granting an interlocutory decree, the judge said: 'Better luck next time.'

Freed from the shackles of marriage and Barrymore's unnatural jealousy, Elaine eventually made it in movies. She made a strip flick called *How to Undress in Front of Your Husband,* calling herself 'Mrs John Barrymore'. Barrymore tried, unsuccessfully, to have it suppressed. However, it was banned for indecency in New York State.

With Elaine gone, fun with the Bundy Drive Boys began to pall. He began cabling Elaine, begging her to come back. He swore to 'straighten out completely' and 'help you in your career'. She did not have to be asked twice.

By this time, Barrymore was in acute financial difficulties. He took any part any producer would trust him with, while Elaine's attempts at acting usually ended on the cutting-room floor. Together they toured in a mediocre play called *My Dear Children*. More often than not, Barrymore forgot his lines, but his ad libs were much more amusing than the original text. They played to standing ovations.

Relations between him and his wife were no better. He suspected that she was being unfaithful with other members of the cast and tried to have her fired. Elaine's mother told the director, Otto Preminger: 'If you fire my daughter, I'll tell the press that Jack tried to rape me.'

Towards the end of the second act of *My Dear Children*, there is a scene where Barrymore puts his wayward daughter, played by Elaine, over his knee and spanks her. He managed to get rid of his frustration then, but one night he went too far, raising welts. She bit his wrist. There was an almighty fight and the management had no choice but to fire Elaine. She got another interlocutory decree and Barrymore got to spank a young Doris Dudley instead.

As they moved on across the Midwest, Barrymore's behaviour got worse with each succeeding night. Though most audiences appreciated his bawdy humour and displays of drunken womanizing, he drew protests from women's leagues of decency. When Preminger asked why he behaved this way each night, Barrymore said: 'Bored, dear boy, bored.'

Orson Welles saw the show and commented that Barrymore knew everything there was to know about acting. He played the audience like a stand-up comedian. When a fire engine went by the theatre, he would say: 'Oh my God, it's my wife.' One night, when he had already used that line and a truck backfired directly afterwards, he came up with: 'And she's got her mother with her.'

By the time they reached New York, these ad libs were the better part of the play and appeared in parenthesis in the edition published in 1940.

The high spot of the show was always the top of the third act where, under a portrait of himself as a young man playing *Hamlet,* he recited a little of the 'To be or not to be' soliloquy. Even veteran actors were seen to cry.

With Elaine out of the way, the management laid on three accommodating young ladies to keep him occupied, but Barrymore still caused mayhem by pursuing the other actresses. He had a wonderful line that he used on the young actress Anne Seymour.

'Won't you come up to my room with me,' he would say, 'and prove to me that I am still attractive to women.'

Everywhere he went he was lionized – and guaranteed to offend. He would invariably turn up to any social gathering blind drunk and pinch any patrician bottom to hand. He would proposition any woman he met as a matter of course.

Barrymore had always made a practice of urinating where he pleased. Once on a studio lot in Hollywood, he had overheard two matrons talking. One said to the other: 'We've been in Hollywood for two days now, and I have not seen anything shocking yet.'

This was Barrymore's cue to urinate against a wall in front of them.

On tour with *My Dear Children*, he made a mission of such micturatory fun. He pissed in cars, out of windows, in a socialite's private lift and was thrown out of the Ambassador Hotel after using a sand box in their lobby.

After the show was over, he would spend the rest of the night drinking. During *My Dear Children*'s long run in Chicago, he became a habitué of the Southside, the Windy City's black ghetto. He was particularly fond of a gay club there and danced with an ersatz Joan Crawford and Dolores del Rio. One night, in the Club Alabama on Rush Street, he ran into Evelyn Nesbit. They wept.

In Pittsburgh, he vomited on stage but still women would come on to him because of who he was.

At the Broadway première of *My Dear Children*, in front of a celebrity audience, Elaine caused a sensation by sweeping down the aisle in a tight, low-cut, off the shoulder, gold lamé dress half an hour after the curtain rose. After the show, she tore into Doris Dudley, accusing her of nursing an ambition to be the fourth Mrs Barrymore.

John heaped abuse on her and set off on a spree, but Elaine managed to keep pace with him as he went from club to club around the city. Eventually, when he was drunk enough, she made her move. She steered him back to her room in the Hotel Navarro on Central Park South. Half an hour later, reporters were knocking on the door. Barrymore answered it.

'I have it on good authority that it is legal in New York State for a man to spend the night with his lawfully wedded wife,' he said. 'Or have I been misinformed?'

A second interlocutory decree was duly torn up. When Elaine reappeared in the play in place of Doris Dudley, audiences booed.

The strain was all too much for Barrymore. He collapsed and was rushed to Mount Sinai Hospital. When the doorman enquired after his health, Barrymore said: 'Don't worry, you can cure a ham, but you can never kill one.'

Barrymore and Elaine flew back to Hollywood where he was to star in *The Great Profile* with veteran Gregory Ratoff opposite Mary Beth Hughes.

'I was sixteen and scared,' Mary said. 'I'd heard that when they met you, they ripped your clothes off.'

The first day on the set, Barrymore came bounding into Mary's dressing-room.

'Are you a good sport?' he asked.

'I think I am,' she said.

Then he grabbed her skirt and ripped it off her. She stood

there with perfect aplomb.

'I think I am going to like you,' he said.

Now it was Elaine's turn to be jealous. When she read the script she discovered that *The Great Profile* was the thinly disguised story of their marital problems on tour with *My Dear Children*.

'Who is this blonde bitch who is going to play my part?' she demanded.

The rows at home got worse. They separated and Elaine was granted a third interlocutory decree.

'How wonderful,' said Barrymore when he heard the news, pouring himself a whiskey. 'It's nothing new for me. After all, there is no great distinction in being called "Mrs Barrymore". There have been so many of them. Now I am free to resume my search for the perfect mate.'

Asked if he had anyone in mind, Barrymore said: 'I saw a lovely, simple child in the Christmas Day parade, but she was only fifteen. I could hardly explain to her parents that I simply wanted to put her on ice for a few years. Anyhow I don't think there's enough ice in the world to keep a Hollywood girl cool. I ought to know.'

But it was Elaine he really wanted. She phoned one night about a trivial matter, when he was dining with the Bundy Drive Boys. After they had resolved the matter in question, he begged her not to hang up. She could tell him how much she hated him, taunt him with the men she was now seeing, just as long as he could hear her voice. But it was no good. She had already hung up.

Barrymore was old and ill. His daughter, Diana, came to look after him. Confined to bed with a damaged liver, he asked her to make a call for him. After she dialled the number, she discovered that she was ordering a call girl. Diana packed her bags. When the young lady arrived, she let her in and while the hooker tripped up the stairs and into Barrymore's bedroom, Diana left. She never saw her father again.

Soon after that Barrymore collapsed during an NBC broadcast and was rushed to hospital with cirrhosis of the liver and kidney damage. Elaine tried to visit him but his brother Lionel blocked her way.

A priest was summoned to read the last rites.

'Do you have anything to confess, my son?' he asked.

'Yes, father,' said Barrymore. 'I have carnal thoughts.'

Astonished that a man so near death should be thinking about sex, the priest asked: 'About whom?'

'About her,' said Barrymore, raising his arm and pointing to the nurse.

John Barrymore died on 29 May 1942, at the age of sixty. Some say that only one visitor came to view him when he lay in the funeral home – a local prostitute who knelt quietly by the coffin and prayed. But in truth it would take more than death to get a man like Barrymore to lie down. Film director Raoul Walsh bribed the funeral parlour attendant, kidnapped the body, smuggled it into Errol Flynn's house and sat it up in an armchair. When Flynn came home, drunk, he saw Barrymore sitting in his front room and let out a piercing scream.

The Bundy Drive Boys were drunk at the funeral, of course. On the way back from the cemetery, Gene Fowler's car got stuck in a traffic jam in the Mexican quarter of Los Angeles. W.C. Fields rolled down the back window and gave a group of passing Mexicans a cocktail shaker of dry martinis and some glasses.

'Have a drink for Jack Barrymore,' he said.

Elaine never remarried.

4

THE SWORDSMEN

Douglas Fairbanks Snr was one of the movies' first great swashbucklers. With a ring in his ear and a flashing blade in his hand, he was a romantic hero and a great swordsman.

As a youth, Fairbanks thought he had a religious calling and yearned to be a missionary in Africa, but by the time he was seventeen in 1900, he realized that on a continent full of dusky maidens in various states of undress he would find it hard to stick to Catholic vows of celibacy and decided to seek his fortune in old New York.

He found a job straightaway as an understudy in a touring theatre company and, in that capacity, began reading Shakespeare. The following autumn he enrolled for a 'special course' at Harvard, but spent most of his time in the gym toning up his athletic frame. He travelled widely – in Europe, the Orient and Cuba – funding his activities by theatrical tours of the United States.

Although the critics panned him and one leading lady said that on stage 'he had a bad case of St Vitus dance', the actress Grace George spotted that Fairbanks had star quality.

'He's not good-looking,' she told her husband, producer William Brady, 'but he has a world of personality – just worlds of it.'

Brady hired him as a leading man. During Fairbanks' first

Broadway run, he met and fell in love with pretty, plump, blonde Beth Sully, daughter of 'Cotton King' Daniel J. Sully. He gave the couple a huge society wedding at Kenneth Ridge, the Sullys' mansion at Watch Hill, Rhode Island.

Sully wanted Fairbanks to give up the theatre and take a respectable job; but when Sully suddenly lost his fortune, Fairbanks, rising star on Broadway, bailed the family out.

In 1915, Fairbanks signed a contract with Triangle Pictures for $1,000 a week and set off for Hollywood where he soon made a name for himself. In 1917 alone, he made five pictures, grossing over a million dollars.

Those who knew him at the time described him as a 'young, vigorous man, as uncompromising as his splendid physique'. They noted particularly that he was 'gallant to women', though his son says that he was 'in so many ways ... a conventional neo-Victorian, particularly in his attitudes toward manners and mores. If facets of his personal life disclosed a touch of hypocrisy, I think one might call it sincere hypocrisy...He felt strongly, until his domestic troubles contradicted him, that "respectability" was a cloak to be worn by anyone in serious public life.'

In other words, he had his cake and ate it.

His wife learnt to accept his infidelity. After all, he was in a business where he was constantly surrounded by beautiful, glamorous, desirable and willing women. Beth herself was losing her looks. As long as he came home occasionally, she was content.

He met 'America's Sweetheart' Mary Pickford at a houseparty in New York, where he was attending the première of *The Lamb*. Fairbanks was with his wife. Pickford was with her husband, the hard-drinking and mean-spirited actor Owen Moore.

Pickford was attempting to cross an icy stream on a narrow and slippery log. Halfway across, she stopped, immobilized by fear. Others at the party shouted encouragement and advice, but Fairbanks in true swashbuckling style, leapt onto the log, swept her up in his arms and carried her to the bank.

Back in Hollywood, their affair took off. People were

amazed at the lengths to which he would go to deceive his wife. Once he told Beth that he was going on a fishing trip when, in fact, he had a tryst with Mary. On the way home, he stopped at a fishmonger's.

Instead of sleeping with his wife, he took to sleeping on the porch, which was well away from the master bedroom. When Beth was asleep, he would slide down an Ionic pillar, roll the car down the hill until it was out of earshot before starting the engine, and drive over to Mary's house. In the morning, he would speed home; but he would then have to push the car back up the hill – no problem for an athlete such as Fairbanks.

Fairbanks life with his wife was not as it should have been. Years later, she told her son's biographer: 'Senior always used to say I should have been his sister not his wife, and I think it is true.'

Occasionally, Fairbanks and Mary would drive out into the countryside. He would wear a hat with a turned down brim; she a veil. Once they were far enough from Los Angeles, they would rip off their disguises and neck like two teenagers in a Model T. They would find a quiet place to stop for a picnic and, perhaps, a little amour *al fresco*.

Mary blossomed under the influence of his love. Her friend Frances Marion said: 'You never thought of Mary as being sexy until Doug. He was so physical. Other actors looked sexy, like Owen Moore, but Doug was the only one with that physique and the drive to back it up. Another thing, he'd listen to Mary. He treated her as an intelligent person. Any woman goes for that.'

When his mother died suddenly in 1916, Fairbanks turned to Mary for comfort. They were in New York and went for a drive in Central Park where he broke down and cried. Later they noticed that the clock in the car had stopped at the exact moment he began to cry.

Their growing passion put them in a dilemma. Both Fairbanks and Pickford were Catholics. To divorce, they would have to renounce their faith. They both projected highly moral images on the screen and they feared that such a move might damage their careers irreparably. Also, Fairbanks was on record as saying: 'If a man is manly, he should marry early and remain faithful to the bride of his youth.'

This was plainly something Fairbanks himself was not doing.

Fate lent a hand when the sinking of the *Lusitania* in 1917 brought America into World War I. Fairbanks and Pickford were asked to go on a country-wide tour together as part of the Liberty Loans drive. As they travelled from city to city their love ripened and gradually they stopped trying to hide it. The match, they soon realized, would be accepted by the great American public.

It was only then that Beth realized that her husband was having an affair with her friend Mary Pickford. She was hurt and confused, not least because everyone else had known about it. She went to the press and named Mary as her husband's lover. No paper dared to print it. Fairbanks condemned the rumours of his affair as German propaganda.

He and Beth divorced quietly in 1918 and he gave her $500,000 in settlement. Almost immediately she married a Pittsburgh stockbroker named James Evans. The marriage lasted a year. Then, to stretch her dwindling capital, like so many other Americans at that time, she took Douglas Jnr off to Paris to take advantage of the favourable post-war exchange rate.

Mary went to Reno in 1920, having first ensured Owen Moore's silence with a fat sheaf of bonds. When the divorce came through, she told the papers that she had no plans to marry again, but Fairbanks swept her up in his arms once more and on 28 March 1920, they were wed.

The wedding was a quiet affair. The honeymoon was not. They stormed the capitals of Europe where the public thronged to see their idols; everywhere, except in Germany where their films had not been shown, they were mobbed.

'They came to mean more than a couple of married movie stars,' wrote Alistair Cooke. 'They were living proof of America's belief in happy endings.'

They returned home to Pickfair, the 'semi-Colonial

Georgian' style (as Fairbanks Jnr put it) mansion that Fairbanks Snr had bought at the top of Beverly Hills just before they married. There they became lord and lady of the manor – but trouble was brewing.

Throughout her career, Mary Pickford had been cast as a prepubescent innocent. There had been no leading men and no hint of romance in her films. But sooner or later she had to grow up.

In 1927, when she was thirty-four, she filmed *My Best Girl* with Buddy Rogers. She was cast as an adolescent falling in love with the boy next door. Fairbanks dropped by on the set one day when they were filming a love scene. He watched for a bit, glowered at the couple, then turned on his heels and stalked away.

'It's more than jealousy,' he told his brother Robert. 'I suddenly felt afraid.'

In fact, the King and Queen of Hollywood had already begun to drift apart. He was a teetotaller; she a heavy drinker. She was tired of globetrotting and did not share his love of the outdoors. He was fed up with being corralled in Beverly Hills. His youth, he felt, was fading and he panicked. He needed to prove that he was still attractive to younger and younger women.

Without warning, she cut off the golden curls that had been her girlish trademark and bobbed her hair in the manner of a flapper. Her next film indicated how far she had moved from the virginal roles that had made her famous. It was called *Coquette*.

As if all this was not enough to make Fairbanks feel insecure, it coincided with the release of *The Jazz Singer* and the coming of sound. The Academy of Motion Picture Arts and Sciences, which he had helped to organize, awarded its first Oscar for Best Actress to Mary for her role in *Coquette*. Mary was drinking heavily, something which at that time he could not stand. His son married Joan Crawford against his wishes. Then along came the Wall Street Crash.

'A strange fever and restlessness settled upon him,' Mary

said later.

He headed off to Scotland, ostensibly to play golf. It was the first time he had undertaken a trip alone.

Mary continued to make films, Fairbanks did not. He had little to do with his days except make mischief. He even bought a remote Tahitian island, where he could enjoy the simple pleasures Gauguin had discovered there, and admire the dusky topless girls who wore grass skirts. He even brought back a young Tahitian girl, Maria Alba, who, he said, was going to co-star as 'Saturday' in his version of *Robinson Crusoe*. Mary Pickford made no comment.

He spent more and more time in the South Seas and travelling. In Europe, he was frequently seen in the company of a 'woman of nobility'. Meanwhile, Mary found God.

Mary eventually caught up with Fairbanks in Italy where, for the first time, they talked about his sexual indiscretions. She went home without him. When he arrived back at Pickfair, he found that she had gone to the World Fair in Chicago with none other than her first leading man Buddy Rogers.

Fairbanks flew after her. In the car on the way to the airport, his brother handed him a birthday present. When he opened the box, a mechanical butterfly flew out. The symbolism was not lost on him.

There was a brief reconciliation, but in June 1933, Fairbanks decided he wanted to go to England. Mary saw him off at the dockside in New York. A few weeks later, he wired her saying that he intended to settle in England permanently. She could keep Pickfair if she wanted, but he would no longer be responsible for the bills.

Mary showed Fairbanks' cable to Louella Parsons who made 'brave little Mary's' plight front-page news. It was the biggest scoop of her career.

Mary sought comfort with Rogers. This annoyed Fairbanks because Rogers was so much younger than him and because he had witnessed their lovemaking on the movie set. The following December, Mary filed for divorce in Los Angeles on the grounds of 'incompatibility'. It was uncontested.

Meanwhile, Fairbanks found himself in the divorce courts in London. In February 1934, he was named as co-respondent in the divorce suit filed by Lord Ashley, the thirty-four-year-old heir to the Duke of Shaftesbury. The 'woman of nobility' Fairbanks had been seen with was Lady Ashley, one-time chorus girl Sylvia Hawkes who was now tall, blonde and thirty-ish. This hurt Fairbanks deeply because, as he admitted to friends, he still hoped to get Mary back. Despite years of flagrant infidelity, he still loved her. Also, his split from her had dented his popularity and he was making a new film to be called, ironically, *The Exit of Don Juan*.

Fairbanks headed back to Hollywood. He and Mary were seen together at their beach-house, Fairford, by several members of the film colony, apparently 'happy and joking'. But appearances were deceptive. Mary said: 'Something was gone. It was as though his spirit had fled.'

They stayed together for several days, and Mary told the press that she was glad that he was back.

'I am sure he will be happy here, now,' she said.

But he returned to England to complete what came to be called *The Private Life of Don Juan*. It was his last film. When Lord Ashley won his divorce, Fairbanks took the former Lady Ashley on a round-the-world cruise. Reporters caught them at the station where they were boarding a train for the port. Fairbanks was in an ugly mood and took a swing at a couple of cameramen.

At Jakarta in Indonesia, Fairbanks jumped ship and headed back to Hollywood, ostensibly to sort out a crisis at United Artists, the company which he had helped set up. There were talks with Mary. Those who knew him thought that all that was needed was a grand gesture to sweep away all the hurt pride and ingrained stubbornness and they would be back together again. Instead, they each waited for the other to make the first move. There was something 'world-weary and dissipated' about him, Mary recalled.

'All Doug ever wanted was a sober Mary,' said a friend, Chuck Lewis. But it was more than that. They were both jealous people.

He could not forgive her infidelity and she could not forgive his.

He sailed for England again, thinking that Mary would never let the divorce become final but she did, in January 1936. He refused to accept it and sailed back to America, intending to go to Hollywood to plead with Mary one last time. From New York, he sent long heartfelt wires. She did not reply. Impulsively, he set sail back to England without telling anyone. When Douglas Fairbanks Jnr went around to the Waldorf, he found his father had checked out, saying that any communication should be forwarded to him via ship-to-shore telegram. The desk clerk said that a wire had come from Mary but it had been mislaid. Fairbanks Jnr excitedly put a call through to his father, telling him about the wire. Fairbanks Snr refused to believe it so Mary called him too, saying that she was willing to discuss a reconciliation. But as he steamed on to Southampton, Fairbanks Snr said: 'It's too late. It's just too late.' On 7 March 1936, he married the former Lady Ashley in Paris.

Fairbanks tried to keep his second and third wives apart, but they met in Hollywood. They were civil. Lady Ashley said that she was sorry to hear that Pickfair was on the market.

'Pickfair has served its purpose,' said Mary imperiously. 'Somehow material things do not mean as much to me as they once did.'

Of course, Mary still lived at the top of Beverly Hills. Lady Ashley may have been an aristocrat in England, but Mary Pickford was still a Queen in Hollywood.

Fairbanks became a producer and, after a lifetime of sobriety, a heavy drinker. He died in 1939. His last words, delivered with a grin, were: 'I never felt better.' From then on the swashbuckling was left to the other accomplished swordsman in the family, his son Douglas Fairbanks Jnr.

Junior was more handsome than his father who, despite his wonderfully developed physique, had narrow eyes, a hooked nose and a tendency towards a double chin. Fairbanks Snr had little time for his son as a child and split from his mother when Fairbanks Jnr was eleven. Around that time, Junior recalled, there was a rumour going around his boys' club that there was a girl in the vicinity who actually kissed. The young Fairbanks sought her out and, indeed, the girl did give him and others 'a quick, undetected peck' between floors while riding in a hotel's open-grilled elevator.

'But even that was enough to inspire our first confessed stirrings of animal desire,' Fairbanks said.

Later he fell for a young girl called Genie, while playing clock golf.

'She had a remarkably beautiful face with a permanent angelic expression and a personality to go with it.' Unfortunately she was paralysed with polio.

He impressed the girls by taking them on to the sets of his father's movies at the Pickford–Fairbanks Studio. The girls from Fairfax High were best, he recalled: 'They had the raciest reputation and were said to be quite willing to kiss a guy the first time out.'

One of them suggested a 'mutual anatomical inspection' on the top of Robin Hood's castle but they were caught by the security guard and thrown out.

Then there was Agnes Hawkins. She was the girlfriend of a fifteen-year-old Eagle Scout whose arms were laden with badges. Fairbanks was still eleven, but he plucked up the courage to ask her out. He took her to a nearby orange grove, told her he liked her a lot and begged her for a kiss. She would be his first real girl and it would be his first real kiss, he said.

'This is possibly the first and last time I told the whole truth to a girl,' Fairbanks recalled in later years.

Not that Agnes was impressed by this unwarranted display of candour. She let the young Fairbanks know that she could not even consider such a thing until he had joined the Boy Scouts.

He set about learning to light camp fires, to tie knots, to read maps and compasses, and to memorize oaths and mottoes. On his twelfth birthday, he was eligible to join the Scouts and went for the tests. He passed them all with flying colours, except one. He had not mastered semaphore. But Fairbanks would not give in easily. He offered to arrange a tour of the studio for the scoutmaster who eagerly accepted. Fairbanks went back to the signal flags and this time he passed.

He had pestered his mother into buying his Scout uniform well in advance. The first day he turned up at school in uniform, Agnes, good as her word, passed him a note. It told him to meet her in the orange grove – 'out of sight'.

He got there early and waited, heart pounding. When she finally arrived, he was so excited he could not speak. They put their arms around each other and she gave him a kiss – on the cheek – then ran off giggling. He was too overwhelmed with ecstasy to chase her. Now he was determined to win her from her Eagle Scout.

She gave him a photograph of herself. He had already noticed other girls' developing figures but in the picture, in the fashion of the times, Agnes was wearing a dress that flattened her chest. Fairbanks took a pencil and shaded in two small girlish breasts. Although he hid the photograph away, his mother found it and tore it up. He was too embarrassed to ask for a replacement.

After school, he lost touch with Agnes but, over fifty years later, when he was opening in a play in Los Angeles, he looked her up. She was married to a doctor called Buckingham and still lived in Pasadena. He sent them two tickets to the first night but they did not turn up.

By the time his mother took him to Paris in his early teens, Fairbanks' head was swimming with the possibilities. He was a keen student of D.H. Lawrence.

In France, Fairbanks made friends with a slightly older boy called Hookie. Hookie had a French girlfriend who could speak no English. He could speak no French, so they took Fairbanks along to translate for them. The girl was twenty-two and very pretty. Fairbanks was tall for his age, so Hookie told him to pretend he was seventeen.

It was a warm March morning and the three of them were walking in the Bois de Boulogne. Hookie wanted to take the girl on a sightseeing tour of the Loire and asked Fairbanks to ask her. But Fairbanks had his own fish to fry. He told Hookie that it would be easier for him to raise the matter with her if he, Hookie, was not there. Hookie naively agreed and let Fairbanks walk off with his girl.

They headed for the thickest part of the wood. The girl was no fool. She knew what he was after. Once they were out of sight of other walkers, she kissed him. Nothing had prepared him for this. Even in D.H. Lawrence people did not devour each other the way she devoured him. Then she suggested that they lay down on the grass. Although he had a thorough theoretical knowledge of how the species was perpetuated, the girl proceeded to give him a tutorial in love's infinite nuances and variations. He was shocked. He had no idea what she was doing, but it did not occur to him to protest. It was all too much for him. The next thing he knew she was slapping his face to bring him round.

'*Est-ce-que ça va, mon cher?*' she asked. '*Tout va bien? Oh, mon pauvre, joi chou!*'

Her lesson had been so intense that he had passed out. When he regained consciousness, she wiped the lipstick from his face and reapplied it to her own and they went to look for Hookie.

Fairbanks was as yet unacquainted with the Machiavellian side of love. He immediately confessed his premeditated duplicity. Hookie did not mind in the least being a cuckold. He laughed and, with Hookie's permission Fairbanks took another few lessons in love from his amorous French girlfriend. Fairbanks' mother spotted the growing circles under his eyes and his wan complexion and concluded that he had been studying too hard. He was to rest, take things easy, spend more time with his friends, or visit museums.

Back in California when he was sixteen, Fairbanks shared another friend's girlfriend. He had gone to camp at Laguna with Hookie when his buddy Freddy turned up with Polly. There was a strict rule that no girls were allowed in the camp, but the friends did not let on. During a gin-drinking session in the back seat of a car, Freddy suggested that she kiss Hookie and Doug. Fairbanks was surprised at her enthusiasm. This time he did not pass out.

'I felt wild, wicked and sophisticated,' he recalled. 'And in the unthinking way of most male animals, I was relieved to learn that she could, after all, stay only one more day and one more night.'

Fairbanks thought that Polly was a good sport. There was nothing delicate or ladylike about her.

'She was a good, happy, amoral sort of a roughneck,' he said.

He had already started making pictures. On-screen, he had even got married, and the studio ordered him to grow a moustache for the part.

Of course, the women at the studio were a constant distraction. They were 'as attractive as the devil'.

'I kept on having romantic crushes and getting over them every few days,' he said. There were 'exciting stolen moments in dark corners, gardens, or the rumble seats of runabouts'.

He was also having a thing with his cousin Flobe – he used to take her dancing or to the theatre – but 'it was still a year or more before I was even remotely serious about any one girl'.

That girl was Helene Costello the sister of Dolores Costello, who was about to become John Barrymore's third wife. Their relationship was as intense as anything he had felt before. For months they were inseparable. Then she went to New York on business and Fairbanks found out how painful the separation of young lovers could be.

When Helene returned, Fairbanks took her swimming up at Pickfair. His father and stepmother were away, so they could use the pool privately. After a long, moody silence, Helene announced that she had something to say.

'My heart began to pound so loud I was sure she could hear it,' he said.

He was sure that she was going to tell him that she had had an affair on her trip; but after a tearful but encouraging hug, she announced that she had got married. Her husband was the renowned Broadway actor Lowell Sherman. He was much older than her and they had decided to keep their wedding secret. Years later, Fairbanks could still feel the shock of that moment.

'I didn't get over this first romantic blow for months.'

Fairbanks was still tending his broken heart when some Japanese friends of his father's came to stay at Pickfair. They brought with them their beautiful sixteen-year-old daughter. Fairbanks respectfully paid court to her. He was allowed to take her out to a movie on Saturday or Sunday, provided he brought her back promptly. After a month, he held her hand; another month and he kissed her on the cheek. Things were progressing swimmingly.

Finally, he got her to himself for a whole afternoon. They went to his father's then empty studio and he took her to his father's holy of holies – the dressing-room, office, Turkish bath complex which was usually off-limits to women. His hands grew clammy as he led her to a sofa. There, impulsively, he kissed her on the lips. She was more than responsive. Next, he fumbled at the pins that held up her hair. It fell softly to her waist. Then, although he was older than her, she seized the initiative. Although it was plain she knew exactly what she was doing, afterwards, he apologized for what he considered was his brutish animal attack. She smiled and patted him on the hand.

'You are very, very sweet,' she said. 'So like your father.'

For the next few days, Fairbanks Jnr found it difficult to speak to his dad.

Lupe Velez, the 'Mexican Spitfire', made quite an impression on the growing Fairbanks and he began to pursue older, more sophisticated women rather than girls.

'If I made an impression on one, I celebrated discreetly and altered course for the next one,' he said. 'It may have been outrageous, but I continued this procedure for some time.'

As a result he managed to avoid any serious entanglements and get, as Charlie Chaplin said, 'the most fun you can have without laughing'.

As part of his pursuit of older women, Fairbanks developed a crush on the actress Gertrude Lawrence, who was ten years his senior. Meanwhile, another older woman was after him.

He was starring in the play *Young Woodley*, when he got a

note from MGM star Joan Crawford, who was three years older than him. She had seen him on the opening night and her note asked him to give her a call. He did and she invited him round for a drink. She was, he said, 'a considerable beauty'. Her mouth, particularly, impressed him. It was 'wide and generous'.

'Her figure was beautiful,' he said. 'When finally I left for San Francisco, I knew I was once again involved, although, as I told myself, not seriously or exclusively. I still thought it all a great lark to go after and be with the most attractive older women, while not allowing my sentiments to run away with me.'

Fairbanks was, however, acutely aware that Crawford was just the sort of honest-to-God girl that he might fall for. He found her approaches to him so flattering that he just melted. It was more than just a crush. In his own words, he 'began to wear her like a flower in my young buttonhole'.

'My interest in other girlfriends had begun to diminish in direct proportion to my increasing absorption with the glowing Miss C.,' he said.

However, this did not stop him trying to get off with Greta Garbo during the shooting of *A Woman of Affairs*, despite the fact that she was at that point still with Fairbanks' friend Jack Gilbert. In fact, Gilbert and Garbo were having a little spat at the time and Gilbert made the mistake of giving Fairbanks a note for Garbo and asking him to be a go-between. Fairbanks used the note to lure Garbo into a dark corner of the studio where he made a pass at her himself. Garbo's response was to ask Fairbanks what was all this she had heard about a 'romance' between him and 'that nice Joan Crawford'. It was, Fairbanks recalled, 'a muffed opportunity'.

Fairbanks tried again on several other occasions. He escorted Garbo to parties. By this time, he was too openly involved with Crawford for Gilbert to be suspicious. One night Garbo got drunk and asked Fairbanks to drive her home to her Santa Monica beach-house. The lecherous Fairbanks thought he was in luck, but Garbo fell asleep in the car.

'I was, damn it, disgracefully proper,' he wrote in his autobiography.

The slow-burning infatuation between Crawford and Fairbanks blossomed into a fully fledged romance. They began to see each other daily. Crawford did her research on Fairbanks' background through the movie magazines – 'I did mine more directly.' Soon, she asked him to stop calling her Joan, which was the studio's invention, and call her Billie, her given name.

Fairbanks' mother was less than thrilled at the relationship and referred to 'that Crawford girl' as 'my son's current chorus-girl fling'. However, when Douglas took Joan up to 'Hollywood's Royal Palace' – Pickfair – she was received graciously, although when they got a little over-familiar in a dark corner during a movie show there, Fairbanks Snr gave his son a dressing down. In fact, neither of Douglas' parents was thrilled at the prospect that Doug and Joan might get married, maintaining that they were not well suited and 'Junior is far too young'.

But Fairbanks Jnr was fascinated by the 'seamy experiences' Joan had had as a stripper, a hooker and a blue-movie star. She urged him to stand up to his parents. Matters got worse. One night, coming back from a late-night session with Joan, Fairbanks found his mother had passed out. When he roused her, she said 'look what you and that dreadful girl have done to me' and sobbed hysterically into her pillow. Fairbanks solved this problem forthwith. From then on, he stayed over at Joan's.

However, his mother's attitude softened when she started 'walking out' with writer Gene Markey, long-time lover of Broadway comedienne Ina Claire, ex-husband of Joan Bennett, Hedy Lamarr and Myrna Loy, and 'one of the few who did not marry Gloria Swanson', according to Fairbanks. Then she got seriously involved with dancer Jack Whiting.

Beth and Whiting were witnesses to Fairbanks' marriage to Crawford in the Actors' Church – St Malachy's – in New York. Although his father was less than thrilled, he had the good grace to send a long telegram congratulating them. Beth and Whiting married a few weeks later.

Back at Pickfair things were frosty. Pickford warned Joan:

'If you ever make me a grandmother, I will kill you.'

During the shooting of *Outward Bound*, Fairbanks got friendly with his co-star Leslie Howard, who had a little fling with an eager studio girl. They were less than careful and she became pregnant. With no money to pay for an abortion, she turned to Howard for the cash. His money was controlled by his wife, Ruth; he could not even cash a travellers' cheque for $5 without her knowing about it. So Fairbanks scraped up the money for the abortion to help his friend out. Howard had to pretend that he had lost two large bets to Fairbanks to pay him back. Ruth cursed him for being so stupid as to bet against a man with such a rich father.

Even though he was newly married, in *One Night at Susie's*, Fairbanks began to take an inordinate interest in his co-star Billie Dove's bust. Howard used to tease him about it.

Fairbanks admitted that he was 'no Sir Galahad' and little things about Joan began to annoy him. Her use of childish sexual euphemisms, for example, got on his nerves. She called a woman's breasts 'ninny-pies', a kiss a 'goober' and making love 'going to heaven'. She called Douglas, irritatingly, 'Dodo'.

He got annoyed when Joan invited Howard Hughes to a party. Fairbanks had overheard Hughes asking someone to try to get him a date with Joan. When he had been reminded that Joan was married to Fairbanks and therefore 'not one of the girls', he said he would offer her 'a very big present'. Meanwhile, Fairbanks had followed in his father's footsteps and developed a roving eye of his own. He was devoted to his wife, he admitted, but he was happy to live by the world's double standards.

'It must not be supposed that I allowed myself an inordinate amount of time for prowling,' he said. He avoided the sort of philandering that would distress or embarrass Joan. 'Nor was anyone in doubt that, all things considered, I was essentially faithful – in my fashion.'

Joan was not that faithful either.

'Certainly Billie, whose own early explorations of life had been more varied than mine, turned over a completely new page of personal conduct during our courtship and early marriage,' he conceded. But 'I have no idea when those enormous hungry eyes first locked onto someone else. The uncertain evidence suggests that it was roughly at the same time that I began rather aimlessly to wander.'

On *Scarlet Dawn*, Fairbanks was led astray both on- and off-screen by Lilyan Tashman. She was married to Edmund Lowe. Fairbanks did not mind that, but he found her accounts of her close friendship with the bisexual actress Tallulah Bankhead 'quite disarming'.

Another friend at that time was Laurence Olivier, who was having some domestic difficulties of his own. To cheer him up, Fairbanks made up a story about a rich girl who had fallen head over heels in love with him. Olivier fell for it hook, line and sinker and became insistent that Fairbanks introduce him to the woman concerned.

Fairbanks kept Olivier at bay by telling him that the woman came from Pasadena, where people were notoriously contemptuous of theatrical folk, and she was never in Hollywood after 5 p.m. In that case, Olivier insisted, they must meet for lunch.

In desperation, Fairbanks found a woman friend who would play along with the charade and, after a couple of lunchtime meetings with Olivier, she got rather stuck on him. Fairbanks now had to arrange an assignation. He borrowed the keys to his uncle's apartment – his uncle was going out of town – but he was not going to let Olivier have all the fun. He was going to hide in the flat in order to watch the proceedings. Then, when they reached a crucial point, he would signal to an accomplice – a burly, cauliflower-eared stuntman – who would burst in.

Everything went to plan. The stuntman burst in, catching Olivier and the woman in a very compromising position.

'What're youse doin' wid my wife?' the bruiser demanded.

Olivier jumped up from the couch to defend himself, then, realizing the size of the man, keeled over in a dead faint.

While Joan was filming *Rain* on Catalina Island, she would not take his calls, so Fairbanks flew over to see her. She was livid that he had dared to come over without warning. There was no accommodation for him and, bewildered by her behaviour, he was grateful to leave.

Fairbanks decided to cheer himself up with a sailing trip down to Mexico with Olivier and a few other friends. The night before they went they got drunk in the Russian Club and hired the orchestra to come with them. They thought it would be fun to have live music out on the Pacific, but the musicians got seasick. Fairbanks tried to lash them into shape Captain Blighstyle, only to provoke a mutiny. They had to return to harbour and drop the green-gilled Russian musicians off.

Meanwhile Joan had headed off 'somewhere' for a rest. When she returned she seemed delighted when Fairbanks suggested they take a belated honeymoon in Europe. Elegant, educated and sophisticated, Fairbanks found himself perfectly at home in the upper reaches of European society. Joan, with her poor Kansas background, did not. They returned home early.

Fairbanks was invited out to dinner with Jean Harlow by his old friend Paul Bern, who announced over the brandies that he and Jean were going to be married. Fairbanks was flabbergasted. He could barely believe his ears. Fairbanks found her very attractive and 'her very loose and revealing décolletage, though something of a professional trademark, was not wasted on me'. Throughout dinner, she had been playing footsy with him. At first he thought he was just flattering himself but then he felt her hand on his knee and her undercover attentions reached the point where he found it hard to follow the conversation.

'Imagine, me, the old bachelor, getting married to the most witty, wonderful and attractive girl I have ever known?' said Bern.

'Look,' said Jean holding out her other hand, 'the ring Paul gave me. Isn't it beautiful?'

Fairbanks stayed away from Bern after that. Harlow made him uncomfortable. He did not even attend their wedding. After two months of marriage, Bern killed himself. He had been impotent.

Things with Joan had grown chilly. She had moved to a Malibu beach-house, without telling him where it was or how he could reach her.

Broadway musical star Clifton Webb made a pass at Fairbanks. He placed his hand on his thigh and told him of his feelings. Fairbanks did not know whether to punch him manfully on the jaw or kick him in the groin. Instead he just laughed. Webb did not speak to him for six months.

Fairbanks in 'the tightest, sheerest green tights this side of the Ballets Russes' played Romeo to Katharine Hepburn's Juliet. He was immediately smitten. He managed to persuade her to have dinner with him, but found himself too tongue-tied to tell her of his feelings. After dinner, he drove her home. She gave him a peck on the cheek when he dropped her off. Fairbanks was overcome with romantic longing. He got no further than fifty yards down the road before pulling over in his small, open-topped roadster, to stare at the night sky and sigh about Kate. No sooner had he stopped than something in the rear-view mirror caught his eye. It was Kate's svelte figure bounding out of the backdoor of her house, across the lawn and into someone else's car. Fairbanks never did find out who his rival was.

Joan withdrew further into her 'personal solitude' in Malibu and Fairbanks found himself helpless to prevent the relationship sliding from intense romance to easy companionship. When she returned to the couple's home, it became obvious that the feelings they had once had for each other were lost. There was gossip, of course. Not wanting to be an object of pity, Fairbanks played the cheery, faithless cad, while Joan played the hard-working, long-suffering wife.

Fairbanks' resentment of Joan's coldness towards him led him into self-indulgence, after-hours prurience and superficial dalliances. But 'when we had guests in our home we gave a passable performance of a civilized couple,' he said.

When she finally confronted him with his 'carryings on', he could confess no more than 'third-degree guilt'. Although she still hoped to save their marriage, she said, they were to consider themselves separated but assured him she was not seeing anyone else.

He said that if she wanted to save their marriage there were better ways than separation. If she gave half as much attention to him as she did to cleaning the house, there might be some hope. She walked out, slammed the door and headed back to her mysterious hideaway.

It was then that a Dane named Jørgen Dietz, the husband of a pretty young extra at Warner Bros, threatened to sue Fairbanks for 'alienating his wife's affections'. Fairbanks insisted that he had not touched the woman. They were prepared to drop the suit for a few thousand dollars.

The studio were delighted.

'That guy Fairbanks has got so many faggot friends that I was beginning to wonder about him,' said Jack Warner. 'This kinda thing is a relief. It'll prove he's no fairy.'

Warner let the papers run the story and paid off the Dietzes, provided they left the country.

Although Joan told the press that she would stick by him '100 per cent', the scandal caused a further rift. One day, while Fairbanks was at the studio, Joan had his things packed and sent to the Beverly Wilshire Hotel. She sent news via his agent that that was where he was now living. He read on the front page of the next day's paper of their 'amicable separation'. Joan had given Louella Parsons another scoop. No one had come to Fairbanks for his side of the story. No one knew where he was. Joan had been thoughtful enough to book him into the Beverly Wilshire under another name.

Fairbanks learnt from the paper that they 'remained fond of each other and respected each other greatly' but it was 'wiser and more honest' to separate openly and legally. However, divorce was not on the cards just at the moment – 'an extended vacation might help to drive us back together again'.

The following day brought a long magazine article about the separation by Joan's friend the journalist Katherine Albert. This must have been prepared months in advance, but Joan's boss Louis B. Mayer had insisted that the story be broken by Louella Parsons as a damage limitation exercise.

Although Joan still insisted she was seeing no one,

Fairbanks heard she was having an affair with New York leading man on *Dancing Lady*, Franchot Tone. He threatened to hire a private detective.

'Try, just try,' she said.

In the end, Fairbanks decided that it really was not worth all the fuss.

'Although I was sad, disappointed, bruised, I was not in the least bit heartbroken,' he recalled.

It was only later that he discovered that it was not only Franchot Tone Joan had been having an affair with, but also the other star of *Dancing Lady*, their mutual friend Clark Gable. It had been going on for more than two years. The affair was conducted in Joan's portable dressing-room, which Fairbanks had bought as a wedding present and which he had only just finished paying for. But Gable was such a nice man that, even under the circumstances, Fairbanks could not really blame him.

'Had our positions been reversed, I wasn't sure I would not have been equally deceitful,' Fairbanks said.

Later, Gable married Lady Ashley, the widow of Fairbanks' father, Douglas' second stepmother.

Joan Crawford and Douglas Fairbanks Junior were divorced on 29 April 1933.

Fairbanks headed for London with his father, where the latter met Lady Ashley. Junior was more taken with a dance hostess he met at the Café de Paris. 'Queenie' O'Brien had been born in Tasmania and educated in India. As a film extra she changed her name to Estelle Thompson; Alexander Korda later changed it again to Merle Oberon.

Fairbanks was present at the Café de Paris when Tallulah Bankhead's latest lover tried to cut her because he was there with his wife. She walked right up to the man and said: 'What's the matter, dahling. Don't you recognize me with my clothes on?'

Douglas finally caught up with Gertrude Lawrence, the object of his teenage crush. At the same time, he was paying intense attention to the beautiful, young Liz Paget.

'I criticized myself – to myself – for inconsistency,' he wrote.

Gertrude proposed marriage which took Fairbanks rather by surprise. He suddenly remembered that his divorce from Joan was not final and that he had to get his finances sorted out – 'but after that ...' There was a third reason for delay which he left unsaid: 'This was my own honest self-appraisal, admitted only to myself, that however smitten I might be by the bewitching Miss L., I had not ever been strictly faithful to anyone.'

But then neither had Gertrude Lawrence. Fairbanks knew that he had a rival for her affections in the shape of Eric Dudley.

She had money problems and said that she was going to spend some time alone, away from everyone, in Majorca. On a romantic impulse, Fairbanks set off after her. He tracked her down to a villa in Formentor. She answered the door herself and looked shocked and frightened when she saw Fairbanks. She began making frantic hand signals, then glancing over her shoulder, she whispered: 'You can't come in. He's here.'

Fairbanks felt terribly let down. She had said that she was going to be alone and here she was with Dudley. He returned to London a sadder and a wiser man.

Years later, he bumped into Dudley at White's Club in London and told him of his impulsive trip to Majorca. He listened with interest, then said: 'But I wasn't there at all. She told me you were there. Now the dear girl's dead and we'll never know who he was.' Gertrude Lawrence had been two-timing both of them.

Fairbanks had to go to Monte Carlo to film *Man of the Moment*. He took the famous Blue Train to the Côte d'Azur and noticed an attractive young woman at the other end of the carriage. She was looking out of the window when suddenly she put her hand to her eye. Fairbanks walked the length of the compartment and offered his help. She had got a cinder in her eye, which he removed with the corner of his handkerchief.

They had a drink together, then dinner. That night they made love, the train swaying beneath them. It was all the more exciting because of the way they had been so suddenly, incomprehensibly, taken with each other.

'It was wonderful,' he said. 'No residue of Protestant

conscience interrupted my natural instincts.'

Fairbanks realized that, after finally bedding his former heart-throb Gertrude Lawrence, he had lost his craving for older women. Now he desired women his own age, or younger.

The Lady of the Train did not give him her name and he did not give her his. The next morning, she left the train to join her husband. It was better that they knew nothing further about each other, otherwise they might be tempted to see each other again. They must just 'always remember the cinder in the eye and the romantic night on the Blue Train'.

As the train pulled out, they blew each other kisses and Fairbanks waved out of the window.

Back in London, Fairbanks' relationship with Gertrude Lawrence had all but petered out, but he was still seeing Liz Paget.

'My trouble was that I so enjoyed the fun and intrigue of romantic attachments that I found myself making a deliberate off-stage play at my new leading lady, Elissa Landi,' he recalled. He was also taken with the villainess of the piece, Coral Browne. Then his Lady of the Train turned up again out of the blue. She was still married but they continued to see each other discreetly.

Marlene Dietrich arrived in London to make *Knight Without Armour* for Alexander Korda. Fairbanks had met her in California, but in London their friendship blossomed into romance. He squired her around chic house parties in the country. In town they tried to be more discreet. At night, when he left her suite in Claridges, he took to leaving via the fire escape, with his collar turned up over his white tie and the tails of his dress coat tied up. One night he was jumping down from the fire escape when he bumped into a policeman.

'Good morning, Mr Fairbanks. Trying out a new trick for your next film?' he said. 'Good idea now, with nobody about.'

All Fairbanks could find to say was an embarrassed: 'Morning.'

Fairbanks found Dietrich's habit of keeping a picture of her former lover, the dead silent star John Gilbert, at her bedside with a lighted candle beside it, disturbing. Gradually she stopped lighting the candle and Fairbanks began to sense that he was now the new man in her life. He tried to arm himself against disappointment by thinking of their affair as only her passing fancy, but slowly she eased his apprehension and he became captivated by her skills as a 'wonderfully unconventional lover'.

The flat immediately below his Grosvenor Square penthouse became available and Marlene moved in. They used the two flats as a makeshift townhouse.

They went on holiday to Austria where – to Fairbanks' horror – they shared a chalet with Marlene's husband Rudi and his mistress Tami. As Fairbanks did not speak German, he found himself excluded and not a little uneasy about Marlene's relationship with her husband. It also disturbed him that she liked swimming nude so that her naked beauty could be appreciated by other men. Fritz Lang, a former lover of Dietrich's, used to tease him about the lack of sophistication revealed by such feelings and assured him of her 'basic fidelity'.

Fairbanks' jealousy eventually ended the relationship. One day, he came across some extremely passionate love letters addressed to Marlene and exploded. She said he had no business going through her private papers. Later, Fairbanks conceded that he had no idea when the letters were written or who they were from, but the damage had been done. After his display of mistrust, their relationship wilted and she went off with German author Erich Remarque.

Back in Hollywood, Fairbanks moved in with David Niven, who had just broken up with Merle Oberon. The house was named 'Cirrhosis-on-Sea' for the amount of alcohol Niven had got through there with the previous resident, Errol Flynn. Niven and Fairbanks spent much of their free time thinking up practical jokes. Once they hired a prostitute to dress up as a doctor and 'examine' Roly Young. They spoilt the joke by trying to spy on them and their guffaws gave the game away.

Fairbanks decided to go back to London to renew a long-standing relationship with an older married woman who, in his autobiography, he referred to only as Mme Y. The liaison had continued throughout other more widely publicized affairs.

'We had few opportunities to meet alone, but when we did these were moments of high romantic beauty,' he said.

The problem was that Fairbanks was an old friend of her husband. His conscience pricked him 'but not enough to resist her or back away from the situation'. They had to be discreet, aware that they risked causing great distress to others. Whatever happened, they knew the affair would come to a sad end – 'we could be considered sophisticated, but never cynical'.

In New York, while waiting for his ship to sail, he fell for the young ballerina Vera Zorina and, quite consciously, made a fool of himself hanging around backstage each night like a regular stage-door Johnny. Fairbanks enjoyed the heat of her young passion right up to the moment he boarded the ship that would carry him once more to his secret love in London. Vera came aboard with him and asked him to take her into an empty cabin before he sailed. Fairbanks was delighted, thinking he was about to get a proper send-off. Instead, she gave him back a ring he had bought her and told him that she was going to marry someone else.

As the liner slipped past Lower Manhattan and out to sea, Fairbanks nursed a bruised heart, but he was not really as distressed as he felt he ought to be. He just wanted to wallow in the pain of unrequited love and, 'as a well-tutored devotee of the double standard, my misplaced faith in women'. After a few assignations with Mme Y., he soon got over her.

Fairbanks and Mme Y. grew reckless. They passed notes to each other at dinner parties and took 'innocent' strolls in the country at weekend house parties. All the time, they were meeting secretly for passionate interludes at a friend's flat. Mme Y. would not even consider divorce and both of them were terrified of scandal, so Fairbanks took to squiring attractive young American Dorothy Fell. They even got engaged to further cover his tracks, but the engagement fizzled out when Dorothy went back to the States.

Fairbanks heard that Mme Y.'s husband had gone away for

a few days grouse shooting in Scotland and he decided to take advantage of the situation. He sent a note around to her house, telling her to meet him so they would have a long, relaxing and intimate time together, this time without the usual pressures. When the note was delivered, Mme Y. was out. The footman who had accepted the note at the door denied ever receiving it. The whole house was searched, but the note never turned up. Discretion being the better part of valour, Fairbanks jumped on board the *Queen Mary* and headed back to New York.

In New York harbour, the customs' inspector found a series of Aubrey Beardsley prints in Fairbanks' bags, seized them as 'pornography' and threw them in the Hudson.

On board ship, Fairbanks had met Anthony Eden and his wife Beatrice. Fairbanks took Beatrice on a tour of Harlem where they were spotted by reporters in the Cotton Club. Fairbanks persuaded the newspapermen to keep quiet. Eden, who had just resigned from the Chamberlain government over appeasement, was making a rousing anti-Nazi speech that night and it would not look good if it was reported that his wife was seen out gallivanting around nightclubs with a handsome movie star.

Fairbanks met his second wife, Mary Lee Hartington, at a houseparty on Long Island. She was in her early twenties and he was much taken by her slim waist. He introduced himself as a schoolfriend of her husband, Hunt, and tried to seduce her in the library. The door, Fairbanks said, got stuck and they had to bang on it and rouse the whole house to get out. Everyone assumed that Fairbanks had locked it to keep his quarry to himself.

Mary Lee's marriage was already on the rocks. She had eloped from Harvard with Hunt when she was nineteen, but he had not been the domestic type. She covered up for his dalliances for appearance's sake. Soon after she started seeing Fairbanks, Hunt announced he wanted a divorce. He wanted to marry someone else.

Fairbanks was thoroughly in love by this time and to win the heart of his future bride, he took her to see his greatest swashbuckling role, the villain Rupert of Hentzau in *The Prisoner of Zenda*.

At twenty-nine, Fairbanks was afraid of marrying again, but in Mary Lee he knew he had found the right person and in the end he was 'happy to surrender my enjoyable, selfish, free-wheeling lifestyle to the bonds of marriage' in 1939.

Within marriage, Fairbanks indulged his interest in the naked female form by sculpting – one of his early nudes had been of Marlene Dietrich. His beautiful cousin Letitia posed for a statue he made as a Christmas present for his wife. He also laid on the strippers for a stag party for the British actors who were leaving Hollywood to go back to Britain to fight.

Marriage suited Fairbanks Jnr. He had three daughters. A discreet man, his autobiography ends after the first years of marriage to Mary Lee. There were rumours in the press, though. One of the most amusing was that, when he heard about the Profumo Affair, he came over to London and managed to get both Christine Keeler and Mandy Rice-Davis into the same bed at the same time. It may, of course, be apocryphal! It seems that, happily married, he finally buckled his swash.

5

IN LIKE FLYNN

Errol Flynn was the greatest swashbuckler of them all, modelling himself from the beginning on John Barrymore. Between his first love, the maid who worked for his family in Australia, and his last, whom he was too much of a gentleman to name, he claimed to have spent between twelve and fourteen thousand nights making love. He died, worn out, at fifty, but his reputation lives on. Since World War II, the expression 'in like Flynn' has been used to denote an easy, if rapid, sexual encounter.

Perhaps it was in the blood. One of Errol Flynn's distinguished forebears was among the crew of the *Bounty,* one of those who preferred the delights of the warm, brown-skinned girls of Tahiti to the kiss of Captain Bligh's lash.

His father, a marine biologist at the University of Tasmania in Hobart, liked to pinch girls' bottoms and few young women were safe from him – certainly not Lily Mary Young, who became his wife. She was underaged when she married him, and already four months pregnant.

A beautiful woman, she refused to breast feed Errol in case it ruined her figure. She had a constant stream of gentlemen admirers who would call round when her husband was at work, and she dreamed of abandoning her husband and running off to Paris. Despite this, she was very puritanical when it came to young Errol's behaviour. With more than a touch of Captain Bligh in her, she thrashed him soundly when she caught him masturbating.

At the age of six, Flynn saw two naked men sunning themselves after a swim.

'I hate hairy people,' he said.

When it was explained to him by a contemporary that all grown-ups had hair on their bodies, he said: 'Daddy and mummy are hairy, but I don't like to kiss them the way I do Millie. She doesn't have a hair on her body.'

Plainly, he had already made a thorough examination of his young friend Millie and what he saw interested him. Like Chaplin, Flynn had a lifelong penchant for dangerously young girls. It may have been something he inherited from his father who was once beaten up by the father of one of his young female students when a biology lesson veered abruptly from theory into practical.

It is not recorded whether Flynn Senior was the father of the young sister born when Errol was eleven. Lily did not want her brought up in a backwater like Hobart, so the family moved to Sydney. The following year, Lily fulfilled her ambition and went to France, where she took a string of lovers, working her way up to the Aga Khan. Flynn Senior, a man of more modest ambitions, satisfied himself with the wife of a local tradesman.

By the time he was seventeen, Flynn Junior was following in his parents' footsteps. His wicked smile was irresistible to women. Many pursued him and not a few caught up. He also experimented in other areas of sexuality, enjoying performing a striptease for his fellow pupils at the Sydney Northshore Grammar School, and relishing the boys' 'circle jerk', a masturbation competition. The first prize was a box of condoms imported from Paris.

Errol also acquired a fiancée, a thirty-year-old maid named Elsie. Flynn claimed that there was nothing very sexual about their relationship, though 'she used to do a bit of grubbing, but I didn't know how to open my fly with a lady present'.

He got a better education from the daughter of the school laundress. They searched around the school for a safe place to consummate their passion and hit on the coal cellar. One night, they were energetically making love on top of the coal heap when the heap collapsed, taking them with it. Hearing the noise from the cellar, the school nurse, armed with a flashlight, found two naked black bodies writhing on the floor. When he was told

Charlie Chaplin

Rudolf Valentino

John Barrymore

Douglas Fairbanks Jr.

Gary Cooper

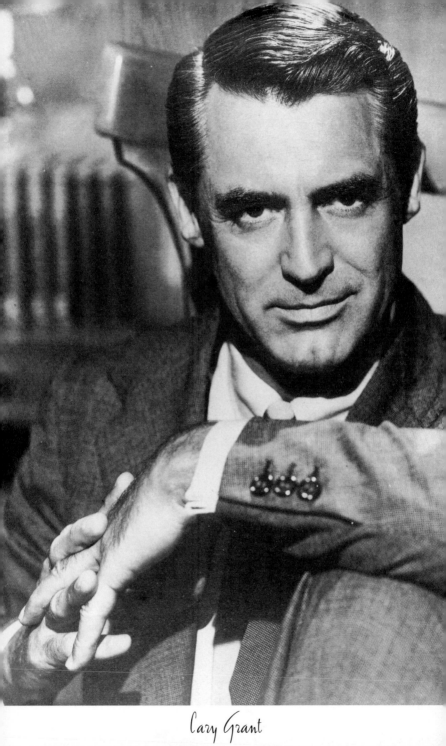

Cary Grant

Rock Hudson

James Dean

who the culprit was, the headmaster expressed no surprise. He expelled young Flynn, whose father congratulated him on bringing his scholastic life to such a spectacular culmination.

He did little better at work, being sacked after two weeks as a clerk for 'borrowing' money from petty cash to back a horse. He did better with the girls. His favourites were the three teenaged Dibbs sisters – Miriam, Naomi and Cecile – who had 'fast' reputations. Girls would go back with him to the stable his friend Ken Hunter-Kerr had converted into a flat. He also used the caves in the cliffs above Bondi Beach for his trysts. These were patrolled by wardens, dedicated to catching courting couples *in flagrante*, and more than once, Flynn despatched his captor with a well-aimed uppercut to the testicles.

Flynn went back to Tasmania to study biology at the university there, but he had no aptitude for it. He learnt more from a hairdresser from Melbourne named Pat Potter. She was a tall, willowy blonde and he was serious about her, but he found he could not confine his attentions to one woman. The relationship ended when he blew the money he had saved for an engagement ring on a horse – not that the horse lost. The outsider came first because the friend who had given him the tip shoved a powerful enema up the horse's bottom. It streaked home streets ahead of the field, but Flynn blew his winnings on chorus girls.

Sex became synonymous with adventure for Flynn. He seduced the daughter of a razor-wielding Italian barber. When he was caught with a precocious fifteen-year-old, he leapt out through the bedroom window and got tangled in an awning. The girl's irate grandmother called the neighbours, who pulled at Flynn's legs and the whole lot came down. In the confusion, Flynn made good his escape, with a sore head and various bumps and bruises.

Back in Australia, this time in Brisbane, he used to visit a fairground fortune-teller who would always tell him that he was going to have a romance with a woman with occult powers. Then they would fulfil the prophecy.

In 1928, there was a Gold Rush in New Guinea. Flynn joined it, but ended up doing little more than getting drunk and sleeping with the native women. He did somehow manage to get his hands on enough money to buy an old yacht which he and his friends used to sail from port to port looking for talent and young native prostitutes. In the German colony of New Britain, Flynn had his first brush with Nazism which held an almost sexual fascination for him.

On another island, he met the Wilson family, whose twenty-year-old daughter Lucy was a child of nature. According to Flynn: 'She looked like some pagan virgin of ancient times.'

While out for a long walk in the moonlight, she suddenly threw off her dress and plunged into a mountain stream. But Flynn was not on form that night.

'I stood on the bank, tortured, knowing it was no use,' he claimed, 'knowing how childlike innocence disarms and that for me there could be no plucking of the lotus.'

In Melbourne, Flynn got his first film part playing Fletcher Christian in *In the Wake of the Bounty*. He got good reviews though the film bombed. It brought him to the attention of a society woman named Madge Parks who introduced him to oral sex. Her ministrations taxed even Flynn's powers. Pausing only to look back at his naked lover – 'a lovely picture, arms outspread, lovely full breasts' – he stole her diamonds and disappeared to Queensland were he got a job castrating lambs.

'All I had to do was stick my face into the gruesome mess and bite off the young sheep's testicles,' he said.

For sport, he seduced the farmer's daughter. The farmer caught them and, stopping briefly to console himself with the 'blonde and lusty' daughter of a hotel keeper, Flynn fled back to New Guinea.

He wrote several articles for the local paper there. One was on 'The Art and Niceties of Seduction'. It advised readers to avoid compromising positions by arranging avenues of escape first. 'Avoid betraying astonishment at the credulity of the victim – even in the dark.' And he likened offering of marriage to using dynamite after having failed to catch a fish with a fly. He also met a Dr Hermann Friedrich Erben who, some say, recruited him as a Nazi spy.

He had a passionate affair with a Melanesian-Polynesian girl. Her Australian husband walked in to find them together and there was a terrible struggle. Later, he met a young native girl. Her hips were slender, her legs long. She wore a grass skirt and her small breasts were bare. When he first saw her, he could only stare.

Her name was Tuperselai and she was about twelve. He hired

her as his servant. She soon became his mistress and they spent their time swimming nude and making love.

Back in Sydney, Flynn announced his engagement to Naomi Dibbs, but after a failed business and threats from cuckolded husbands, he jumped on board a ship and made his way around the world to England.

His travelling companion was a Dutch-American called Dr Gerrit Koets who told Flynn: 'Women are sexier and dirtier than men, bless 'em, and far more perverted – never forget that. They're all sisters under the skin and the foreskin too.'

Flynn took on board much of Koets' amorous philosophy.

In the Philippines, 'the girls came, the girls went'. He indulged himself in the brothels of Saigon. In Hong Kong, he picked up some oriental techniques, and in Macao, he met the beautiful Ting Ting O'Connor.

'At that age, I was under the ridiculous assumption that the man went on the make for the woman, not the other way around,' Flynn remembered. She invited him up to her room and slipped off her embroidered silk underwear. For a moment, he could not move or think but she took it all in her slender stride. 'I know now that nothing I could have said or done or any way I might have looked would have made the least bit of difference, as her frail little hand reached out like the tentacle of a diminutive octopus and dragged me into the sack.'

On another occasion, he made love to her under the influence of opium 'in ways and manners that I would never have believed myself capable of'. Next day, he put it all down to a dream.

On board a ship bound for Ceylon, he met a Japanese girl named Mayako – 'the most spectacular sight you ever saw, slender, with a twenty-inch waist and long-legged'. She had TB and was married to a Swiss boor who was taking her to a sanatorium in his homeland for a cure. Flynn decided that as she was gravely ill she should have one last fling before she died. He also decided that if she was dying she would probably want one – 'I was right'.

Unfortunately, her husband caught them unclothed. He tried to strangle Flynn. Failing in that aim, he chased him around the ship with a gun. A shot alerted the ship's officers, who disarmed him.

Next stop were the whorehouses of Calcutta. Then he had a

week in the brothels of Ethiopia, then on to the bordellos of the South of France. In England, penniless, he checked into the Berkeley Hotel. When he could not pay the bill, he feigned appendicitis and was rushed to an expensive West End nursing home. He could not pay for that either, but consoled himself with his nurse – 'a truly lovely girl, aged twenty-two' – who became his saviour.

He told her to lock the door because he wanted to tell her something, then he recounted the whole story. By the end, she was shaking with laughter and offered to help him out – Daddy was rich. The one proviso was that he stayed on as her patient for two more days.

'My lovely young caretaker nursed me back into a condition of primal animal vitality,' he said.

After three days, she whispered the word 'marriage' in his ear and said she feared she might be pregnant, and Flynn realized it was time to leave his haven. He fled the nursing home and the city, and got a job as leading man in rep in Northampton. There he was extremely unpopular with the local men who feared he would walk off with all the pretty girls, which he did.

After the evening performance, young girls aged between thirteen and sixteen would wait at the stage door for him and follow him back to his digs. Outside he would line them up and pick one to take up to his room.

He also had a rich admirer who invited him to her country home for the weekend.

'I was stunned to find myself, late one evening, caught on this bear rug,' he said. 'She had this half-nelson on me. She was so visibly repulsive that I truly felt I was being raped.'

He managed to break free, fled to his bedroom, locked the door and slept chastely alone that night.

He fell for his co-star in rep, Elinor Joyce – 'very young, endowed with a beautiful body and hardly a brain in her head'. They lived together briefly until he moved to another touring company in Malvern. There, actor Geoffery Toone recalled, young and nubile girls flung themselves at him.

'He always reached his target, but never bragged,' said Toone. 'At one time he chose two girls and did not know they were sisters. He was successful with both of them and I don't think either sister found out that the other had slept with him.'

Spotted on the stage, he was signed up for the low-budget movie *Murder at Monte Carlo*. It was enough to bring him to the attention of Jack Warner and he was on his way to Hollywood.

Flynn sailed from Southampton to New York on the *Paris*. He spent his time hanging out in his revealing trunks around the swimming pool. The women he met on board ship were not just willing, they were insistent. A fellow passenger on the *Paris* was the movie actress Lily Damita.

Once in New York, Flynn went uptown to a club in Harlem.

'The girls were positively stunning,' he said, 'in all shades, from dark to white.'

He asked a particularly enticing young woman to dance. Back at his table, he put his hand on her thigh. She did not complain. He moved higher. There was no resistance. He moved still higher and 'finally to the highest – and, my God! There I was paralysed, holding in my hands ... I didn't know what to do.'

He made his excuses and left.

In Los Angeles, Errol stayed at the Knickerbocker Hotel. The studio had no work for him at first, so he took the opportunity to renew his acquaintance with Lily Damita. This allowed him to be seen in all the right places. She was five years older than him and a star. At the Coconut Grove, the Trocadero or Chasen's, Lily would slip him money under the table. Soon he made this career move permanent and moved in with her. They lived in a house on top of Lookout Mountain. She introduced him to Dolores Del Rio – 'one of the most beautiful women I have ever seen' – and the painter Diego Rivera. Flynn was particularly taken with Rivera's young wife. She wore a *zarape* – a Mexican drape dress – that was so flimsy you could see right through it. She wore nothing underneath.

Even though he was living with Lily, Flynn had not mended his ways. Actor Victor Jory invited him to a New Year's Day party in San Marino where he sat by the bar making passes at married women.

'I'm going to kill that son-of-a-bitch,' complained one man. 'He just had his hand up my wife's dress.'

Jory threatened to throw him out if he did not confine his attention to single women. Flynn boasted that he was an Irish Olympic boxing champion. Unfortunately for Flynn, Jory was a champ in British Columbia and the Army. They fought. Flynn lost.

'How's about introducing me to some single women?' he said as he picked himself up off the floor.

With no work to do, he would spend his days with Lily or picking up pretty girls and taking them back to a hotel, where he would make love to them repeatedly until it was time to go home for dinner. If he stayed out later, Tiger Lil, as he called her, got jealous and would throw vases and ashtrays at him.

Even though he was on salary, Flynn soon began to build up bills. So he did what any man would do, under the circumstances. He married Lily. Nothing changed. He kept up his freewheeling sex life, even flaunted it. He would get one of her servants – Jim Fleming, who became a life-long friend – to drive over to the drugstore to buy condoms. When Flynn went to bed at night, he would drop them on the dressing table with his keys and money.

'She'd know they were for other women,' said Jim. 'She'd get wildly upset and throw things.'

But Lily did have her uses. She introduced him to Charlie Chaplin, Paulette Goddard, Lupe Velez and other Hollywood beauties.

'Lupe had a unique ability to rotate her left breast,' Flynn noted. 'Not only that, she could counter-rotate it, a feat so supple and beautiful to observe that you couldn't believe your eyes. Beyond that, her breasts were probably the most beautiful that even Hollywood had ever seen.'

Lupe was a neighbour and one day Flynn dropped by to see her. She invited him into her bedroom. He took off his clothes and lay on the bed. After a few minutes, he looked up to see what Lupe was doing. She was kneeling in front of an altar with a huge crucifix on it. She prayed for a considerable time, until his patience had nearly run out. Then she crossed herself three times and let nature take its course.

Despite this intimate knowledge of Lupe's unique anatomical feats, there was no falling out between the Mexican Spitfire and Tiger Lil.

'They were friendly, as far as women can be friendly – the same kind of friendship that a female octopus or giant squid has for another of the same species,' said Flynn.

Lupe was endlessly demanding. She would turn up out of nowhere insisting on sex. It was always the same. As she stripped she would sing a beautiful Mexican love song, then fall on her knees beside the bed to pray to the Madonna. After the Ava Marias and some toying with invisible beads, she would launch into the act.

Nevertheless, Lily got Flynn his first big swashbuckling role. When Flynn heard that Robert Donat had dropped out of *Captain Blood*, he asked Lily to put in a good word for him. She talked to Jack Warner's fiancée Ann and Warner was soon telling everyone he already had the greatest *Captain Blood* under contract.

Flynn's way of saying thank you was to take a spin around the ports of Southern California, ostensibly to look at yachts but actually to chase girls.

In the screen test, he played a hot love scene with Jean Muir. It was plain that he knew what he was doing and he was hired immediately. In the movie, Muir was replaced by the virginal Olivia de Havilland.

Flynn, disappointed, consoled himself with waitresses and carhops. Once he put a dead snake among Olivia's clothes. When she found it, she wept. Such pranks were no way to a girl's heart.

'If only he had been gentle and considerate,' said Olivia, 'if only he had known how to woo me and win me.'

Indeed, it is clear that she was physically attracted to him, but was too uptight to show it.

Now that he was a star he needed a new wardrobe in keeping with his status. Lily gave him $5,000 for clothes. He blew it playing poker.

Dr Erben turned up in Hollywood, spouting his Nazi views. Lily disliked him.

'She felt he was encouraging Errol in his promiscuity,' said Jim Fleming.

Erben's Nazi connections almost got Flynn deported. When the State Department investigated, they found that Flynn was working, quite illegally, on a visitor's visa – even that had run out. Jack Warner used the Hays Office in reverse. He got morality watchdog Will Hays to use his influence in Washington to sort things out.

Fame made Flynn self-conscious and unwilling to pick up girls himself, so he got his friend Johnny Meyer to do it for him.

'He'd book into motels, make love to the girls and move on,' said another friend, Jack Kniemeyer.

They went on a trip to Tijuana, where the girls came running.

When they heard Errol Flynn's name they would fling themselves at him. Flynn was in heaven.

'I was living the life of a married bachelor,' he said, 'male pals around me, starlets for fun and the little woman at home.'

On one occasion, Meyer, Kniemeyer and Flynn were in Del Mar for a tennis tournament. They arrived back at three o'clock in the morning. Lily was waiting with a magnum of champagne.

'You son of a bitch,' she yelled, hitting Flynn over the head with the bottle. She knocked him cold. Next morning he appeared on court with a large white bandage around his head.

Flynn liked to collect souvenirs from his lovers, jewellery – even wedding rings – and items of underwear. He kept these around the home, never bothering to hide them properly. He took more risqué pleasures with underaged girls, usually between thirteen and sixteen. His relationships were furtive and intense. He also went for boys between seventeen and nineteen. He managed to conceal his bisexual tendencies by indulging them south of the border in Mexico.

In Cuernavaca, Flynn also indulged his voyeuristic tendencies. There were places men could go to watch women making love through peep holes in the wall; there was a nightclub which featured live sex acts on stage; and, for a price, you could see men and women having sex with animals. Flynn liked to watch other men making love, often in groups, while he made love to a woman.

In Hollywood though, 'the pretty women everywhere dazzled me'. Lily grew more jealous and more violent and Flynn learned to keep his gaze 'as fixed and glassy as one of the guards outside Buckingham Palace' when she was around – otherwise 'I continued philandering among Hollywood's beautiful girls'. The only moments of peace he got with Lily, he recalled, were in bed.

Inevitably, he got the clap and to escape Lily's wrath he headed off to the Spanish Civil War. He loved the passionate Spanish girls and fell for Estrella, who had long legs, a narrow waist, alabaster skin and seemed to symbolize Spain for him.

'When she stood up naked, she seemed as bewitching as a siren,' Flynn said. 'She was young and I hold nothing against youth.'

Lily caught up with him in Europe for a passionate reconciliation. When they returned to the States, they took a second honeymoon on his yacht the *Sirocco*. In Cuba, he went ashore to play tennis. She stayed on board. He saw a beautiful young woman in her twenties who excited his interest. A friend called Pancho Arranyo informed Flynn that she was from one of the best families. Flynn knew that rich Cuban women were haughty and unapproachable, and he had better look elsewhere for his entertainment. Pancho said that he knew where the most beautiful girls in the world were – a whole house full of them. He knew the madam.

When they reached the bordello, Flynn had to concede that the girls were the most beautiful girls in the world. Soon Pancho was lying on the bed smothered in naked girls. Flynn ordered champagne for everyone..

It was soon five o'clock and Flynn knew he would be in the doghouse. Lily would be pacing the deck of the *Sirocco*. He had to go back that instant if he was to avoid another terrible scene with her. But the champagne was making him braver by the minute. Before long he was thinking: 'If I could just get that one with the big breasts and the little feet.'

Then there was a commotion in the street outside. When he looked out of the window, all the girls from the convent across the road were out on the street. When they saw him, they started shouting: 'Bravo, Errol.'

Flynn realized that if his presence in a Cuban brothel made the newspapers, he would be in trouble with Lily and the studio. He dressed and climbed out of a back window to escape. It was an eighteen foot drop and he ripped his white sharkskin suit. He slipped, fell in through a window and landed at the feet of a large black lady. A burly Cuban man came to see what the fuss was about and pulled a gun on him. Flynn tried to explain but could speak no Spanish. Then a little girl arrived.

'Capitán Blood,' she cried. 'Capitán Blood.'

They showed him to the door and he fled back to the *Sirocco*. When he arrived, he had a lot of explaining to do.

Flynn did not see it as man's natural state to be monogamous – or woman's for that matter.

'Women try to make the man a personal prize,' he said. 'The way I see it, if you love someone, you will love him enough to see him free and unfettered.'

As for Lily's possessiveness, Flynn believed that it had ruined their relationship from the start – 'I have seen this trait wreck more lives than it has helped.'

Lily had every reason in the world to be jealous. At a fancy-dress party at William Randolph Hearst's San Simeon home, Flynn ditched Lily and made off with the young socialite Eloise Ann Onstott, searching for a private rendezvous. They found an alcove near the swimming pool. There were no chairs or benches, so they had to make do with the floor.

'She had lovely hard breasts and a lascivious mouth,' Flynn recalled. 'It was dark, but light enough for us to see each other clearly. It was maddening, sudden.'

Then he heard a noise and looked up. There was a balcony overlooking the alcove and they found they had an audience of fourteen security guards.

Starlets threw themselves at stars in the hope of improving their careers – 'a lot of promises were made'. Flynn generally made it clear that there was to be no part in his next movie before they started, although he wasn't above working out a routine with director Raoul Walsh. If he saw a girl he liked, he would call Walsh over. Walsh would look at her and say: 'You're dead right she would be perfect for the part of the sister.'

The girls were usually eager to show their gratitude. When the script came through, he would say: 'Look what that lousy producer has done, he's cut your part down to one line.'

On the set, anytime Flynn saw a woman he wanted he shouted 'star perks'. This was a warning to others to keep their hands off.

He even tried it on with Jack Warner's fiancée Ann, who had helped get him his first break. They had a wager on a game of ping pong. If he won she was to go to bed with him.

'She never paid up,' he complained.

An actress Flynn did help was Linda Christian. He met her in a bar in Mexico City and was immediately taken with her opaque cat-like eyes, her wide shapely mouth and 'a figure that might have been sculpted'. He mentioned that he was on his way to Acapulco.

'Wonderful,' she said, 'I have always wanted to go there. When do we leave?'

She wanted to break into movies. By the time they got back to Mexico City, Flynn had her on a six-month contract at $100 a week plus expenses. He spent $900 getting her teeth fixed and did get her into the movies. Later, she married Tyrone Power.

During the shooting of *Four's a Crowd*, Flynn complained that he had nothing to wear and stripped naked in front of the associate producer as a protest. Location shots were done in the Bahamas and Flynn took off to one of the remoter islands where he could pleasure himself with both sexes without it getting back to the gossip columnists.

While they were filming *Dawn Patrol*, Flynn began to spend more time at David Niven's house 'Cirrhosis-on-Sea' where he smoked and chewed hashish, drank and chased girls. Sometimes they would drive down to Hollywood High School and check out the young girls – 'jailbait' or 'San Quentin quail', Flynn would call them. Otherwise, he would be on the *Sirocco* and only very rarely at home with Lily. He even put Johnny Meyer on the payroll as his full-time pimp. As well as expecting him to pick up girls for him, Flynn also asked Meyer to find out if any of the young male stars he met at parties was gay. Flynn was attracted to the dark good looks of Tyrone Power, who was a well-known bisexual. They conducted a prolonged affair even though Power had recently married the French actress Annabella. Flynn was very much the male in the relationship, Power the female.

They met in out of the way motels and at the homes of homosexual friends. One of them, Edmund Goulding, would lay on all-male orgies for them, but Power would not join in. He was too shy and sensitive. There were also bisexual orgies, which Flynn enjoyed very much, joining in with a man or woman as the fancy took him.

Meyer went on to perform a similar job for Howard Hughes. According to Meyer, although Hughes kept some of the world's most beautiful women under guard all over Los Angeles, he rarely visited them or had sex with them. On the quiet, Meyer would fix up rent boys for him. Once, he even set up a date for Hughes with Flynn himself.

On *Dodge City*, Flynn was still trying to get into Olivia de Havilland's pants.

'I think I was still in love with him, and perhaps he with me,' she said.

He failed after turning up on the set one morning with a twisted ankle, the result of a daring escape from a girl's flat when her husband had turned up unexpectedly. Flynn asked Jack Warner not to put Olivia de Havilland on his next picture so he could have a crack at a more compliant leading lady.

Flynn practically lived on board the *Sirocco*. He liked to take his shirt off and pose bare chested when tourist boats came by. When he was anchored at Wilmington, one young woman got her water taxi to circle the *Sirocco* six times. When Flynn flexed his muscles for her, she came up alongside and clambered aboard.

Her husband was most put out when the water taxi returned without her. He demanded to know where she was. The boatman told him. He took the taxi back out to the *Sirocco* and hailed Flynn. Two minutes later, the young woman dived over the side and swam towards the water taxi. The husband ordered the taxi back to harbour, leaving his wife to swim the two miles to shore.

Flynn was not the only one who used the *Sirocco* for recreation. A gang of friends, known as the Shit Club, would gather on board under the insignia FFF – Flynn's Flying Fuckers. They would have a contest to see how many young girls they could get through. They kept track on a scoreboard and the winner would get a lapel badge in the shape of an erect penis and testicles.

During the filming of *The Sea Hawk*, Flynn took co-stars Flora Robson and George Sanders to a famous whorehouse downtown. Robson was fascinated by the madam who was swathed in jewels. Sanders was photographed with two prostitutes, wielding a cricket bat.

During World War II, Flynn's patriotism was questioned. Unlike other British and Commonwealth actors in Hollywood, he did not join up. He even had an affair with Gertrude Anderson, a young Swedish nightclub singer who was a Nazi sympathizer.

Rows with Lily got worse. Hedda Hopper who lived next door complained about their shouting. Despite the rows, or perhaps because of them, his appetite for underaged prostitutes of both sexes did not let up.

Lily became pregnant in September 1940. She announced the happy event in a most delightful way.

'Flynn,' she said, 'you think you have screwed every dame in Hollywood, but now I've screwed you, my friend. You will have a child.'

She sure did. In the divorce settlement she got half of everything he owned plus $1,500 a month plus tax.

Financially, he never recovered.

'Even if I worked all my life exclusively for her,' he said, 'I could never meet the tax on the tax on the tax.'

When she gave birth, he was in Hawaii with Gertrude Anderson, spying on Pearl Harbor naval base it has been alleged. He returned shortly after his son Sean was born to drive mother and son home from hospital, he explained, for publicity purposes. The six-year marriage was over. Flynn saw little of his son, though he was plainly concerned about his moral education. When he was twelve, he took him to a brothel and sent him $25 which Sean was to spent on 'condoms and/or flowers'. Sean Flynn went on to become a minor film star, then a photographer. He was lost on assignment as a photojournalist in Cambodia during the Vietnam war.

During World War II, Flynn was classified 4F, which meant he would not be called up. He explained that 4F entitled him to 'Find women, Feel women, Fuck women and Forget them'.

Flynn moved into a dream home he had built on Mulholland Drive. The front room was dominated by an obscene mural, painted by John Decker whom Flynn had met through his hero and drinking buddy John Barrymore. The bookshelves were crammed with pornographic literature. In the bedroom, the huge bed was covered in Russian sable and surrounded by black satin curtains with gold question marks on them. It was a monogram he would later have sewn on to all his things.

The legendary playboy Freddy McEvoy was a friend of Flynn's. McEvoy claimed to be the only man ever to give Woolworth heiress Barbara Hutton an orgasm. He ran a stable of studs for rich women and supplied Hutton with a husband, the superstud Porfirio Rubirosa, for a finder's fee of $100,000.

McEvoy's contribution to Flynn's new establishment was a Russian servant called Alexandre. One night when Flynn came home to find a pair of enchanting twins in his bed, one blonde, one brunette, he called Alexandre and demanded and explanation. The Russian was unrepentant.

'What sort of house do you think this is?' asked Flynn. He looked at them again.

'If you know what's good for you, Alexandre,' he said, 'you'll get one of them out of here.'

McEvoy got married eventually to the twice-widowed and

extremely wealthy Beatrice Cartwright.

Life magazine wanted a spread showing Flynn surrounded by young girls on Catalina. Young hopeful Peggy LaRue Satterlee jumped at the chance. The photographer brought her to the *Sirocco*, which was moored there. They spent the day swimming and sunbathing and that evening they went to a restaurant. Back on board, Flynn went to Peggy's cabin.

'At first, she said no,' he told Jim Fleming. 'Then she said yes. We happily went to bed.'

When Peggy went home, she told her mother what had happened. Mrs Satterlee took her daughter to the doctor who examined her and declared that there was evidence of 'forcible entry into the vagina'. Next stop was the D.A.'s office.

Flynn arranged for a payment to be made to a member of the District Attorney's staff. His lawyer, Jerry Giesler, warned Flynn to be very careful for the next few months. When Flynn complained that this was going to be difficult as the well-developed Peggy looked much older than her fifteen years, Giesler said: 'You'd better check their birth certificates next time.'

Flynn played safe by going down to Mexico with a beauty named Tara Marsh, a former lover of Goebbels. She also claimed to have slept with Hitler, who – far from being impotent, she said – was a normal male despite having one testicle shot off during World War I.

Flynn could not be careful for long. At a party in Bel Air, a drunken girl named Betty Hansen plopped herself down on his lap and snuggled up. He took no notice and continued his conversation. When they went through to dinner, Flynn stood up and dumped her unceremoniously on the floor.

After dinner, he found her on the sofa. She had been sick. He took her to the bathroom. Upstairs, she threw herself on the bed. He could not resist. He took her clothes off and made love to her. Afterwards he invited the two friends she had come with – nightclub singer Lynn Boyer and dancer Chi-Chi Toupes – to join him in the shower.

The next day, seventeen-year-old Betty told her sister that Flynn had seduced her. She was taken to Juvenile Hall and the D.A. dusted off the Satterlee case again.

Two weeks after the party, Flynn was woken by the police who told him that he had been accused of 'the felony of having intercourse with a minor'. He was charged with statutory rape.

Flynn was taken to Juvenile Hall where Betty identified him as the man who had had sex with her. He was also arraigned for forcibly raping Peggy Satterlee on the *Sirocco* – twice.

The press and public went hysterical. Friends rallied around but the prognosis was not good. There were plenty of people who knew that Flynn had had sex with both girls. The public believed him to be a charming seducer, but both girls were undeniably under eighteen, the age of consent in California.

Jerry Giesler was a wily trial lawyer. He took a chance and picked a jury of nine women and three men, reasoning that women loved Flynn. The D.A., surprisingly, accepted this.

In court, Betty Hansen wore a tight sweater with a poodle on the front. The way it moved during her testimony sent titters through the courtroom.

She told the court that she thought Flynn was undressing her to put her to bed because she was unwell.

'Did he remove all your clothing?' asked the Assistant D.A.

'All, except my shoes and stockings.'

'And then what happened?'

'He undressed himself.'

'Did he remove all his clothing?'

'Everything except his shoes.'

'What happened next?'

'We, well ...'

'What happened next, Miss Hansen?'

'We had an act of intercourse.'

'You state that you had an act of intercourse with Mr Flynn right there in that upstairs bedroom?'

'Yes.'

'And this act was forced on you. I mean to say, it was against your will.'

'It was against my will.'

'When you said before that you had an act of sexual intercourse with Mr Flynn – you meant, didn't you, that Mr Flynn inserted his private parts into your private parts?'

'Yes.'

'Please speak up so everybody can hear you, Miss Hansen.'

'Yes, it was like that.'

'How long would you say the act of sexual intercourse took?'

'A half hour. Maybe fifty minutes.'

Afterwards she said she went into the bathroom to use a douche bag.

Giesler undermined Hansen's testimony completely. He got her to admit she was provocatively dressed. He pointed out that one minute she had said that she had thought Flynn was a nice man helping her to undress because she was ill; the next that he had forcibly undressed her. She also admitted that she thought Flynn might help her get a job in the movies.

Then Giesler asked if she had ever had sexual intercourse with her boyfriend, Armand Knapp, a messenger at the studio. She denied it. He then asked her if she had been held at Juvenile Hall, charged with performing oral sex on Knapp – oral sex was a felony in California. The Assistant D.A. leapt to his feet. Giesler pressed on.

'Did you not admit, Miss Hansen, under oath before the grand jury that you have performed two acts of sexual perversion with a man?' he asked.

The courtroom exploded.

Sobbing helplessly, Betty Hansen admitted having oral sex with Knapp – and she was suspected of having performed oral sex on several of his fellow messengers.

The case was far from over. Peggy Satterlee took the stand. She told how, on the first occasion, Flynn came to her cabin and got into bed with her. He had pulled her underskirt up and her panties down and had sex with her. Afterwards, he had brought her a glass of milk and had called her J.B. – jail bait – knowing she was underage. After a day's swimming and photography, she told the court she had been sitting on deck looking at the moon. Flynn had remarked that it would look prettier through a port-hole. She went to his stateroom and got on the bed to look at the moon. When she tried to get off, she said, he pushed her back on the bed, removed his trousers, pulled down her pants and had sex with her.

'Did Mr Flynn insert his privates in you?' asked the Assistant D.A.

'Yes,' said Peggy.

On both occasions, she claimed, she resisted.

Giesler established that Peggy worked in nightclubs as a showgirl and frequently said she was twenty-one to get work.

With the help of a renowned astronomer, he demonstrated that Peggy could not possibly have seen the moon through the port-hole of Flynn's stateroom. It was on the wrong side of the boat. Giesler also got Peggy to admit that she had extra-marital relations with another man and an illegal operation – that is, an abortion.

Flynn had five shots of vodka to steady his nerves before he took the stand. He denied everything calmly point by point. Betty had not sat on his lap; he had not gone upstairs with her; he had not had sex with her; he had not called Peggy jail bait, nor laced her milk with rum; he had not been to her cabin; he had not slept with her; he had not taken her to his stateroom to see the moon; and he had not had intercourse with her on either occasion.

In summing up, Giesler said that his handsome, rich, famous, movie star client was as pure as the driven snow. His two accusers, he said, were lying to avoid prosecution for other felony charges.

The jury was out overnight. The women all believed Flynn was innocent. Rape in a narrow bunk four foot off the ground on board the *Sirocco* was impossible, they held. Two of the men thought he was guilty. Eventually, the men gave in. Flynn was found not guilty. He was not wearing a hat, but touched his hair as a salute to the ladies of the jury.

'I yielded with a smile to the now complete legend of myself as a modern Don Juan,' he wrote.

The rape trial had forced the war off the front pages. Afterwards, women pursued him more assiduously. His popularity soared at the box office. Ironically, the next two films out were *Gentleman Jim* – which some joked should be called simply *Jim*, because he had not taken his shoes off before having sex with Betty – and, oh yes, *They Died With Their Boots On*.

Although Flynn appeared to take it all in his stride, he was deeply damaged. His lust for young girls – and boys – was not going to subside. In any sexual encounter now he felt vulnerable. He had a printed notice put on his front door which read: 'Ladies: Kindly be prepared to produce your birth certificate and driver's license and any other identification marks.' One of the Shit Club scrawled on the bottom: 'Preferably on your thigh.'

What Flynn really craved was the safety of the love of one woman who would adore and idolize him – a woman like Lily

Damita. What he got was Nora Eddington.

She was the daughter of Captain Jack Eddington of the Los Angeles County Sheriff's Office. Her mother was Mexican. Stuntman Buster Wiles brought her up to Flynn's house for a party one night. They were attracted to each other right away, but Nora was not a pushover.

'I was a virgin and already had a beau,' she said. 'Errol was charming, but I didn't want to be involved.'

However, she kept coming back. Flynn took time out to educate her about literature and music, but she knew when she left his house in the evening that he would get in 'professionals' for himself and other guests. Hookers were hardly going to go to the police complaining about rape.

Despite this outlet, Flynn grew increasingly frustrated at Nora's unwillingness to go to bed with him. One night, after a party, when he was high on booze and cocaine, he got her into his bedroom and stripped off her clothes. Then, Nora told author Charles Higham: 'Suddenly he was thrusting into me. It was like a knife. I felt I was being killed. I screamed and screamed. He went on and on. I couldn't push him out. There was blood everywhere. It was on the sheets, on the walls. Alex came rushing in, convinced there was a killing going on. He was horrified. At last, Errol got off me. Later, when he realized what he had done, he wept and begged forgiveness.'

And Nora did forgive him. She consented to be his mistress, though he had two others at the time.

'He was changing women as fast as Alex was changing the sheets,' she said. 'I wanted to love Errol to death and then alternately to kill him every time I learned about those other girls.'

One of them was a model from New York. She tried to kill herself on Mulholland Drive and Flynn told her enough was enough. Just to be near him, she started sleeping with Alex.

On a trip to New York, Flynn met a fresh-faced struggling young writer named Truman Capote. Flynn suggested going to El Morocco but when they got there, he said: 'Let's forget about El Morocco. Why don't we go back to your place?'

Capote explained that he lived in a tiny walk-up. Flynn said he did not care as long as it had a bed. Years later, Marilyn Monroe asked Capote if he had enjoyed it.

'If it hadn't been Errol Flynn, I wouldn't even have remembered it,' he said.

Flynn was fighting a paternity suit when Nora became pregnant. At first, he suggested an abortion. When she refused, he suggested they marry to legitimize the child, then divorce straightaway. He would give her $75 a week child-support.

Nora went to her mother's in Mexico for her confinement and Flynn took up with her cousin. Eventually Flynn turned up in Mexico and they married by proxy in Cuernavaca. The next day, promising to return for the birth, Flynn headed back to Los Angeles for another round of his paternity suit with twenty-three-year-old Shirley Hassau, the wife of a sailor.

She said that he had made love to her in the front seat of a coupé and was the father of her three-year-old child. Flynn said her claims were ridiculous. He never made love in the front seat, only in the back seat – and only with the greatest discomfort in a coupé. He was six foot two.

Of course, Flynn did not return for the birth of his daughter Deidre. He headed for Jamaica instead. He did not even admit to the marriage until three months after the birth when Nora returned to Los Angeles. Even then, it did not seriously restrict his freedom. He bought Nora a house in Hollywood and continued his bachelor existence in Mulholland Drive.

'This is the only way I would be married to anyone,' he said, 'separate houses, separate lives, separate people.'

Nora seemed happy enough, too. After all as Flynn wrote in his autobiography: 'The man who for a woman fits the bill is the one who pays the bill.'

Mulholland Drive became the scene of a constant orgy. Mickey Rooney recalled turning up there for a dinner party with Wallace Beery.

'When we knocked on the door,' Rooney said, 'it was opened by a pair of exquisitely beautiful twins, and they were absolutely nude.'

Pornographic movies were regularly shown. He had a two-way mirror installed in one of the bedrooms so he could watch guests making love. He would get friends to bring women and have sex with them in there, and give them a big round of applause at the moment of orgasm.

Famous Los Angeles madam Lee Francis would have fleets of hookers shipped up to the house. They played 'musical whores'.

Each man would perform with each of the prostitutes in turn. The last one to climax was the winner.

Flynn took to writing semi-pornographic novels and bought a new yacht, the 118 foot *Zaca*. He had a king-sized bed installed in his bedroom with a large mirror facing it. He loved his new yacht so much that he made a film about her called *The Cruise of the Zaca*.

He gave the actor Sterling Hayden a sailing lesson once. Hayden told Flynn that he had first heard about him from a man named Mackenzie in Port Moresby: 'He said you owed him money.'

'He's a bloody liar,' said Flynn. 'I had a, shall we say, 'social disease' at the time. After I left, it seems his wife came down with it.'

Flynn also spent time freewheeling around the Caribbean, Mexico and South America. He particularly liked Jamaica. The beautiful girls reminded him of the Melanesian and Polynesian girls he had known as a young man. It was this that persuaded him to buy an estate there.

He nearly got arrested in a cathouse in Panama. The moment he walked in he was mobbed by near-naked girls who put themselves in every imaginable position to get near him. They asked if he wanted to take any of them to bed. He replied, gallantly, that he did not think he could afford any such beautiful women. Ten minutes later the place was raided by a shore patrol, but fortunately Flynn had left to rush a friend to hospital. The friend had been bitten in a sensitive place by a hooker unwilling to perform oral sex.

In Acapulco, Flynn picked up a beautiful nightclub hostess called Choo-Choo. She had exquisite breasts and legs, but when she stripped off it became clear that she was a man. Flynn renewed his affair with Tyrone Power, but it was a rocky relationship. Power wanted things done to him that Flynn found distasteful. His homosexual activities were confined to oral sex. Flynn also seduced beachboy Apollonio Diaz, who was having an affair with actress Mari Blanchard. Later, Apollonio dated Power's early love, Lana Turner.

In Argentina, Flynn met and fell in love with Eva Peron. He told a friend in Hollywood: 'Eva and I were lovers for a long time. At one time, when I was in Buenos Aires, Peron found out about it. He told me if I didn't get out of the country in twenty-four hours I would be found dead in my room.'

Nevertheless, the affair lasted until her death in 1951.

In Hollywood, Flynn would occasionally spend an evening with his wife, talking again of literature and music. Nora recalls these as idyllic times and they had a second daughter, Rory, when Deidre was eighteen months old.

The birth of their second child brought about a change in Flynn. He wanted to give his marriage a proper try. He had a nursery built on to the house on Mulholland Drive. Nora moved in on the proviso that he did not bring any other women to the house or to the *Zaca*. She knew it was futile to try to prevent him from seeing women elsewhere. But Flynn could not even live up to those limited conditions. He entertained his leading ladies on his yacht and once, not knowing Nora would be there, a friend brought a girl with whom Flynn had slept in Jamaica, up to the house. Flynn pretended he had never met her before, but Nora was not fooled. She had seen her in *The Cruise of the Zaca*.

By the age of thirty-eight, Flynn had a heavy drug problem and was beginning to lose his potency. One night he went to a party with a beautiful girl and got so drunk he passed out. The host discovered that the girl was a very expensive hooker. Flynn had hired her for the night and not even used her.

He allowed his homosexuality to surface nearer to home, too. He picked up a young male hitchhiker and installed him in a cottage in the grounds of the house on Mulholland Drive.

However, during the shooting of *The Adventures of Don Juan*, Flynn was up to his old tricks. When he was late for a scene, director Vincent Sherman stormed into Flynn's dressing-room to find Flynn stark naked with a girl in full period costume on top of him.

Another time, Sherman went into Flynn's dressing-room to find Flynn naked except for a towel. Flynn whipped off the towel and a giant dildo jumped up at Sherman, giving him the shock of his life.

By now, Flynn's marriage was on the rocks. Nora took off for Palm Springs where she started dating singer Dick Haymes. When Flynn found out about it, he grew jealous. While he went off to indulge himself in the fleshpots of Europe, she obtained a divorce in Nevada and nine days later married Haymes. Flynn responded by getting engaged to Princess Irene Ghika, a member of the Rumanian royal family. She was so distressed by his behaviour that she slashed her wrists. He left her and went to India to film *Kim*.

Flynn greatly enjoyed watching the erotic dances of India and he experimented with aphrodisiacs. A Eurasian girl called Flower of Delight attached herself to him and he also latched on to the daughter of a British diplomat in the Maharaja's Palace in Jaipur.

'You can't be serious,' said director Victor Saville. 'She's staying in the Maharani's quarters. That's sacred.'

The women's quarters were heavily guarded. Undeterred, Flynn managed it.

At the end of filming, Flynn gave a massive party. He had a giant gold pyramid constructed by the props department. Lounging on it were sixty of the most beautiful girls in town, bought and paid for and completely available to any member of the cast or crew who wanted them. He even laid on a special girl to look after their clothes. Flynn himself looked on as a judge. At the end of the evening, he awarded a special gold FFF medal to the man who had given the most spectacular performance.

The co-star of his next movie, the western *Rocky Mountain*, was the stunning blonde Patrice Wymore. They were thrown together on location in Gallup, Kansas. She had only been given a corner of a tent to dress in. Generously, Flynn allowed her to change in his trailer.

'We were like two kids, having fun,' she said. 'I was twenty-four and Errol was forty-one but we both felt we were sixteen.'

They married on 23 October 1950 in Monaco. At the reception in the Hôtel de Paris, Flynn was served with a warrant for his arrest. He was charged with having unlawful intercourse with sixteen-year-old Denise Duvivier on board the *Zaca* which was moored in Monte Carlo harbour.

Hauled in front of a magistrate, Flynn faced his accuser. He was horrified. She had long black hairs on her legs. She claimed that they had had sex in the shower on board the yacht. Flynn maintained that was physically impossible and invited the magistrate out to the *Zaca*. Inspecting the scene of the alleged crime, the magistrate accidentally nudged the tap and got drenched. But, he noted, he was soaked with salt water. Duvivier had claimed it was fresh. Case dismissed.

While he was away, Lily Damita tied up most of Flynn's property in Los Angeles for nine years' back alimony. Not that she was hurting. She lived a lavish lifestyle in America and Europe and had refused a number of parts in films. Nora was also in the courts demanding $885 a month in child support, so Flynn spent more of his time on his estate in Jamaica.

'Jamaica is a woman,' he explained.

He was visited there by the writer Earl Conrad who helped ghostwrite Flynn's autobiography. He noticed that young blonde nymphets would seek Flynn out. Seduction was easy.

'They have seen me on the screen and they've passed beyond their fantasy life into trying a direct confrontation,' Flynn explained. 'What they want is a little romance: some sweet talk, a bit of gentle fondling, a work-up, something to remember the situation by. It doesn't have to be too much, but some dalliance. When the moment is right, you plunge into the mattress.'

Often, he couldn't be bothered even with that. He preferred the local girls who were supplied to him by a pimp. The pimp would line them up in the driveway each day and Flynn would look down from the second-storey porch where they were working on his book and pick one out. Once he had paid the pimp, he would shout down: 'You – the tall one – come up and show me a good time.'

The encounter would last five or ten minutes.

He would also pick up prostitutes in the street, respectable women, too. He would offer them a job as a nurse at a top rate of pay. They would nurse him once or twice, only to find that he was perfectly well.

'I'm probably oversexed,' he explained.

Filming *Crossed Swords* in Italy, Flynn became very ill with hepatitis. He was warned off sex and alcohol and taken to hospital.

'But Errol was still Errol,' said friend Johnny Bash. 'He had two girls going up there for oral intercourse every hour on the hour and bringing him champagne which he put in the flower vases. The flowers died, of course.'

So, nearly, did Flynn. A priest was called and he made his peace with God. The girls were cancelled. The champagne stopped. Ten days later he was back at work.

Flynn indulged himself with the handsome boys who hung around the Spanish Steps. They would often latch on to him when he was drunk. Once they had seduced him they would demand money. If he did not pay, they said they would go to the newspapers. One boy, called Claud, even accompanied Flynn on a romantic cruise down the Adriatic coast.

Patrice put up with this, but gradually it caused a gulf between them. He wanted a woman to fight with. Her understanding was intolerable to him. When she became pregnant, he fled.

Flynn returned to Patrice for the christening of their daughter Arnella on Jamaica. Then he flew to England to film *Lilacs in Spring*. He visited Northampton and told an audience that he had spent the happiest period of his life there. In Blackpool, he judged a beauty competition, but instead of shaking the winners' hands, he goosed them one by one.

In *The Warriors*, Flynn played the Black Prince. One afternoon, he was standing on top of the battlements originally built for *Ivanhoe* when he saw two girls arriving by car. He clambered down the battlements, had a word with them and clambered back up again.

'Good news,' said the Black Prince addressing his men. 'I'm on with both of them tonight.'

In 1956, while Patrice was away on a singing tour of Europe, Flynn went to Cuba to film *The Big Boodle*. He enjoyed the prostitutes there and loved to watch the sex shows. His marriage to Patrice finally came apart. He sued *Confidential* magazine for libel, for alleging that he had left his bride on their wedding night to have sex with a prostitute. After that, he continued to travel the world, visiting gay brothels and sleeping with prostitutes.

While Flynn was playing his old friend John Barrymore in *Too Much, Too Soon*, he met fifteen-year-old Beverly Aadland who had lied about her age to get a part in *Marjorie Morning Star* which was being filmed on the adjoining set. Beverly claimed that she was a virgin when she met Flynn, though actor John Mohlmann claims to have been there first. His seduction of Beverly was much like that of Nora Eddington – a violent rape. Beverly's show-biz mum Florence dried her daughter's tears and hushed the whole thing up.

Soon Beverly and Flynn were an item. Her youthful vitality made Flynn his old self again. In his diary, he recorded that his favourite pastime with Beverly was 'a prolonged bout in the bedroom'. His career revived. There was even talk of him playing

Humbert Humbert in *Lolita* – a case of life imitating art if ever there was one.

Flynn called Beverly 'Woodsie' because she reminded him of a wood nymph. On her seventeenth birthday, Flynn announced their engagement. They would be married just as soon as he divorced Patrice.

They travelled widely together. In Paris, Flynn took her to a lesbian nightclub he had once visited with Lily. Beverly danced cheek to cheek with a bull dyke. Flynn objected and picked a fight with the dyke, who flattened him with one punch.

'If they hear about this in Hollywood,' said Flynn, flat on his back, 'I'm finished.'

Flynn developed cancer of the tongue. After a painful operation in New York's Presbyterian Hospital he went back to Cuba to film the excruciating *Cuban Rebel Girls* with Beverly. The film purports to show the struggles of the young women guerrillas who rallied to Castro's cause. While he was there he managed to conceal from her an affair with a young male admirer.

Flynn had a heart-attack in July 1959 and was told he had a year to live. He grew tender towards Beverly. One night, at a sophisticated party, she slipped and fell in the pool, ruining her dress. In her embarrassment, she ran to the bathroom in tears. He followed and held her close to comfort her.

'I never saw such tenderness in a man's eyes,' said a friend.

Soon after that, he died. He was just fifty. The coroner said he had the body of an old, old man.

Fourteen months after his burial, Beverly's mother sued Flynn's estate for $5 million. He had deprived her daughter of her youth and introduced her to 'his unhealthy, unwholesome and perverted philosophy of wringing every pleasure out of life, regardless of cost', the petition stated. He had 'debauched and corrupted her through repeated or persistent immoralities' and he had led her 'along the byways of immorality, accustomed her to frenzied parties, subjected her to immoral debauchery and sex orgies, and aroused within her a lewd, wanton and wayward way of life, and deep unripened passions and unnatural desires inimical to the interest, welfare and fulfilments of her normal youth'. So he had given her a pretty comprehensive education, then.

The case was dismissed. Besides, after everything had been accounted for, there was not much left. Apart from his films, his only enduring legacy is his wonderfully frank autobiography *My Wicked, Wicked Ways*. You said it, Errol.

6

LESS-THAN-ABLE GABLE

'God knows I love Clark, but he's the worst lay in town.' So said Clark Gable's third wife, Carole Lombard – and she should know, she had very broad experience to draw on when making any comparisons.

Gable's lover for more than thirty years, Joan Crawford, concurred.

'He wasn't a satisfying lover, I often tried to distract him from the bedroom,' she said. 'But he had more magnetism than any man on earth.'

His reputation as a great lover depended on the sheer number of women he slept with. But he was more than aware of his own shortcomings. When he was given the opportunity to sleep with Gary Cooper's long-time lover, the Mexican spitfire Lupe Velez, he refused, saying: 'Forget it. She'll be blabbing it all over town the next day what a lousy lay I am.'

On the whole, he preferred going with prostitutes.

'Because they go away and keep their mouths shut,' he said. 'The others stay around, want a bit of romance, movie love-making. I do not want to be the world's greatest lover.'

The number of women he is reputed to have bedded is inflated. Gable himself said: 'Hell, if I'd jumped on all the dames I'm supposed to have jumped on, I'd never have had time to go fishing.'

But he was quite sanguine when his reputation for being no good in the bedroom got about.

'I guess I'll just have to practise more,' he said.

And practise he did. Even when he was married to Carole Lombard, whom he loved more than the world, he was always going to bed with someone else. He had one great secret when it came to women – himself. Gable knew he was king and he knew why.

'When I make love to a woman on the screen, I rough them up a bit before they beg for a kiss,' he said. 'I don't open doors for them. They open doors for me. Light my cigarettes too. A dame won't admit she likes it, but men are getting away with a slap and a boot. It's reality. So I'm king for showing them how to treat a lady.'

Women loved it. Marilyn Monroe got goosebumps all over when Gable accidentally touched her naked breast.

'Any woman who is not attracted to him is dead,' said actress Joan Blondell.

He took advantage of that. Screenwriter Anita Loos said Gable had 'that old early American male idea that you must take on any girl that comes your way'.

In Europe during World War II, an army buddy asked why he was going out with a real dog and Gable replied with a shrug: 'Well, because she was there.'

Not that he did not have his fair share of beauties, too. His name was linked romantically with nearly every one of his co-stars, from Grace Kelly, through Ava Gardner to Jean Harlow. Once, when looking at an MGM publicity display showing the studio's stars, he said: 'What a wonderful display of beautiful women and I've had every one of them.'

But he had a dark secret – on-screen, he was the quintessential male, but as a struggling young actor in Hollywood he had slept with Twenties' star William Haines to further his career. The bisexual director George Cukor knew about it. During the filming of *Gone With The Wind*, Cukor would tease Gable by calling him 'dear' on the set. Gable responded by calling him a 'fairy' to his face and getting him sacked from the picture.

Producer David O. Selznick put it about that Cukor was a 'woman's director' and, at Gable's insistence, had been replaced by 'man's director' Victor Fleming, a well-known hetero who was fresh from affairs with Norma Shearer and Clara Bow.

William Clark Gable was born on 1 February 1901 in Cadiz, Ohio. His mother died as a result of childbirth. His father was a wildcatter – a roustabout with his own rig – who considered that acting was sissy.

At fourteen, Gable had his first girlfriend, a redhead named Thelma Lewis. At six foot, he may have been tall, but he was not good-looking.

'His ears were too big,' Thelma said. 'He wasn't interested in school, except for playing the horn in our band. Clark wasn't a good dancer either, all feet.'

He was no good at sport and started appearing in school plays. His father, noticing signs of incipient sissiness, sold his rig and bought a farm in Hopedale, Ohio, where Clark was to pitch hay and learn to be a man.

Fortunately, Gable's father found a new wife, who mellowed him. He let his son take a job as a time keeper in a rubber factory in Akron. Until then Clark had never been to a movie before and he also went to the theatre for the first time. He loved it so much he took a job as a callboy just for tips. He sewed on buttons, slept in the theatre and showered at the YMCA.

Unfortunately, when the stock company left town, the next one would not employ him. He joined his father working on the oilfield near Bigheart, Oklahoma, chopping wood and handling a jackhammer. They slept in a tent which was sweltering in the summer and freezing in the winter. The wildcatters were serviced by visiting prostitutes – young girls mainly, but old before their time. Clark had to have his share to prove himself to his father, but he was appalled to discover that one woman he took to be a blonde turned out, in reality, to be a brunette.

The life of a roustabout was more manly than Clark could handle. When he heard that a new repertory company was being formed in Kansas, he quit the oilfield, determined to be a sissy.

Unfortunately, the thespians of Kansas City did not think he was nearly sissy enough. They hired the strapping Gable to help hoist the tents. In an attempt to rise in his chosen profession, Gable slept with an older woman in the company who, he claimed, had only one eye.

The tent show folded in the middle of a blizzard and Gable jumped train at Bend, Oregon, where he got a job in a lumber company near the tracks. He had no gloves and toughened his hands with lard and vinegar. This gave him his large masculine hands. He never needed gloves after that.

He headed on to Astoria where, after selling ties in a department store, he made his stage debut on 23 July 1922 – as Eliza, the Negro cook, in *When Women Rule*.

Gable met petite, twenty-two-year-old Franz Dorfler when he went to audition for the Astoria Stock Company. He was flirting with another girl when he offered Franz a sip of his soda. She refused, but he insisted on walking her home. On the way, he turned on the charm. She was the most beautiful girl he had ever met, he said. It was love at first sight. By the time they reached her front door, she was all but convinced that he could not live without her.

He failed the audition, but kept on turning up. Soon he was telling everyone that Franz was his girl and got jealous if she so much as talked to another man. The company was preparing to tour, but there no way that Gable could go with them.

'He had nothing, absolutely nothing, to offer the stage,' said the company's director Roland Jewell. 'He barely got on and off the stage without a great deal of difficulty.'

Clark begged Franz to stay behind with him, but she was not going to give up her chance. Instead she convinced Jewell to take Gable – for no pay. He did, at least, know all the parts and could stand in for others if they got sick. His big chance came when one of the actors quit, but on his first night on-stage, he fell over.

'It was a disaster,' said Jewell, but he had no choice but to keep him on until the end of the run. The only thing Clark had to recommend him was that he was always immaculate.

Franz felt sorry for Gable and encouraged him. They spent a lot of time together, sharing their deepest thoughts and ambitions. He stole his first kiss.

'I was shocked,' she said. 'But I liked what he did so impulsively. It was wonderful because we could share each other. He was my first beau, and I was his first girlfriend. We had been looking for each other.'

Franz was two years older than Gable but she felt that she had time to wait for him to master his craft. At Seaside, Oregon, where they shared a small cottage with another couple, taking turns to sleep on the beach, Gable proposed. Franz accepted. They planned to save their money and build a career together.

The touring company folded and they went to stay with Franz's parents. They were less than impressed with this drifter their daughter had brought home and, when marriage was mentioned, they actively discouraged it.

They sent Franz to Portland. Gable chased after her. By the time he got there, she was in Seattle, where she had been offered a good part in a play. For the time being, Gable gave up the theatre and took a job as a telephone linesman to earn enough money to marry. Franz encouraged him to take singing lessons. Then she wrote telling him that a drama coach, Josephine Dillon, who had once appeared on Broadway, had moved to Portland. Meanwhile, Jewell had formed a new company. He had signed up Franz, but there was no job for Clark.

Gable was desperate to keep up with the woman he wanted as his wife. He sought out Josephine Dillon and enrolled in her classes. He was, she noted, truly awful. One afternoon, he dropped around to her house and told her of his overwhelming desire to be a movie actor – until this time he and Franz had always set their sights on Broadway. Josephine was impressed with his burning ambition. And she was overwhelmed when, as he was leaving, he turned and said: 'You're a fine looking girl.'

No one had ever said that to her before.

Gradually, her interest in other students dwindled and they left. She lavished all her attention on Clark, describing him as a 'gorgeous skeleton'. Until this point, he had been utterly faithful to Franz. Now, he found that he was attractive to all sorts of women, particularly older, wealthy ones. He gave a poetry reading at Portland's Women's Club and found himself besieged.

Josephine herself was thirteen years older than him. She mothered him and, despite her growing feelings towards him, took messages from his middle-aged lovers and encouraged him to go out with girls his own age. The last thing she needed, she concluded, was a frustrated student who might suddenly throw it all up when she had put in so much work.

Franz reappeared in Portland with the touring company. She was as eager to marry as ever, but Gable had cooled. He even told her that a doctor had advised him never to get married, but would not say why. She asked Clark if there was another woman. He said no, which was true – there were many other women.

Franz suspected there was something going on between Clark and Josephine. There was an uneasy rivalry between the two women, but Franz felt distinctly upstaged by the former Broadway actress. Josephine resolved the situation by moving to Hollywood and opening a drama school there. In the meantime, now that Gable was trained, she arranged a job for him in the stock company alongside Franz. With her rival gone, Franz thought she could rekindle their romance but Gable avoided her, dating other women all over town. After a couple of months, Josephine sent the $50 fare from Portland to Los Angeles. Gable told Franz cheerily: 'I'm going to Hollywood.'

Franz threw his love letters in the fire and cried every night for years.

By this time, Josephine was deeply in love with Gable, but she would not give herself to him physically. Instead, she worked tirelessly to teach him and polish him for the big break which she was convinced was just around the corner. She bought him a car for $60, so that he could make the rounds of the casting agents and studios. He waited on line at the studio gates with thousands of other bit-part players, to be turned away more often than not.

On 18 December 1924, they married to save money. That way, they could live respectably in her one-bedroomed bungalow, without Gable wasting cash on a hotel room. Both insisted that the marriage was 'in name only' and remained unconsummated.

They were devoted to each other and clung together through hard times. He would queue for hours each day for a walk-on part that would yield just $3 a day. But when he suggested that, like others, he slept outside the studio to be nearer the gates when they were hiring in the morning, Josephine would not let him. They needed their evenings together for his lessons.

Josephine tried to cultivate friends who might help Gable. She would take him to parties where he would quickly scan the ladies' jewellery. Soon he would be dancing cheek to cheek with the wealthiest woman there. Josephine became jealous. This led friends to conclude that their relationship was not as platonic as they insisted. They were living together under one roof, in one room, sleeping in one bed. Those who knew Gable knew that he was perfectly capable of having sex with anyone, then turning over and going to sleep.

Suddenly he got a bit part in the silent film *White Man* at $15. He began to go out more on his own. She asked no questions, but in an attempt to keep him home she put him through his paces over and over again. In the end, he would run out into the night, slamming the door behind him.

Taking a break from the movies, Gable got a part on stage as a spear carrier in *Romeo and Juliet*. He so impressed the forty-one-year-old leading lady Jane Cowl, who played the star-crossed teenaged maiden, that she upped his salary and took him on tour.

Another mature lady of the theatre, producer–director Lillian MacLoon, offered him a part in *What Price Glory?* When the leading man left, Gable replaced him. At first, Josephine would accompany him to the theatre, but when sparks flew between her and Lillian, Josephine was banned.

On tour with a play called *Lullaby* in San Francisco, Gable bumped into Franz again. They spent a lot of time together. Their kisses were long and passionate, and he grew jealous of the other men in her life. However, he somehow forgot to mention that he was married. Then, when their feelings got too intense, he ended it.

'I regretted seeing him again,' she said, 'because I realized how much I still loved Clark.'

The relationship ended abruptly when he stood her up.

When Gable appeared in Los Angeles, Josephine would come every night and criticize his performance. He retorted that there were plenty of other women who liked what he was doing up there. She dismissed his easy way with his leading ladies and warned him to put out of his mind the admiration of 'a few flighty girls'.

His teeth, Josephine decided, were a problem. They had not been capped. It was expensive but she worked out a deal with the dentist and went on paying for years to come.

His new smile worked a treat on Billy Haines, MGM's popular leading man and closet homosexual. Gable knew which side his bread was buttered and extended his sexual favours to Haines for a favour in return. He appeared with Haines in *The Pacemaker, The Plastic Age* and *North Star*.

Joan Crawford, a friend of Haines and a lover of Gable's, explained: 'Jobs were hard to get. If you didn't know somebody, forget it. There was a lot of that sort of thing going on in dark corners.'

When Haines' homosexuality got to be a problem, the studio ordered him to drop his boyfriend, Jimmy Shields, and arranged a marriage to Pola Negri; but before the wedding, he was caught with a sailor in the YMCA and there was nothing the studio could do to save him. He went on to a distinguished career in interior decorating.

While waiting for his next movie part, Gable took a minor role in the play *Madame X*, which starred forty-four year old Pauline Frederick. She had made over forty films. Critics loved the way she used her eyes and hands. Gable was struck by her professionalism and glamour; she by his terrible teeth. She insisted that he get them capped properly, at her expense.

To reimburse her, he would keep her company each night in

her mansion on Sunset Boulevard. Gable commented that Pauline was 'a woman who acts as if she's never going to bed with another man'. Although she was twenty years old than him, she wore him out. Gable complained of stomach problems at the time because of all the oysters she forced down him to keep him going.

He moved out of Josephine's bungalow into an apartment of his own. Then he played opposite Lionel Barrymore in *The Copperhead* and, in *Chicago,* upstaged Nancy Carrol who had just won a $5,000 a week contract at Paramount. He was playing one of his favourite movie roles, a reporter.

Then the parts dried up. In desperation, he turned to Josephine. She got him a job with a stock company in Texas. When he phoned from Houston with news that his salary had been raised to $200 a week and he was playing leads, Josephine rushed to his side, but her interference was again an embarrassment to him. Besides having Mrs Gable around was inhibiting his social life. Already little girls queued up at the stage door for his autograph. Gifts from admirers arrived daily and silk-gowned socialites fawned over him at the posh parties he got invited to. Gable and his harassed director begged her to go back to California.

Back in Los Angeles, Josephine turned down a movie offer from Dorothy Davenport on Gable's behalf, without even consulting him. He was furious and asked her for a divorce. She consented, but insisted that they stick by the deal they had made back in Portland. They were partners until he had made it on Broadway.

So she went to New York to fulfil her side of the bargain. She did the rounds and landed him a role in *Machinal,* a new play produced by Arthur Hopkins. She wanted to hang around to coach him during the rehearsals, but he had had enough of her meddling.

'He signed the contract with Hopkins, got himself a good agent, and phoned to say he was through with me,' Josephine recalled. 'I said I was going back to California and that he had better become a good actor, as he could never be a man.'

The critics raved. *The New Yorker* referred to him as a 'great lover'. He tried to pull his leading lady Zita Johann, but she refused him.

'He had impact on stage, but no impact on me,' said Zita.

But he was not to be pitied.

'Clark was always out with women,' recalled another member of the cast. 'I don't know where he slept because he never slept in his own bed.'

The heiress Jana Langham was a great fan of Gable's in Houston but when she turned up in New York, her forty-five-year-old mother Ria said: 'Guess who I've been seeing a lot of? Clark Gable!'

'I was very happy for her,' said Jana.

Ria Langham was halfway through a divorce herself. Everyone assumed Gable was after her for her money. It did not matter, though. She could afford him. Besides, it was acknowledged, he was very, very handsome.

By this time he had developed his fashionable, thin moustache and he sported a derby and a gold-tipped cane that Ria bought him. He looked wealthy, but after *Machinal* closed he went through a bad patch and was soon deeply in debt.

Again, he knew which side his bread was buttered. Marriage to Ria would sort everything out. He set out for Los Angeles with Mexican divorce papers for Josephine to sign. She refused, arguing that a quickie divorce might cause problems in the future. Instead, she would file for divorce in California on the grounds of desertion. She would ask for no property and no alimony. The divorce would be uncontested, but he would have to wait a year for it to become final. When it did, the penniless Gable and the wealthy Ria married secretly.

Gable was happy to live off Ria's money, but she wanted him to pursue his acting career and encouraged him to take the lead in the play *The Last Mile* in Los Angeles. He took the part reluctantly, convinced that he was going to be a flop and back in New York in a matter of weeks. Instead, he was a great success. His salary rocketed to $300 a week. Movie agents beat a path to his door but, after years of struggle and rejection, he wanted no part in the film industry.

However, *The Last Mile*'s producer ran off with the box-office receipts and Gable let Hal Wallis' sister Minnie take him to see a Hollywood casting director. He got a part in *The Painted Desert*, a B movie, for $750 a week. He played a cowboy. Minnie signed him to the part assuming, as a farm boy, he could ride a horse. He could not. Minnie quickly arranged lessons.

Warner turned him down for a gangster role in *Little Caesar* because his ears were too big. He was relieved and was getting ready to jump on the train back to New York when Ria and two of her children turned up on the coast. She wanted to stay in California, but he did not want to play house. If he had to stay, he would much rather spend his time hustling the film industry with Minnie.

Hollywood was abuzz with the advent of sound. Many of the silent stars fell by the wayside and the studios were desperately searching for a new batch of leading men. Gable had no fear of the talkies. For years, Josephine had been giving him voice lessons. MGM signed him for $650 a week and, after the sneak preview of his first talkie, *The Easiest Way,* they were convinced they had found a new star.

The studio was not too pleased that Gable had a wife. They liked their stars to be single and 'available'. If a star was married, it had to be to a glamourpuss. Ria was too old.

Gable tried it on with his leading lady, Constance Bennett, but was rejected.

'She didn't know I was alive,' he said.

Then Franz turned up in Los Angeles.

'You're my only friend here,' he told her. 'I'm a very lonely guy.'

This time he told her about the break-up of his marriage to Josephine, but neglected to tell her about his new marriage to Ria. She read about it in a fan magazine and was broken-hearted once more. Although she outlived Gable, she never married.

On *Dance, Fools, Dance*, he was teamed with Joan Crawford. They were afraid of each other. He was afraid that she would make him look a fool because she was a star. She was afraid of him because of his stage training. But when they met, the attraction was instant.

'Call it chemistry, call it love at first sight or physical attraction. What's the difference?' she said. 'The electricity between us sparked on the screen, too. It wasn't just acting. We meant every damn kiss and embrace. God, we both had balls in those days.'

Joan constantly warned other actresses about falling in love with their leading men. They should not take the romantic scenes to heart and they should leave their feelings behind when they left the set.

'Boy, I had to eat those words,' she said, 'but they tasted sweet.'

Ria wanted to socialize with Clark's leading lady and her dashing husband, Douglas Fairbanks Jnr. Most of all she wanted an invitation to Pickfair. Gable was unenthusiastic.

'But Pickfair appeals to anyone who has an ounce of class,' Ria said.

'That's why it doesn't appeal to me,' said Gable.

Besides, Crawford's marriage was already on the rocks. Fairbanks wanted her to give up acting, though it was her life, and she resented the fact that he spent his days socializing around Hollywood swimming pools while she sweated it out in the studio.

With Gable everything was different. They both came from the same impoverished middle-American background and both had made it through sheer determination.

'He told me it wasn't his thing to get involved with married women,' said Crawford. 'I was the exception, but we were both in and out of affairs, marriages and divorces all the time. We outlasted them all.'

It was a love affair that lasted a lifetime.

The strain was already showing on Gable's marriage. Often Ria would go to bed alone, while he stayed up late studying scripts. The truth was he could not raise a laugh for her. Joan was using up everything he had.

In his next movie, *A Free Soul,* Gable gives rough sex to his boss's wife, Norma Shearer who, at that time, was married to Irving Thalberg. Thalberg himself said: 'Gable's the man every woman wants and the man every man wants to be.'

The public wrote in, in their thousands, asking to see more of 'the guy who slapped Norma Shearer'. On the screen, as in life, Gable became, not the man who chased after women, but the man women chased after.

In 1931, MGM discovered that Gable's marriage to Ria was not legal in California. The studio had a problem. They had played down her role. Now, to avoid a scandal, they were going to have to arrange a wedding.

It was a quick, private affair in front of a judge, but as they were leaving the courthouse, the newlyweds were cornered by reporters. Under their relentless questioning, Ria broke down. So Mrs Gable was not the sophisticated, worldly wise socialite they had taken her for.

The marriage threw the spotlight on Josephine, too. The press hounded her for the intimate details of her life with Gable. She called MGM and threatened to sell her story to the tabloids unless Gable came up with some money. Her silence cost him $200 a month.

Next, Gable was teamed with Garbo. He was afraid that she would act him off the screen. He held his own, though.

'I was more at ease in our love scenes than at arm's length,' he said.

After ten movies, the Gables moved to Beverly Hills. This put him in the middle of the Pickfair set to which Ria craved entry. Gable endured it to be near Crawford. They were falling deeply in love.

Joan confided in her old friend Billy Haines, who was discreet enough not to mention his doings with Gable. He did, however, remind her of how much she looked like Gable's old lover Pauline Frederick. Crawford was a great admirer of Pauline's. She knew she could not rival the older actress's performance on the stage, but had no doubt that she could outperform her in bed.

As a long-term lover, she was far from exclusive. During Gable's feud with Josephine, Hearst newspaper writer Adela Rogers St John stoutly defended Gable against his former wife's claim that she was the fount of his talent. St John dismissed Josephine as an 'old lady schoolteacher'. Adela was also the screenwriter on *A Free Soul*. She was ten years older than Gable. They became lovers and the affair continued for many years. When confronted with the rumour that she bore him a child, she said simply: 'What woman would deny that Clark Gable was the father of her child?'

Reunited for the filming of *Possessed,* Crawford and Gable found their emotions had reached a new intensity. They were compared to Garbo and John Gilbert during *Flesh and the Devil*. When, during love scenes, the director said 'cut', they did not stop.

'It was like peeking into someone's bedroom,' said one observer.

'We were madly in love,' Crawford said.

She was in a turmoil. She was worried about her future in movies, her marriage to Fairbanks and, most of all, about her love for Gable. He was well known for the one-night stands that made his married life bearable.

Jokingly, Crawford brought up the idea of marriage. Gable took her seriously and said he thought that they should begin divorce proceedings right away. Crawford kept her head firmly glued to her shoulders. She knew that the Hollywood rule was 'never marry your leading man until you have filmed three pictures with him'.

Hollywood was buzzing with rumours about Gable and Crawford. Ria knew that confronting her husband would only make matters worse, so she took a trip to New York with her children, courtesy of MGM.

As far as Gable was concerned, Ria's trip was a separation and he saw Joan day and night. They were being so recklessly public with their love that Louis B. Mayer had to step in. The affair would do neither of them any good, he explained.

'But I love Joan and I intend to marry her,' said Gable.

'What about all the others you are sleeping with?' said Mayer. 'Besides, Joan is good for only one thing. I admire her as an actress, but she's a slut.'

Crawford, too, protested she was in love. And Gable's other peccadilloes?

'If we were married, that would change,' she said.

'I know different, and so do you,' said Mayer. 'And I'm not so sure you know what it is to sleep in only one bed either.'

Mayer forced them to break it off, otherwise he would ruin their careers. MGM would drop them and he would make sure that no other studio would touch them. Gable was even forced to call Ria in New York and beg her to come back.

As a consolation prize Crawford got to play in *Grand Hotel* with Greta Garbo and John and Lionel Barrymore. She recalled meeting Garbo: 'We came face to face, noses almost touching, and my knees went weak. She was breathtaking. If I ever thought of becoming a lesbian, this was it.'

But still, behind Mayer's, Ria's and Fairbanks' backs, they found ways to be together.

Gable also found a little consolation of his own on *Polly of the Circus*. It was an awful film, but it co-starred William Randolph Hearst's blonde mistress Marion Davies. When Hearst was busy, the ex-Ziegfeld girl liked to play away. Gable frequently accepted invitations to dine *à deux* at her Santa Monica beach-house. She rewarded his attentiveness with a property near Palm Springs.

The MGM publicity machine made sure that the magazines were full of the happy couples – Gable and Ria, Crawford and Fairbanks. They mouthed platitudes in public; in their few snatched moments, Gable and Crawford cried, loved, tore into Mayer, and made love again.

When Mayer realized what was going on, he sent Crawford on a second honeymoon to Europe with Fairbanks, all expenses paid, and cast Gable opposite Jean Harlow in *Red Dust*. She had married MGM producer Paul Bern only to discover, on her wedding night, that he was impotent. She flung herself at Gable. During the scene when she bathes in a rain barrel, she refused to wear a bathing costume and flaunted herself naked in front of him on the set.

Their on-screen love scenes were unselfconscious. They made love as if the camera was not there. Even when the camera was not rolling, they could not stop touching each other. Few who saw them believed that they were not having an affair.

During the filming of *Red Dust,* Bern killed himself over his impotence and the scandal enveloped Jean, but with Gable's guiding hand, she made it through to the end of shooting.

Crawford and Fairbanks returned from Europe and joined in the merry social round. The Fairbankses and the Gables dined frequently and kept up appearances. Behind everyone's back, Crawford cursed Gable for his affair with Harlow.

'It's either her or me,' she told Gable. 'And if you choose her, don't ever speak to me again.'

But there was nothing she could do when he was cast opposite Jean in *Hold Your Man*. Again, the two were dynamite on-screen and commiserated with each other off it.

'That frustrated tart is bedding down with him,' Crawford told a friend.

To Joan's further chagrin, Gable managed to fit in a number of casual flings. Meanwhile, he was loaned to Paramount for *No Man of Her Own* opposite Carole Lombard, who was happily married to actor William Powell at the time. She bought a ham with Gable's name on it and told everyone: 'I'm one leading lady he did not seduce.'

Gable and Crawford worked on *Dancing Lady* together, which sent Fairbanks into a sulk. Joan announced their divorce and pressed Gable about their marriage plans. Gable was in no hurry. He was afraid of what Ria might do to him in the divorce courts. He took two months off to have an appendectomy and his rotten teeth replaced by dentures. It was also rumoured that he had become a Mason and would bed only girls whose families were Masons.

Crawford was considering marrying Franchot Tone, while Mayer punished Gable by lending him out for *It Happened One Night*, with Claudette Colbert. Even Gable could get nowhere with her. She was one of Marlene Dietrich's lesbian 'sewing circle' and she refused even to show a leg during the famous hitchhiking scene – until she realized that the stand-in's legs were not as shapely as her own, that is. However, Mayer's punishment backfired. *It Happened One Night* was a surprise success. It won four Oscars, including one for Gable as best actor. Now Mayer had to give him good pictures.

The first was *Men in White* with Myrna Loy.

'No, we weren't lovers,' said Myrna. 'He wasn't my type, even though I found him extremely attractive. I heard he was always on the make at the studio, snapping garters left and right.'

One night, when Gable and Ria gave Myrna a lift home, he walked her to her front door and, while she was unlocking it, Gable gave her a 'monkey bite' on the back of the neck. She shoved him off the porch into a hedge.

After that he did not talk to Loy again off the set. Instead, he began a pretty serious thing with actress Elizabeth Allan, who was playing a student nurse.

He was sent on a tour to promote *Men in White*. Everywhere he went, women fell at his feet. More than once Ria walked into their hotel bedroom to find Gable kissing and fondling a young woman. She pretended to be near-sighted.

For his sins, Gable was teamed with Myrna Loy again in *Manhattan Melodrama*. Then he was cast in *Chained* with Joan Crawford and her current beau, Franchot Tone. The attraction between Gable and Crawford was too strong to be resisted.

'We grabbed every chance to be alone,' she said.

This was too much, even for Ria. Now fifty, she could not compete with the twenty-eight-year-old Crawford and withdrew to Houston.

Gable told Crawford that his marriage was over, but they knew they could never marry. The studio was against it. Nevertheless, Crawford pledged her undying love. So did Gable. In that case, why had he been sneaking up to see Mary Pickford on the servants' day off Joan asked. And why had he been seeing Carole Lombard now that her divorce from William

Powell was coming through? Gable admitted ashamedly that both women had turned him down. Years later, Mary Pickford conceded that she had indeed turned Gable down because she was so upset over her separation from Fairbanks, but she regretted it later.

'I must have been out of my mind,' she said.

On *Call of the Wild*, Gable fell for twenty-three-year-old Loretta Young. She had been in pictures from the age of fifteen. At nineteen, she had eloped with twenty-nine-year-old actor Grant Withers. The courts annulled the marriage. During the filming of *Man's Castle*, Spencer Tracy left his wife and moved into a hotel with Loretta, who was thirteen years his junior. She later announced that they could not marry as they were both Catholics and the affair ended.

Despite her broadminded attitude to sex, Loretta was prudish about swearing and installed a swearbox on the movie set when she was working. It was five cents for a 'damn'; ten cents for a 'hell'.

'How much for a "fuck"?' Robert Mitchum once asked.

'Oh Robert,' she said. 'That's free.'

During the filming of *Call of the Wild*, director William Wellman lost his temper with Gable because he was paying too much attention to 'monkey business' and not enough to making movies. The gossip columnists hinted that Gable and Young were melting the snow on location in Washington state on the cold winter nights. After the end of filming, Loretta Young went to Europe.

Gable was teamed up again with Jean Harlow on *China Sea*. During the filming, Harlow divorced her husband of two years' standing, cameraman Harold Rosson. Gable went on to South America to meet up with Loretta. She returned to Hollywood with a baby girl she had 'adopted' – even though it is against Californian statute for a single person to adopt. She said she had found the girl in a San Diego orphanage, but the child had suspiciously large ears and grew up to look like Loretta.

Gable went to New York where he was seen about town with a number of wealthy ladies. He confirmed that his marriage to

Ria was at an end. They were formally separated and the judge awarded her half his earnings. Meanwhile, Joan Crawford eloped with Franchot Tone. The marriage did not last long and the following year Gable and Crawford resumed their affair.

In the meantime, Gable indulged himself with starlets, extras and high-priced call girls. To protect his male stars, Mayer laid on a service. Covertly MGM ran an establishment called The Cat House. It was staffed by former starlets who were checked regularly for venereal disease. This way, Mayer could protect his stars' health and reputations and avoid the complications of divorce and blackmail.

'He was like a kid in a candy store,' said Crawford of Gable at this time. 'At a party, he would size up every woman in the room. Within minutes he knew which one was leaving with him, even though he had not met her yet.'

His approach was subtle. He would walk up to the woman he had picked and say something flattering about her hair or dress, without taking his eyes off her face.

'He didn't have to say anything sexy,' said Crawford, 'because he reeked of it. Maybe he did some chasing but few girls ran the other way.'

One particular girl who worked as an extra recalled how he operated on the set.

'Within fifteen minutes, he knew I was from Cleveland, how old I was, where I lived in Hollywood, and how many room-mates I had,' she said.

Then he said that he wanted to go over his lines for the next take and suggested they go back to her place after work, so he would not be disturbed by reporters and autograph hunters. Her roommates could go to a movie.

Back at her place, he poured a drink, entered into some harmless chit-chat, then asked her about her movie ambitions. He told her how cute she was, then kissed her and enfolded her in his arms.

He fondled her breasts, then suggested they take their clothes off. She was impressed with his muscular body. There was no romancing, no petting, no foreplay and no kissing during the act, which lasted less than a minute. Then he asked whether he could take a shower.

After that, he talked a little about getting her bigger parts and left, without even a goodnight kiss. The next night, he went with another girl. The girls on the set talked about it, swapped notes and they all said the same thing – that Gable was the most exciting man in the world and that he was the cleanest. He took five or six showers a day and shaved his armpits and his chest.

He was just as scrupulous about his women. They had to be spotless. When he discovered that a girl was not a natural blonde, he would suggest that she bleach her pubic hair too. After that, he would never see her again.

The next week he went with the same extra again. He gave her a big wink and said what a lucky guy he was. He never got her a screen test, but the cachet of sleeping with Gable got her more extra work.

Once he invited her over to his suite in the Beverly Wilshire. She spent a week's pay on a sexy negligée for the occasion. He told her to come around the back of the hotel, where he had a private entrance.

He took her suitcase for her, but left it by the door instead of taking it into the bedroom. After a few drinks, he had her on the floor, then disappeared into the shower. She was just about to hang up her negligée, when he came out of the bedroom wearing a collar and tie.

'I have to rush off to a meeting. Glad you could come over. I guess you're anxious to get back home for dinner,' he said, handing her her suitcase and bundling her out of the door. She forgave him the next day after a wink and a smile.

Sometimes, he would fool around in bed and talk, but that was usual. The affair went on through a number of pictures and even continued when he was seeing Carole Lombard.

Not every woman was so compliant, though. When a maid walked into his hotel room to find Gable naked in bed, he said: 'Why don't you join me?'

'How much?' she asked.

'I would think just being with me would be payment

enough,' said Gable.

The maid disagreed, and left.

By 1936, Merle Oberon was in Hollywood. She had moved out of the Café de Paris and into movies by the simple expedient of marrying Alexander Korda. Her career in Hollywood blossomed because she became the mistress of the legendary producer Joe Schenck, one of the founders of United Artists and Twentieth Century Films, who smothered her in diamonds and furs. When Gable met her, she was also bedding Leslie Howard and David Niven.

Gable thought that she was the most exotic creature he had ever met. For her, love was not just a quick one on the floor before being bundled out of the door. It was a banquet. The stage had to be set with champagne and caviar, incense, soft music, candlelight, exquisite lingerie and satin sheets.

Gable's relationship with Carole Lombard was tempestuous from the start. She had turned him down when she was going through her divorce from William Powell. He had once steered her out of a party at Victor Hugo's in Beverly Hills and got her halfway back to his hotel before she demanded to be taken back to the party.

At a ball given by millionaire John Hay Whitney, she had stormed off the dance floor, very publicly rejecting him. Gable was still a married man making no attempt to get a divorce and she had no intention of being one of his 'quickies'. Gable was persistent and Lombard began dating him occasionally.

Knowing how much Gable loved his Duesenberg convertible, Lombard bought a second-hand Model A Ford for $15, had it painted with big hearts and sent it to Gable on Valentine's Day 1936. He phoned her up and asked for a date. He turned up in his tuxedo – and the Model A – and drove the evening-gowned Lombard to the Trocadero.

Lombard was simultaneously dating scriptwriter Robert Riskin, and running around town, dancing till dawn. Gable continued his discreet affairs. If she spotted Gable flirting with other women, she would give men the glad eye. She always gave as good as she got and Gable, though taken aback at first, liked a challenge.

The press began to take an interest in their affair. When asked whether he was in love with Lombard, Gable replied: 'No, I just like the way she wiggles her derrière in a tight satin dress.'

She told reporters: 'Clark's not circumcised, but that's all right.'

Gable began to take her on hunting and fishing trips, previously reserved for the boys. She swore like a trooper, told the dirtiest jokes and caught the biggest fish.

The whole affair soon became impossibly public. Her house was besieged by reporters and it was awkward for her to be seen spending too much time at his hotel. So they moved into houses close by each other in a secluded corner of Bel Air. With their busy schedules, it was the only way they could see each other, he told friends. For the first time, the King was exhibiting signs of being in love.

In 1937, an Englishwoman named Violet Norton claimed that Gable was the father of her daughter Gwendoline. She had recognized him when she had seen *It Happened One Night*. Gable managed to prove that he had never been to England.

'As affairs go, the one she described had to be a long-distance project,' he said.

Lombard remarked that he had his work cut out to make it at close range. She thought that the Norton affair was the funniest thing and used to hang pictures of her and the 'love child' over the bathroom mirror or under the toilet seat.

During the filming of *Saratoga,* Gable's co-star Jean Harlow died. She was about to marry William Powell, Lombard's ex. Gable and Lombard were shaken and it brought them closer still. A number of young actresses had to be auditioned to stand in for Harlow – to be shot from the back – to complete the film. Gable ran his eyes over the young blonde hopefuls as if he was auditioning for his own personal seraglio. Mary Dees got the part and remained one of Gable's favourites. Virginia Grey, who failed on this occasion, turned up in a number of other Gable movies.

Lombard began to spend a lot of time on the set with Gable, which inhibited his activities with his co-stars and extras. She would hold on to his arm, to show that he was hers. Once she left a little present with a note for him in his dressing-room. He showed it around. It was a woollen cock warmer that Carole had knitted herself. Everyone noted that it was rather small.

On the set of *Idiot's Delight*, Lombard noticed a chorus girl flirting with Gable.

'Get that whore outta here!' she yelled.

The girl was fired.

She also managed to keep him out of the grips of his co-star, the recently widowed Norma Shearer, who had had her eyes on Gable for some time. Lombard was determined to marry Gable, but he was not ready to divorce Ria, fearing that she would take him to the cleaners. Soon his hand would be forced.

In 1938, while Gable was up for the part of Rhett Butler in *Gone With The Wind,* the magazine *Photoplay* printed an article headlined: 'Hollywood's Unmarried Husbands and Wives'. It complained that Robert Taylor and Barbara Stanwyck, George Raft and Virginia Rice, and Clark Gable and Carole Lombard were all openly living together as lovers but had not bothered to marry.

The article caused a scandal, which was compounded when Ria gave an interview saying that Gable could have a divorce any time he wanted – provided he was 'businesslike' about it. Mayer insisted that Gable open negotiations with Ria. Meanwhile, Gable and Lombard – using Lombard's money – bought Raoul Walsh's ranch in the San Fernando Valley as a marital home.

Everyone believed that Gable would bed Vivien Leigh during the filming of *Gone With The Wind* – certainly there was high-voltage sexual electricity between them – but there was also too much aggravation. Gable resented Leigh's poor time-keeping. She considered it unprofessional that he left the studio at six o'clock each evening – factory workers punch time clocks, not actors, she said. He thought it was wrong for an English girl to be given the most American of roles. She got on with the soft, understanding George Cukor. He favoured Victor Fleming, Cukor's replacement who was more of a man's man. Leigh hated Gable's bad breath – he ate onions deliberately – and the smell of liquor around him nauseated her. When he kissed her, he said, he thought of a steak.

So instead of bedding his co-star, he fooled around with a 'blonde, petite, cute' bit-part player.

In January 1939, Gable got his divorce. On his first day off from filming, he and Carole took the 400-mile drive to Kingman, Arizona, where they married. The following day they held a press conference. The day after that he was back on the set.

On the ranch in the Valley together, Gable and Lombard were idyllically happy – except for one thing. They had no children.

'They were forever checking sperm and tried every position known to humans,' said a friend.

'We'd do it in a pile of manure if we thought it would make any difference,' said Carole.

It seems that Gable's low sperm-count was responsible for their infertility, but Carole took the blame, not wanting to ruin his rugged, masculine image. As time went on, he managed to keep up his reputation as a womanizer through his own efforts. It caused not a little marital strife.

Clark loved to regale Lombard with details of his affairs. Once he told her about having a girl in a swimming pool.

'It's not an easy thing to do,' he said.

'I know,' said Lombard.

Gable turned white.

'How can you talk like that,' he said, 'a nice girl like you.'

Carole took her mind off things by signing for as many pictures as she could. She thought if she kept busy, she might get pregnant and warned friends not to drop around on Sundays because she and Gable were making babies.

She also went horse riding, because the doctors told her that it would shake up everything inside, but she was unimpressed with the experience.

Gable was cast opposite 'Sweater Girl' Lana Turner in *Honky Tonk*. Lana denied they had an affair but rumours were so rife that Lombard had to be barred from the set. Gable and Turner were teamed up again on *Somewhere I'll Find You*, which caused even more domestic strife.

'Clark was nuts about Lana,' said agent George Nichols, 'but I honestly don't think she was a threat to his marriage.'

Nevertheless, Lombard issued some ugly threats. Generally, she took it all in her stride. When she left on a war-bonds sales tour of her home state, Indiana, she left a blonde dummy in the bed with a note saying: 'So you won't be lonely.'

Lombard was so eager to get back to Gable that, against the advice of her numerologist, she took a flight home rather than wait for the train. The plane crashed.

As a joke, Gable had put a male dummy in bed with the blonde one. It did not seem so funny after the telegram came saying: 'NO SURVIVORS. ALL KILLED INSTANTLY.' Gable had not even been at the airport, waiting for his wife the night she died. He had been busy elsewhere – with another woman, it was said.

The night after the crash, he went for comfort to his long-term lover Joan Crawford. She said he cried and got drunk. Guilt at making love to someone else at the very moment Lombard, the love of his life, died was said to account for much of his grief.

'He had every right to drink during that terrible ordeal,' Crawford said, 'but he kept right on hitting the bottle. He was in another world and never came back to us.'

Carole's death had left him with a death wish. He bought a motorcycle and had a near fatal accident before the studio forced him to give up the bike. At the ranch, Gable kept Lombard's bedroom exactly as it was the day she left for Indiana, even though he invited long-term lover Adela Rogers St John there.

When Lombard died, Gable was still filming *Somewhere I'll Find You* and the studio asked Lana Turner to comfort Gable through his grief. He visited Crawford regularly, often staying until dawn. Although the first heat of passion had gone out of their relationship, they still made love occasionally.

He joined the US Army Air Corps, in the expectation – and the hope – that he would not survive the war. After training in Florida, he returned briefly to the ranch. At a farewell party, he met up with Lombard-lookalike Virginia Grey, who was seen on his arm again after the war.

Posted to England, he was mobbed by women. One woman, who had no underwear on, leaped on him and he had to shout for help.

He contented himself with one-night stands and daredevil stunts. Those who flew with him reported that he had a death wish but somehow he survived and returned home to the ranch to find Virginia waiting for him. Thoughtfully, she had moved into a property nearby. But the pain had not gone. When he attended the naming of a ship called *Carole Lombard*, Gable broke down.

Once he got back down to work, the old Gable began to re-emerge. When he met MGM actress Kay Williams, he lost no time.

'Why don't we go upstairs and get undressed?'

'Why don't you go shit in your hat?' she replied.

Soon they were dating regularly.

He was also seen around with thirty-year-old former model Anita Colby. In West Palm Beach, he was seen with millionaire divorcee Dolly O'Brien and, in Oregon where he had bought property, he spent time with Carol Gibson, a mean hand with a fishing rod. And there was always Joan Crawford.

Cast in *The Hucksters,* Gable was not happy with the script and demanded changes. Mayer complained that he was castrating the script, castrating the book and castrating the project.

Gable said: 'Hell, no. If I wanted to castrate something, it would be you.'

Gable was still not happy, even after the changes were made, but agreed to be in the movie because he had been cast opposite twenty-four-year-old Ava Gardner. She was not happy either, but agreed because Gable was in the picture. They hit it off right away, though both maintained a stable of other rides.

He added eccentric Standard Oil heiress Millicent Rogers and Jones Sausages heiress, the blonde athletic golfer Betty Chisholm to his growing harem. Some of his earlier conquests had bolted, though. Dolly O'Brien and Kay Williams had both married again, and Lana Turner was in love with Tyrone Power. Gable was lonely and drinking too much, more conscious than ever that he was no good at making love.

He would spend time enjoying the fun and games at Errol Flynn's house, along with Robert Taylor and Spencer Tracy. Anne Sheridan compared the two Hollywood legends, Flynn and Gable: 'Flynn was the most beautiful man I had ever seen. Flawless. But he didn't have the startling effect that Gable did. I have yet to figure it out. Errol made my heart beat faster, but the first time I saw Gable, my heart stopped beating.'

Gable dated Paulette Goddard and the young starlet Nancy Davis, who later married Ronald Reagan. Millicent Rogers turned up in Hollywood, determined to marry Gable. When she discovered that he was seeing other women she dropped him and became a recluse.

Dolly O'Brien, now on the loose again, whisked him off on holiday. He proposed to Anita Colby. She turned him down, believing that he had only asked her to marry him out of loneliness. Then his relationship with Crawford went public. He was nearly fifty; she was in her mid-forties. They had both been around the block a few times.

'We understood each other,' she said. 'That was the problem. We understood each other too well.'

Virginia Grey doggedly hung on and the newspapers expected an announcement at any time, but Gable still decamped on fishing trips with Carol Gibson and went golfing with Betty Chisholm. He added the British writer–producer Joan Harrison to his stable of fillies.

Newcomer Shelley Winters and Yvonne de Carlo went to Flynn's house for a drunken dinner party with Flynn and Gable. Winters threw herself at Gable, but he went off with de Carlo, leaving her to entertain Flynn for the weekend.

Flynn suggested that he give a party in her honour. She

would turn up with Gable. The two men would have a fight. The press would have a field day which would launch her career. They double-crossed her. During the fight, Flynn had someone call the police. Winters was arrested, handcuffed and led away in tears. Winters was livid, but next day the stunt was splashed all over the front pages and offers began rolling in.

At a party given by his former agent Minnie Wallis in the summer of 1949, Gable met Douglas Fairbanks Snr's widow Lady Sylvia Ashley. They began dating occasionally. Then in December, he was seen drunk at a party given by agent Charles Feldman. She was all over Gable and he was not slow to respond.

'It was really something to see a woman take advantage of him,' said another guest.

The next day, Gable announced that he was going to marry Lady Ashley. Three days later, they got spliced. Gable was still drunk.

They went to Hawaii for their honeymoon with MGM publicity chief Howard Strickling in tow. It was plain to Strickling that the couple had nothing in common. Gable remained drunk throughout the trip.

When they returned, Gable phoned Virginia Grey to apologize. He was drunk, he explained. It had all been a terrible mistake.

'Don't ever phone me again,' she said.

Gable's friend Robert Taylor immediately moved in on the grieving Virginia. Joan Crawford was merely amused.

'If I had still been married to Douglas Jnr,' she said, 'Clark would have been my father-in-law.'

The marriage did not fall apart immediately as everyone imagined. Lady Ashley put Carole Lombard's remaining possessions in storage and redecorated the ranch in pink – a colour that Gable detested. His gunroom was turned into a French parlour and the house was extended. Even though she was wealthy in her own right, she spent his money on expensive clothes. Continental cuisine replaced plain American food and the dinner guests – the Nivens, the Colemans, the Boyers –

were distinctly European.

After years of dissolute living, Gable responded positively to this change in regime. He glowed with health. However, the sight of Gable carrying Lady Ashley's terrier, Minnie, with its diamond-studded collar turned many a strong stomach.

Minnie had to come too when he went to film *Across the Wide Missouri* in Colorado. Lady Ashley transformed the cabin they were assigned by hanging frilly lace curtains and landscaping the garden. Breakfast was served on bone china and eaten with the best silverware. Cocktails were served in cut glass. She could not get the hang of the cookouts where the cast and crew ate dinner at long tables, although it gave her a chance to wear her 'western outfits'. She had bought one for each day and one for each night of filming.

Back in Los Angeles, Gable offended his wife by falling asleep at the opera in his white tie and tails. Everyone else was greatly amused.

When Gable was offered *Lone Star* with Ava Gardner, he had no intention of letting Sylvia spoil it and told her he wanted a divorce. She took a holiday in Nassau. When she returned the locks had been changed. In May 1951, she filed for divorce in Santa Monica. Gable was, once again, with Gardner.

'Ava makes me feel like a man,' he said.

Fearing that Sylvia was about to hit him with a crippling divorce settlement, he withdrew all his money from the bank, threw it in a suitcase and headed for Lake Tahoe, where he countersued under Nevada law.

In Carson City, he met young brunette divorcee Natalie Thompson. She returned with him to Los Angeles, but Gable was not really interested in a steady relationship. He set about restoring the ranch to the way it had been before Sylvia. Carole's things were taken out of storage and returned to their rightful place.

Gable settled with Sylvia for $150,000, paid over five years. She went on to marry Prince Dimitri Djordjadze. Royalty was much more her style.

Gable was pleased to be cast in *Mogambo* opposite Ava

Gardner, but this time around, she was well and truly married to Frank Sinatra. The film was a remake of *Red Dust*, which he had made with Jean Harlow whose nude scene in a rain barrel remained etched on his brain. This time they would film in Africa. On the way, he stopped in London to film *Never Let Me Go* opposite Gene Tierney. Her mother told Gene: 'You could have Gable if you set your mind on it.' But Gable had already fallen in love with twenty-seven-year-old blonde Suzanne Dadolle, a Schiaparelli model in Paris. He spent weekends with her and danced in the street with young French girls on Bastille Day.

He had another treat awaiting him in Nairobi – his other co-star, twenty-four-year-old newcomer Grace Kelly. Grace had been mugging up on Swahili. She called Gable *Ba*, the Swahili for father – Carole Lombard always called him 'Pa'.

'Would you like a nibble of my *ndizi*?' she asked.

'I'd never turn down an offer like that,' he said.

She explained that *ndizi* was Swahili for banana. *Mogambo*, she said, was Swahili for passion. He was beginning to get the gist. She also told him that she had fallen in love with him when she had seen *Gone With The Wind*.

Gable was not impressed by Grace at first, though he realized that she was not the posh Philadelphia girl she made out to be. Once on location, he discovered that there were no available white women for thousands of miles and quickly warmed to her. In the bush, they took long walks together. They ate together and she read poetry to him, like an elderly married couple. One night Donald Sinden, Grace's husband in the movie, stumbled into Gable's darkened tent to find the two of them in bed together.

The news got back to Hollywood. Louella Parsons cabled her congratulations. Gable wired back: 'THIS IS THE GREATEST COMPLIMENT I HAVE EVER HAD. I'M OLD ENOUGH TO BE HER FATHER.'

After the filming was completed, they took a holiday together on the Indian Ocean. Gable was rather overwhelmed with the way Grace gave herself so completely. He had decided not to get married again – he could not afford the alimony. Besides, he was bored being with just one woman.

Grace flew to London, via Rome, with Ava Gardner. Gable went back to Paris and Suzanne Dadolle. They met up again in London for post-production. Grace wanted him to fly back with her to New York, but he wanted to stay on in Europe. It might be his last chance to see the sights. Besides, why should he rush home to an empty house? At Heathrow Airport, Grace burst into tears. There was little doubt that she loved Gable very much.

Gable was back in Paris with Suzanne Dadolle when the news came through that his divorce from Lady Ashley was final. Reporters asked whether she would be wife number five. She said: *'Oui.'*

That was the end of Suzanne. He fled to Holland to film *Betrayed* with Lana Turner. It was his last film for MGM.

Back in the US, Grace Kelly continued pestering Gable. He explained that he was too old for her. Besides, he and Robert Taylor were having too much fun. They would head off to some farflung town, get drunk, pick up waitresses and have sex with them in cheap motels. Gable never got bored with picking up girls in bars. He said it was a challenge to him.

Although they pretended to be Hollywood stuntmen, Gable did not really care if he was recognized, just as long as he could get one more girl into bed.

He continued seeing Betty Chisholm and Adela Rogers St John, Virginia Grey let him back into her life, and Joan Crawford's door was always open, even though she was now dating the vice-president of Pepsi-Cola.

Gable filmed *Soldier of Fortune* with Susan Hayward. They laughed at how they had never got it together before. At Hollywood parties Gable had always lusted after her. Her friends had always told her that he could not keep his eyes off her, but she had not believed them. She was shortsighted and could not see his lecherous looks for herself, and he would not make an approach without some sort of response.

Kay Williams had divorced and they began dating again. She came to visit him when he was filming *The Tall Men* in Mexico with Jane Russell. There was talk of an engagement and on 11 July 1955 Gable and Kay married before a justice of the peace in Minden, Nevada. Three months later, Kay announced that she was going to have a baby, but she contracted a viral infection and miscarried.

Despite the temptation of playing opposite Sophia Loren in *It Started in Naples*, Gable remained faithful. Even more of a temptation was Marilyn Monroe on *The Misfits*. She would never have done the film if Gable had not been in it and was determined to seduce him.

She made her first move during a morning after scene, where he comes into the bedroom to find her completely nude under a bed sheet and kisses her.

'I was so thrilled when he kissed me, we had to do the scene over several times,' she said. 'Then the sheet dropped and he put his hand on my breast. It was an accident and I got goose-bumps all over.'

At night, Marilyn said she dreamed of nothing else but having sex with Gable. She dreamed that they were kissing and cuddling. Gable was an obsession.

'Whenever he was near me, I wanted him to kiss me and kiss me and kiss me,' she said. 'We did a lot of kissing, touching and feeling. His wife caught us smooching once. I never tried harder to seduce a man.'

Gable, it appears, did not give in; nor did he go to Reno with director John Houston and the crew. He listened with envy to their tales of drinking and whoring. It was just the sort of thing he would have done a few years earlier.

Gable was delighted when he heard that Kay was pregnant again. She had kept quiet about it until the four-month danger period was over. He also began to have fun with Monroe, kissing her on the lips and pinching her bottom. He even talked of doing another film with her, but it was not to be. The day after he finished filming *The Misfits,* he had a heart-attack. Two days later, he died.

7

FLYING THE COOP

Gary Cooper was a man of few words – two actually, 'yup' and 'nope'. Tallulah Bankhead said she left the stage for Hollywood for the money and 'that divine Gary Cooper'. But during her seduction, she complained, he never said a word. A friend pointed out that he might have said 'yup' but certainly did not say 'nope'. He was like that with all his women – and there were hundreds of them.

Howard Hawks summed up Cooper's seduction technique: 'If I ever saw him with a good-looking girl and he was kinda dragging his feet over the ground and being very shy and looking down, I'd say: "Oh-oh, the snake's gonna strike again."'

Then there was his stamina. The Mexican spitfire Lupe Velez boasted of how well endowed he was and another woman in a position to know, Clara Bow, said he could 'go all night'.

There were also rumours that he swung both ways. He was seen in the company of prominent homosexuals and some men on the gay circuit claim to have been intimate with the tight-lipped cowboy. Certainly, Coop was not all that he seemed.

Although he was born in Montana in 1901, his parents were British. His mother wanted a daughter and dressed the young Coop in dainty frocks. He played with the girls because his mother did not want him to get dirty. Years later, he admitted playing with dolls, though he was adamant that he had never owned one.

His parents became naturalized American citizens and his father, who became a prominent judge, bought a cattle ranch called the Seven Bar-Nine. The young Gary was sent away to public school in England. He may well have followed his older brother to Oxford had World War I not panicked his mother into calling her boys home.

The wartime labour shortage forced Cooper to go to work on his father's farm. He was a reluctant cowboy and hated the work. Local girls were sweet on him, but he was too shy to ask them out. He lost his virginity to a whore on the Omaha cattle trail.

After graduating from high school, he took a job driving a tour bus. The female tourists seemed to prefer his bus and the other drivers thought he was earning extra tips working after hours.

Cooper soon realized that he did not want to spend his life as a bus driver or as a cow poke – he wanted to be an artist. He went to study art at Montana State College in Bozeman, where he also tried his hand at acting. He attracted a number of local girls and proposed to one of them, Doris Virden. The problem was he did not have enough money to marry, so he dropped out of college and hopped on a bus to Chicago, where he aimed to become a commercial artist. Things did not work out and he nearly froze to death in the unheated YMCA.

Doris wrote to tell him that she was going to marry an Iowa druggist instead. Cooper also heard from two friends – Jim Galen and Jim Calloway – who had moved to Los Angeles that they had found work riding horses in the movies. California, Coop decided, would at least be warm and he set off for Hollywood. He got some extra work, did some drawing and worked as a tour guide, showing wild-eyed hopefuls around the sights of Hollywood. They were mainly beautiful girls who got excited when he showed them the studios where John Gilbert and Valentino worked, and he used to joke with a friend that he was bedding some of them.

He eventually caught up with Jim Galen, who was working on a western. Galen got Cooper a job as a stunt rider at $10 a day. In his first year and a half, he appeared in fifty films.

By this time, his father had been elected to the Montana Supreme Court, but the state was in the grip of a recession and he and Coop's mother moved to California. When his mother saw the state of him, his clothes dirty from falling off horses and his tiny squalid room, she decided that she and her husband would settle in Hollywood, so she could look after her darling son.

Cooper would go to the movies and study the actors.

'Look at that fellow Valentino,' he would say. 'When he looks at a girl, he's thinking of taking her clothes off. You know that when he walks up and kisses her, he is sort of halfway beyond that kiss already.'

He dated secretaries and script girls from the studios. He borrowed his parents' Buick to take them out. When he finally pulled Sam Goldwyn's secretary, he paid $65 to make his own screen test. She showed it to Goldwyn. He was uncertain, but when he showed it to a group of girls working at the studio, they slavered. So he gave Cooper an acting job on *The Winning of Barbara Worth* at $50 a week. Cooper promptly fell in love with the star, Hungarian actress Vilma Banky. The love was unrequited.

When he saw the movie, Goldwyn was furious. Cooper could not act, he said. *Variety* disagreed. So Cooper moseyed on over to Paramount who signed him for $150 a week.

Cooper's first Paramount party was a dour affair. Everyone was discussing who would be the next 'sheik' now that Valentino was dead. Then Clara Bow arrived. She stirred things up, moving around the room from man to man. When she reached Cooper, she looked him in the eye and said: 'Let's scram. This party is taking the snap out of my garters.'

She took him straight back to her house in Beverly Hills. They stayed there all night. Her friends said that few men could satisfy her but there were no complaints with Coop.

From then on, his mother and father saw little of him at

home. They saw a lot of him in the gossip columns, though. They said he was Clara's beau. Was he living with her his parents asked when he dropped by?

'Sometimes I fall asleep there,' he said.

Word got around that Clara called him 'Studs' for his nocturnal abilities. This notoriety won him the lead in both *Arizona Bound* and *The Last Outlaw*. He bought himself a red Chrysler roadster. He also got a bit part in *It* and Clara demanded that he play opposite her in her next movie, *Children of Divorce*. Rumour had it that Cooper was building his career on his talents as a gigolo, not as an actor. His parents were appalled. It was true, of course.

The first day on the set of *Children of Divorce*, he had to make love to Esther Ralston. Cooper froze. Veteran director Frank Lloyd, who had been called in to coax her first dramatic performance out of comedienne Clara Bow, asked: 'What's up?'

'I don't know what to do,' said Coop.

'Hold her and kiss her,' yelled Lloyd.

'But, sir,' Coop mumbled. 'I don't know this girl very well.' Lloyd fired him.

Cooper jumped in his car and drove off into the Mojave Desert. He wanted to quit the movies. When Lloyd saw the rushes he changed his mind, but Cooper was nowhere to be found.

William Boyd was called in to replace him. On the set Hedda Hopper said loudly: 'That's the last time I want to hear about Frank Lloyd being able to get a good performance out of anybody.'

Lloyd took up the challenge. He called the police who found Cooper at the bus station, getting set to go back to Montana. But it was not until he was firmly ordered to do so by the studio that Cooper resumed filming.

'You see, it's real hard for me to smooch with a filly I hardly know,' Cooper explained.

'Don't worry,' said Lloyd. 'Tomorrow you will be kissing Clara.'

He was no better. Clara complained that he made love to her on the set as if she was a horse.

The film was a disaster for both Cooper and Bow; only Esther Ralston got good reviews. Nevertheless, it did not do Cooper's career any harm. The studio upped his salary to $300 and promised him that he would only appear in cowboy movies from now on.

Meanwhile, Gary had fallen totally in love with Clara. They liked to make love out of doors, on the beach at Malibu, in the mountains above San Bernardino, in the walnut groves of the San Fernando Valley. Then he went and spoilt it all by asking her to marry him.

'Why take all the fun out of it?' she said. Her feelings quickly cooled and she resumed her affair with Victor Fleming.

Cooper consoled himself with nineteen-year-old Carole Lombard, whose tongue was as salty as Clara's. Soon Clara decided she wanted him back because he was one of the few men who could satisfy her in bed. To cool his desire to get married, she told him that she could not have children, because she 'did not have all the bits down there'. She got him a part in *Wings* so he could go with her to San Antonio where it was to be filmed.

Clara was the only woman on location so along with Cooper, there were plenty of other men visiting her tent. Her fiancé Victor Fleming, who was filming near by, even dropped by for a session. Cooper fumed with jealousy.

During his one big scene, unthinkingly, he picked his nose and asked for another take.

'Coop,' said director 'Wild Bill' Wellman, 'you keep right on picking your nose and you'll pick yourself a fortune.'

In Cooper's next film, *Nevada,* he played opposite the torrid starlet Thelma Todd. She was available and eager, but Clara kept him on a short leash. However, she was so active herself that she could hardly keep an eye on him all the time and in his next movie, *Beau Sabreur*, he fell for his co-star, the dark, sharp-featured Evelyn Brent.

Known as the 'Queen of the Underworld' for her gangster

roles, she was a hot property. She was even more sexually adventurous, but more discreet, than Clara. Cooper took her to dinner with his folks, who approved, and the studio promoted their 'engagement'. To be seen out and about with a star like Evelyn did him no harm, though he was still at Clara's beck and call when she wanted a 'great lay'.

Evelyn knew better than to marry an actor like Cooper at whom girls constantly threw themselves.

'I think it was his shyness that attracted them,' she said. 'He brought out the mother instinct in women.'

When his affair with Evelyn wound down, Paramount teamed him with Fay Wray and promoted them as the 'glorious young lovers'.

With Wray, then with Colleen Moore, he began to play screen lovers. It was Colleen who spotted that he was going to be a big star. Asked why, she said: 'Because there is not a girl in the front office who did not come down to look at him.'

During the filming of his first talkie, Cooper would fall asleep during takes, his services as a lover were so much in demand. Next came *Wolf Song*. Director Victor Fleming cast his own current girlfriend, Lupe Velez, opposite Cooper. She was also dating the crooner Russ Columbo, who sung love ballads in the film. Lupe fell hopelessly in love with Cooper from the first moment she saw him. Within twenty-four hours, she had found her way into his bed. Fleming caught the sexual chemistry on film. He even shot a nude bathing scene which did not make the final cut.

When Evelyn Brent got married, Cooper's mother was upset. Evelyn was her favourite. Despite his active love life, Cooper was not a little put out himself. Very publicly, he moved in with Lupe. His mother was heartbroken. Lupe said that Cooper had bought her a ring. He denied it. It was said that she had gone shopping for a trousseau in New York and for three years it was rumoured that they had secretly married.

They would have done if Cooper's mother had not taken against Lupe, who she called 'that Mexican thing'. She was hot and passionate but, unlike the other girls he had bedded in

Hollywood, she was faithful.

'I make love when I'm in love,' she said.

It was not a trick that Cooper could pull off, not with Clara still making demands.

The real problem was that Cooper and Lupe fought. Frequently he would turn up at the studio black and blue, and had to be patched up by the make-up man. He said he gave as good as he got but that is unlikely. Lupe was provoked by his passivity. She once said: 'I think I will kill my Gary because he does not get angry when Lupe is angry with him.'

She could easily have done it. She kept a stiletto in her garter and a gun in her bedside drawer. Once, when he was trying to take a break from her, she caught up with him at the railroad station and shot at him through the window of the departing train. It was never ascertained whether she was trying to kill him, or just wound him. The studio brushed the incident under the carpet by saying that Lupe just broke the window so that she could have one last goodbye kiss.

Cooper admitted that he was in love with her – 'or as much in love as one could get with a creature as elusive as quicksilver'.

She would make obscene phonecalls to him on the set to arouse him.

'He didn't even blush,' a friend said.

Lupe was not the blushing kind either. At parties she would throw her dress over her head, revealing that she wore no underwear. This was not exactly the kind of publicity Paramount were courting for Cooper.

When Cooper's parents went back to Montana for a visit, he moved Anderson Lawler into their house. Lawler was well known in homosexual circles. They had pet names for each other. Lawler called Cooper 'Jamey' and Cooper called Lawler 'Nin'. The studio devised the cover that Lawler, who was from Virginia, was coaching Cooper to give him an authentic accent in *The Virginian*.

Cooper was also close to Dick Arlen, a married man who put on all-male parties for Paramount's bachelors. The boys would take off for the weekend at Lake Arrowhead or Catalina. No women were allowed, but several prominent homosexuals were in tow. The studio tried to discourage these events when pictures of the boys swimming in the nude began fetching high prices in the back alleys of Los Angeles.

When Clara Bow heard about Lawler, she broke it off with Cooper once and for all.

'The whole thing makes me sick,' she said. 'One has to draw the line somewhere.'

Before *The Virginian*, Cooper was teamed up again with Evelyn Brent in *Darkened Rooms*. Even though he was still hurt, he could not turn down the picture or he would be put on suspension. Things were awkward on the set, but Cooper found plenty to distract him. Director Stuart Heisler, who had known him since his *Barbara Worth* days, said: 'Coop was probably the greatest that ever lived. They fell over themselves to get him to take them to bed. He couldn't stop screwing around. The women wouldn't let him. They'd go lay down for him in his portable dressing-room by the sound stage. I guess he had the reputation for being a wonderful lay.'

The Virginian made Cooper a star and put him in line for *Morocco* with Marlene Dietrich. Cooper instantly fell for her. The problem was the director Josef von Sternberg was in love with her, too. Although he had been brought up in New York, von Sternberg decided to direct the picture in German to give him the advantage with Marlene. Cooper got sick of this. He grabbed von Sternberg by the neck, hoisted him off the ground and said: 'You goddamned kraut, if you expect to work in this country you'd better get on to the language we use here.'

From then on, the picture was directed in perfect English.

Paramount wanted to cast Cooper and Dietrich in *Dishonoured*, but Cooper refused to work with von Sternberg again.

When Cooper's parents returned from Montana, he moved into Greta Garbo's old house at 1919 Argyle Avenue. Lawler helped him settle in.

Cooper was looking forward to working with Clara again on *City Streets*, but she was brought down by a scandal. During the trial of her maid Daisy DeVoe for attempted extortion, it was revealed that Clara was a nymphomaniac who had been through half of Hollywood, including on one notable occasion the entire University of Southern California football team. She was forcibly retired. Daisy also said that she had woken up one morning in her mistress' bed alongside Clara and Coop. After the trial, Cooper's parents refused to speak to him.

Cooper, typically, rode out the storm in silence, but his affair with Clara was well known and being one among so many lovers did not reflect well on him. Lupe was also causing grief. She began to be suspicious of his relationship with Lawler – and she was not one to keep her mouth shut. Cooper began to fear that he might suffer the same fate as Clara. He had to clean up his act. Pressure from the studio and his mother's silence eventually forced him to drop Lupe, leaving him gaunt and on the verge of a nervous breakdown.

Carole Lombard nursed him through *I Take This Woman*. Later, when Clark Gable and Cooper used to go hunting and fishing together, Gable asked about it.

'He got pale as hell,' said Gable.

Lombard had told Gable about the romance during a drunken row.

'She used to throw it in my face and that was hard to take, especially since I didn't know the whole truth until years later,' Gable said. 'I have to admit I was jealous.'

It was particularly hard to take when you compare the two men's reputations as lovers. Cooper and Gable did not go out hunting and fishing so much after that.

After *I Take This Woman*, the studio arranged for Cooper to take a long vacation in Europe to recuperate.

In Rome, he visited the Conte and Contessa di Frasso, whom he had met briefly at a party at Pickfair. The Conte was in his fifties; the Contessa, New York beauty Dorothy Taylor, was in her twenties. They both discreetly took lovers. The Contessa's charms became obvious to Coop. Soon he was pictured everywhere with her, minus the Conte. Paramount figured that if he was well enough to be seen out and about with an attractive young woman, he was well enough to work and ordered him back. The Contessa did everything she could to keep him. She dressed him in the finest Italian clothes, taught him about wine and art, took him riding and referred to him in front of everyone as 'Big Boy'.

When Paramount took him off salary, she contemplated buying the studio, but when the Contessa mentioned marriage, Coop thought it was time to return to Hollywood. She gave him a big send off – a huge party which overflowed with royalty and heiresses. The press mistakenly reported that the party was to announce the Contessa's divorce from the Conte and her engagement to Cooper. The studio went ballistic. When he arrived back in America, Cooper had to stress to the newspapers that he was good friends with the Conte as well as the Contessa di Frasso.

In New York, Cooper was seen out with Anderson Lawler and the man-eating bisexual Tallulah Bankhead. Coop and Tallulah spent the night together and next day, the press were announcing their engagement. Lupe Velez was in town, too, and Cooper apparently tried to stage a reconciliation. He asked her to marry him. This time, Lupe rejected him. She told the press that Cooper had dropped her because of the disapproval of his mother and pressure from the studio. She was not taking him back now. Reading that he had finally split from Lupe, his mother flew to his side. The Contessa di Frasso was also reading the headlines and going quietly crazy.

Hollywood was gearing up for the return of Coop when suddenly he jumped a ship to Africa. He had decided to use the last of his savings to go on safari with notorious homosexual Jimmy Donahue, cousin of Woolworth heiress Barbara Hutton. Four days after he arrived in Tanganyika, the Contessa turned up. The studio took him off salary again.

After bagging over eighty animals, Coop and the Contessa went back to Rome to relax. Then they outraged the American public even more by taking a Mediterranean cruise as a three-some with her husband, the Conte.

'Europeans are so open-minded,' said the Contessa's close

friend Elsa Maxwell. 'Americans could learn from them. After all this is 1932, not the Dark Ages.'

While gambling in Monte Carlo, Cooper heard about the shake-up at Paramount. Jesse Lasky had been kicked out, Victor Fleming had gone to MGM, and the studio had a new star – one Archie Leach who the studio renamed Cary Grant. Cooper was furious.

'That guy has my initials backwards,' he said.

Now it really was time to get back to Hollywood. But Cooper had one more sensation to cause. He arrived in New York with the Conte and Contessa di Frasso, before flying on to Hollywood alone. He was so broke that the Contessa had to pay for his ticket.

Back in Hollywood, he had to borrow money to rent a house. He was quickly back on the payroll with his salary upped to $4,000 a week for two pictures a year. The first was *The Devil and the Deep* with Tallulah Bankhead. She had liked what he had done for her in New York and had turned up in Hollywood.

Cooper tried to give her a wide berth. He could not get Lupe out of his system and dated her on the quiet. Publicly he knew that he had to keep his nose clean. Besides, the Contessa's bosom pal Elsa Maxwell was on hand as a chaperone.

When the Conte and Contessa turned up on the coast, Tallulah went on the offensive. At a party, she called the Contessa an 'old whore' and got a glass of wine in her face. At another party, when Cooper failed to show up, Tallulah said he must be 'worn to a Frasso'.

The Conte spent a great deal of time out of town, so Cooper had free access to his wife. Seeing the glamorous girls around town, she realized that she faced some stiff competition and went on a diet.

During the shooting of *A Farewell to Arms*, Cooper's co-star, Helen Hayes, said that she would have left her husband and gone away with him if Cooper had asked.

In 1933, Cooper met dress designer Irene Gibbons, who took over from the legendary Adrian as wardrobe mistress at MGM. Although she was married to screenwriter Eliot

Gibbons, she began an affair with Cooper which lasted, on and off, for many years. A year after Cooper died, Irene slashed her wrists in the Knickerbocker Hotel and jumped from a window of the fourteenth floor to her death. Cooper was the only man she had ever loved, she had told Doris Day.

Irene's brother-in-law was Cedric Gibbons, the art director at MGM and husband of Dolores del Rio. Cooper had met Gibbons when he had been hired out to MGM to make *Today We Live* with Joan Crawford. On Easter Sunday 1933, Gibbons invited him to a party he was giving for his niece, twenty-year-old debutante Veronica Balfe, known to one and all as Rocky. The Contessa did not go – she could not bear daytime parties – which was just as well. The gorgeous, raven-haired Rocky told Cooper that she had been mooning over his pictures since finishing school back east.

When Cooper started dating Veronica, the Contessa realized that she had to take decisive action. The *Los Angeles Times* announced that she was going to Reno to establish residency in Nevada so she could divorce the Conte.

'This time that Coop has got himself in a fix,' said Lupe.

'Then, like all men who didn't want to get married,' Rocky said, 'he disappeared for three months.'

Cooper began dating a young German actress by the name of Wera Engels. Scandal broke when he started seeing minor Paramount actress Judith Allen. He did not know that she was married to wrestler Gus Sonnenberg. He had neglected to ask.

Meanwhile, Veronica Balfe was seen out with Gilbert Roland. Lupe married Tarzan, Johnny Weissmuller, and the Contessa was seen out with the Conte again. They headed back to Italy, via New York, but before she went, she invited both Lupe and Veronica to lunch at the Vendome, a chic restaurant which catered for celebrities.

'It's only a vacation,' the Contessa told the reporters at the station. 'Gary plans to join me as soon as he can.'

But Gary had other plans. He planned to marry Veronica. He knew he had the sort of reputation that would not impress her parents. His latest love triangle did nothing to help and he regretted sowing his last wild oats so publicly.

In a way, he was tired of womanizing and longed to settle down and have children, though he had doubts about his ability to be faithful. Nevertheless, he bought a new house and began seeing Rocky again. He took her on a hunting trip to Arizona. Louella Parsons said they had eloped. Veronica came back with a fifteen-carat, square-cut diamond engagement ring on her finger.

'Rocky is the ideal girl for me,' Cooper told the newspapers. 'She can ride, shoot, and do all the things I like to do.'

He also said 'a woman's place is in the home' and 'one career is more than enough for one family'. That put paid to her $75, rising to $750-a-week contract with Sam Goldwyn at RKO.

They married on 15 December 1933, just two weeks after their engagement. The word 'obey' was omitted from the service. They honeymooned in Arizona. Veronica's parents and Cooper's secretary came along. His parents also joined them for the Christmas holiday. Everybody was very happy, except for Lupe. She was the cause of many rows between the newlyweds. Back in Hollywood, Lupe threw a drink in Rocky's face in a nightclub and Cooper had to restrain her.

'I believe Gary held on to Lupe,' said Clara Bow. 'Otherwise, he might have been a widower instead of a groom.'

Veronica was not exactly taken with her new home. It was a ranch in Van Nuys where Coop intended to raise a few head of cattle. She was a city girl. Hollywood insiders gave the marriage a year at the most, but Rocky tried hard.

The Contessa turned up again, like a bad penny. She marched up to their table when they were eating in Vendome and started chatting. She expected Rocky to invite her to sit down and stood talking for twenty minutes before she finally turned on her heels and went.

This endeared Rocky to Lupe, who felt that the young girl needed someone in her corner when dealing with a woman of the world like the Contessa. Lupe, Rocky, Weissmuller and Cooper went out as a foursome, which made Coop uneasy – all the more so when rumoured problems in Lupe's marriage were laid at his door. Still Rocky and Lupe presented a united front against the Contessa.

Rocky invited her out to lunch at the Mocambo. When the Contessa arrived she found Lupe at Rocky's table. Very publicly, Rocky returned some emerald cufflinks the Contessa had given Cooper, while Lupe egged her on.

Hollywood was impressed. So was Coop. He even gave up disappearing with script girls for an hour or so while filming. The Contessa eventually divorced and went on to hitch up with Bugsy Siegel. When Siegel was shot in 1947, the Contessa said that Bugsy was the love of her life.

Sam Goldwyn paid Cooper $100,000 to appear in *The Wedding Night* with Russian beauty Anna Sten. Gone was Coop's customary shyness. Their love scenes were among the most convincing he ever played, despite director King Vidor's complaints about his acting.

Then there was Marlene.

Cooper was filming *Desire* with Dietrich when John Gilbert died. When she collapsed at his funeral, it was Cooper who carried her to her seat.

The fact that Cooper was married made him more attractive to leading ladies. If they were encumbered with a husband or boyfriend themselves, his marital status ensured that he would handle any off-screen dalliance with the utmost discretion. Things were unlikely to get serious or out of hand. Certainly, he could not keep his eyes of British blonde Madeleine Carroll – reputed to be the most beautiful girl in the world – during the filming of *The General Died at Dawn*. Cooper also had a crush on another avid admirer, Paulette Goddard, Charlie Chaplin's 'wife', who played with him and Madeleine Carroll in *Northwest Mounted Police*.

And there were always script girls. One said that he made her 'feel as if we were the only women in the world. My two husbands never made love to me that way.' The other script girls she spoke to said he made them feel the same way. Cooper, she said, did not like quickies. He told her so himself. It was an insult, he said. Of course, he indulged himself – but he hated himself for it. Sometime he lived with the guilt for, well, days. Plainly, he was a sensitive man. He had suffered in silence through the Clara Bow trial, she said. She remembered particularly his long, beautiful fingers, which he used 'gently but firmly'. Not on the script, I take it.

She knew Rocky and thought her beautiful. She also knew the stars he slept with – Marlene, Madeleine, Tallulah, Anna – and the other script girls, secretaries, hairdressers, wardrobe girls, extras and 'I don't doubt he had a man occasionally'. Certainly Cecil Beaton claimed to have slept with him on his first visit to Hollywood.

This had its dangers. He had a casual affair with a girl who took it to heart. She was also dating one of Bugsy Siegel's boys, who put a contract out on Coop. When George Raft heard about it, he was told that he had better hustle the girl out of town, fast, 'otherwise this actor winds up on a slab'. Raft went around to her apartment, packed her things, took her to the station and put her on the first train east.

'I don't think Coop missed her,' said Raft, 'but she almost cost him his life.'

He never told Cooper about it, even after they become good friends on *Souls at Sea*.

Cooper's extraordinary sex drive was the talk of Hollywood and Rocky kept him on a very long leash. Plainly she was doing something right because 15 September 1937 found Cooper and Frank Capra pacing up and down the waiting room of the Good Samaritan Hospital, chain-smoking. Capra's third daughter had been born the day before and he stayed on with Cooper when Rocky went into labour. She gave birth to a healthy, almond-eyed girl they called Maria.

'Having a daughter is the thing I'm proudest of,' Cooper said in later life.

That did not mean he would go home nights. He fell for Merle Oberon on *The Cowboy and the Lady*.

'His eyes gave him away,' said a friend. 'Miss Oberon was definitely his type.'

She was no shrinking violet. Despite being panned by the critics and bombing at the box office, *The Cowboy and the Lady* mysteriously remained Cooper's favourite film.

F. Scott Fitzgerald's girlfriend Sheila Graham flew with Cooper to Dallas for the première of *The Westerner*. When she got air sick, he lay her on a bunk and offered to rub her tummy. At the hotel, she went into the bathroom to freshen up. When she came out, she found him waiting for her in the bedroom.

Cooper was, of course, famed for being laconic. He needed few words to express his inner feelings. Once he found himself at a loose end in New York with a press agent, after an appointment had been cancelled.

'What shall we do now?' asked the agent.

'Let's go look at the tits of the pretty girls on Fifth Avenue,' said Cooper. The agent discovered that it was a pleasant enough way to spend a few hours.

The earth moved for Cooper and Ingrid Bergman when they shot *For Whom the Bell Tolls* in the Sierra Nevada. They were both ripe for a torrid affair. Living in log cabins on location in the mountains was the perfect romantic setting. They had twelve weeks away from the pressures of home and Hollywood.

They managed to get together again to film *Saratoga Trunk*. They were even seen out together in public, but Bergman's jealous husband Petter Lindstrom put a stop to it. She stoutly denied any involvement. The day after the end of filming, Cooper could no longer get her on the phone.

'Ingrid loved me more than any woman in my life loved me,' Cooper said.

By this time, Rocky was inured to Cooper's philandering. She invited Bergman and Lindstrom to dinner and their children played together.

Long after, Bergman admitted the affair.

'Every woman who knew him fell in love with Gary,' she said.

However, Cooper's marriage was rocked to its core by the spectacular suicide of Lupe Velez. Long divorced from Johnny Weissmuller, at thirty-six, she had become pregnant. She could not stand the shame of being an unmarried mother; nor, as a devout Catholic, could she go ahead with an abortion. So she dressed in her finest silver lamé gown and invited two close friends over for dinner. They dined on the best Mexican food and doused their cares with pitchers of Margueritas. When they had gone, she laid out her most expensive sheets in her flower-festooned, candle-lit bedroom and downed twenty-five Seconals with her favourite five-star Mexican brandy. Then, a mortician's delight, she lay down, crucifix in hand and waited to die – the perfect picture of a Hollywood suicide.

Sadly her stomach was not used to this volatile mixture. She awoke feeling unwell, dashed to the toilet and threw up. With the barbs down the pan, she would have survived, but she slipped on the vomit-greased floor, smacked her head on the rim of the toilet and died with her head down the bowl. Coroner's verdict: death by drowning.

Whatever corner of Hollywood heaven Lupe now occupies – she would not be in purgatory because her suicide bid, however heartfelt, was a failure – I hope she can look down and appreciate the full pathos of the situation.

Before she died, Lupe had told the proud father of Maria that the child she was carrying was his. Cooper was devastated.

At forty-seven, Cooper was to play opposite twenty-two-year-old Patricia Neal in *The Fountainhead*. She had been warned that Cooper was a womanizer, but although she was on her guard when she met him in the office of director King Vidor, she could not help herself.

'He was the most gorgeously attractive man. For me it was love at first sight,' she said, 'and that love never died.'

On location in Fresno, Vidor took them to a Basque restaurant.

'I could tell they were falling in love,' he said. 'It was a big, terrific romance. Outside of work, I hardly saw either of them.'

Back in Hollywood, things were more awkward. Rocky visited the set a couple of times.

'I think she was aware of what was going on, though I am not sure,' said Vidor. 'It was uncomfortable for all of us.'

In the autumn of 1948, Pat Neal went to England for three months to film *The Hasty Heart* with Ronald Reagan. When she returned to the U.S., the Coopers just happened to be in New York to greet her. She played with Cooper again in *Bright Leaf*.

By late 1949, Rocky realized that Pat was no passing affair. Although Pat did not want to break up the happy home, she wanted marriage. When she bumped into Dorothy di Frasso, the Contessa said: 'Good luck. You're going to need it.'

'I felt sorry for all of them,' said Jack Warner's wife Ann. 'Rocky was very smart. During that period, she wasn't nasty, she looked good, and she made her own life. She went out with a few boys, and she acted cleverly ... If Pat were conniving, she might have been able to break up the marriage. Pat was so in love with him, and Gary with her. She satisfied him a great deal.'

Rocky was seen out with Ethel Merman's ex, millionaire Bob Six. There was talk of marriage. Meanwhile Cooper took Pat to Cuba to get the seal of approval from his old friend Ernest Hemingway. Hemingway took a stern moral line in front of his wife Mary, but he was having an affair with twenty-one-year-old Adriana Ivancich behind her back at the time.

Back in Hollywood, Pat became pregnant. At first, both she and Coop were delighted, but Rocky was a Catholic and was refusing a divorce. Pat feared that her mother might commit suicide if she had a baby out of wedlock. There was no alternative. In October 1950, Gary drove Pat to the doctor's to have an abortion. They wept.

In her autobiography, Pat wrote: 'For thirty years I cried over that baby. If I had only one thing to do over in my life, I would have had that baby.'

With Rocky away in New York, anxious not to flaunt his affair, Cooper would turn up at parties alone; but he spent most of his free time in Pat's apartment.

'I can stretch my legs and put on slippers and relax,' he said. 'We don't need parties.'

His discretion did not help Pat. Warner Bros dropped her contract and it was rumoured that she was being hounded out of town by irate wives.

Although divorce was not on the cards, a property settlement was being discussed. Then Rocky found help from the most unlikely ally – Grace Kelly.

On *High Noon*, newcomer Grace made a play for Cooper. The movie began with a wedding scene. All Coop had to do was say 'I do', take Grace in his arms and kiss her. The scene was shot over and over again. Cooper kissed her at least fifty times.

Grace made no secret of the fact that she preferred older men and with Cooper she was star struck. Cooper was taken with her too and watched her intently during her close-ups. At the end of one take, she plopped herself down on his lap and planted a kiss on his cheek. He blushed under his make-up and wiped her lipstick off with a handkerchief. When she tried to kiss him again on the other cheek, he whispered: 'Not here.'

Cooper was planning a fishing trip with screenwriter Bob Slatzer. Grace asked whether she could come along. When Cooper tried to ignore her, she placed her hand on his knee and asked again.

Later, when Cooper was lunching with Slatzer, Grace blew a kiss in their direction.

'That was for you,' Cooper told Slatzer. 'Why don't you do something about it?'

'And compete with you?' Slatzer protested.

'I'm twice her age.'

Slatzer said he would not let that stop him.

'It hasn't, but I don't need it,' said Cooper.

He may not have needed it, but he got it anyway. Grace came over to the table and reminded Cooper that they had a love scene to do. There was an embarrassed silence.

'Coop, you're one lucky guy,' Slatzer said eventually.

'Isn't he?' said Grace.

Cooper chewed hard on his food, swallowed and said: 'Yup, guess I am.'

Cooper later told Slatzer that he was having an affair with Grace; not that it was not obvious.

'Just the way she looked at him, you could tell she was

melting,' said Slatzer. 'She'd embarrass him sometimes by coming over and putting her arms around him and being obvious in front of other people.'

Because of Pat, Cooper made a point of not being seen out with Grace. Nevertheless the affair made the gossip columns, partly because his attentions to Grace sent *High Noon*'s other female star, the fiery Katy Jurado, into tantrums of jealousy. Grace also dated Slatzer. Slatzer had never known Cooper to ask a personal question, but on a fishing trip Coop said laconically: 'I guess I'd be kinda outa school if I asked you if you'd been to bed with her.'

'You would,' said Slatzer.

'I shouldn't ask a thing like that,' Cooper said, but he could not help himself.

'He was eaten up with the idea that she might have gone to bed with me,' Slatzer said.

Later, Cooper said in an interview that Grace 'gave the impression she was a cold fish with a man until you got her pants down and then she'd explode'.

Gary and Rocky were legally separated. When agent Charles Feldman gave a big party for Dolly O'Brien, Rocky arrived with Peter Lawford. Cooper turned up with Pat, who wore flowers in her hair. They did not suit her.

The older woman knew how to handle herself in this situation. She danced every dance and never let the smile slip from her face. Pat was stiff and awkward. When she did get up and dance, Cooper took the opportunity to go over and have a word with Rocky. Everybody held their breath.

'I would not be surprised if it was then and there that Pat accepted the fact that things would not work out,' said gossip columnist Hedda Hopper, who was at the bash.

The next day Cooper flew to New York to have an operation on a duodenal ulcer that was bothering him. He did not want Pat to accompany him. Later, she called the hospital.

'It's all over, Gary,' she said and hung up the phone. The affair had lasted three years.

Later, she tried to reconcile with Cooper, but he was hesitant and she put the phone down on him again. She returned to Broadway and later married the children's writer Roald Dahl.

Rocky was now seen on the town with a string of men, including Robert Wagner, Rock Hudson and athlete Howell van Gerbig. Cooper went to Samoa to film *Return to Paradise* with Roberta Haynes, whom Cooper had met as a bit player on *High Noon*. He had used his influence to get her the lead in *Return to Paradise*. She was suitably grateful, though Cooper denied an affair.

'The medication I'm taking makes me impotent,' he said. No one believed him.

Back in Hollywood, Cooper hung out with Gable and Robert Taylor. They drank too much and frequented a whorehouse. Cooper was also seeing Kay Williams, who later married Gable.

At the Cannes Film Festival, he ran off with Prince Rainier of Monaco's mistress Gisele Pascal. They were seen having a romantic dinner in Paris. When asked if they were in love, Cooper declined to comment.

'You see, my wife might not appreciate it,' he told reporters. 'She's coming over here with our daughter next week.'

When Rocky and Maria turned up, all three toured the Continent together, playing happy families.

On his next film, *Blowing Wild* with Barbara Stanwyck, Cooper was injured during a stunt and returned to the family home in Brentwood to recuperate. Rocky nursed him.

Filming *Garden of Evil* in Mexico, Cooper was seen out accompanied by French model Lorraine Chanel. He denied that they were going to be married.

'I'm seeing quite a few girls,' he said.

Director Henry Hathaway confirmed this, but was disappointed by his choice.

'He was still highly sexually charged and needed a variety of girls,' said Hathaway. 'But they were floozies. After Pat Neal, he went after anything because Coop didn't want to get involved.'

His shyness had disappeared. There was now nothing discreet about his approach. He would make a pass at a girl, leave the studio with her and park his car in front of her apartment.

Nevertheless, he moved back in with Rocky. They told the press that they had both learned a hard lesson. But they had separate bedrooms. Cooper was ill and lonely. He pined for Pat. She missed him too. On her wedding night, she recalled that tears rolled down her cheeks.

'I could feel my heart break,' she said. 'I so wanted to be married, but to another man.'

Three years later, they ran into each other in New York and had a drink together. Nothing had changed.

Now fifty-five, Cooper had done with romance, but if young women – 'fillies' he called them – wanted a roll in the hay, that was fine by him. One night, he met a girlfriend of supporting actor Sonny Tufts, took her home and spent the night with her. She told Tufts that he was quite something for an old man. She had been expecting a quickie, but when he got up and went to the studio the next morning, she had to stay in bed and take a rest.

'And she was capable of handling three men without taking a deep breath,' said Tufts. Cooper later apologized to Tufts for taking one of his 'fillies'.

In January 1956, *Confidential* magazine ran the headline: 'Gary Cooper's lost weekend with Anita Ekberg'. He had met her at a party and gone back to her apartment. Somehow Rocky understood.

She even understood when he took the lead in *Ten North Frederick*, which many Hollywood insiders called 'The Gary Cooper Story'. Playing the Pat Neal part was radiant redheaded fashion model Suzy Parker – though those on the set said she was more of a Grace Kelly than a Pat Neal. Rumours of a torrid affair continued until they were finally topped by Rocky's seventy-year-old stepfather, Paul Shields. Suzy was seen on board his yacht, cruising down the East River.

Cooper saw Pat Neal one last time when he was filming *The Wreck of the Mary Deare* at Elstree Studios in England. They had a brief conversation on the set when she came to visit Charlton Heston, with whom she had been at college.

Those who knew him said that Cooper really gave up on life after he lost Pat Neal. He lived for Maria, and Rocky's support gave him the strength to go on. He died of cancer on 14 May 1960. When Pat heard the news, she said just two words: 'My love.'

8

CARY ON CAMPING

Nothing about Cary Grant was quite what it seemed. He was not the Ivy League New Englander he appeared to be on-screen, but a working-class boy from Bristol. His name, of course, was not Cary Grant, but Archibald Alec Leach. He was not a sophisticated, eligible bachelor, as the women who succumbed to his charms discovered; he would beat, abuse and sometimes injure them; nor was he a heterosexual.

Archibald Leach was confused from the beginning. Mysteriously, his birth was not registered until three weeks after he was baptized. His parents had him circumcised, a procedure rarely practised outside the Jewish community at the time. In later life he told friends and actress Mary Brian, his then fiancée, that he was Jewish and he secretly supported Jewish causes.

His parents had lost their first child shortly after the baby's first birthday and may have adopted Archibald in his place. Archie's dark good looks were ascribed to a mysterious strain of gypsy or Spanish blood, for which there is no evidence.

Archibald himself was a little confused about whether he was a boy or a girl to start with. His mother insisted on keeping him in dresses, like Gary Cooper.

'I wonder why little boys are ashamed to be mistaken for little girls?' he said in later life. 'Why do they take such pride in being little boys?'

Rather than being proud, he was ashamed. Even as a small child, he objected to being bathed naked in front of his grand-mother.

His home life was not happy. His parents rowed. His father, a suit presser, constantly disappeared with other women. His mother did what she could with the little money he gave her. The loss of her first born had left her slightly unhinged. She blamed Archie for taking the place of the dead child and punished him on the slightest excuse, often with a sharp rap across the knuckles.

School offered no haven from this harshness. He lived in fear of the cane – ferocious thrashings were meted out by his spinster teachers. They also put him through his paces with compulsory physical training in the freezing yard, an ordeal for a withdrawn and sensitive boy.

His father was a stage-door Johnny who used to hang about at the theatre to pick up actresses and chorus girls. When he took six-year-old Archie to the pantomime, he was enthralled. The producer, Robert Lomas, needed a child extra and Archie's father signed temporary guardianship of the boy over to Lomas. The next stop for the troupe, and Archie, was Berlin, where he got a graphic education in the facts of dressing-room life. The troupe was seen by New York impresario Jesse L. Lasky and, just turned seven, Archie found himself on board the *Lusitania,* heading for Broadway.

While the rest of the troupe performed in a 'profane bur-lesque' called *Hell* – the girls caused an outrage dressed in flesh-coloured tights – Archie learnt to walk on stilts.

Soon after he returned to Bristol, he came home from school one day to be told that his mother had died suddenly from a heart-attack and had been buried immediately. In fact, his father had had his mother committed to a lunatic asylum and moved his mistress, Meg Bass, into the house.

At the age of nine, Archie fell in love for the first time with the pleasingly plump daughter of a local butcher. He could not pluck up the courage to address a word to her, but would walk past her house looking nonchalant. The act was ruined when he found her playing with her dolls in the garden. As he went past, he craned around for one more glimpse of his beloved – and walked straight into a lamppost. That was the end of the affair. He could never bring himself to walk past her house again.

Archie went off to secondary school, where his slim build, dashing good looks and long eyelashes began to have an effect on women. When he could, he continued working in the theatre as a call boy and as a magician's assistant on a trick which involved semi-nude women.

He was expelled from school when he was found in the girls' playground. Many of the girls cried at the news. Immediately, he rejoined Bob Lomas' burlesque troupe. After appearing as the back end of a cow in pantomime, Archie got another crack at Broadway when the troupe sailed again for Manhattan. On the *Olympic*, Archie met Douglas Fairbanks Snr and Mary Pickford who were returning from their honeymoon in Europe. As they sailed into New York harbour, Archie remembered catching sight of the Woolworth building. Twenty-one years later, he would marry the granddaughter of its founder, the heiress Barbara Hutton.

Like the rest of the troupe, Archie lived in straitened circumstances in New York, but he was helped financially by Francis Renault, a muscular drag queen who worked under the name 'The Last of the Red Hot Papas'. It is thought they were lovers.

Another alleged lover was Jack Orr-Kelly, a chorus boy and tailor's assistant who went on to become a Hollywood set designer. They moved into a loft in Greenwich Village together with Charlie Phelps, also known as Charles Spangles, a gay steward from the *Olympic* who had jumped ship to be with his friends. It was Archie and Orr-Kelly who were the couple in this ménage.

At nineteen, Archie could not hold his drink. At one party, he spent the evening drinking cider and had to be laid to rest in a spare room. Thoughtfully, his friends tucked a young woman in with him.

'We awakened to find ourselves falteringly, fumblingly and quite unsatisfactorily attempting to ascertain whether those blessed birds and bees knew what they were doing,' he said. 'Up to that time, it was my closest contact with wine and women. I cannot add that it was an occasion for song.'

The girl lived in Brooklyn, which seemed an awful long way to travel. So he dropped her.

Archie toured the country with burlesque shows. On one trip to the coast, he renewed his acquaintance with Douglas Fairbanks Snr, who showed him around the set of *The Thief of Baghdad*.

When work was slack, Archie worked as a sandwich-board man – on stilts – in Times Square and Coney Island. There were also rumours that he worked as a gigolo, servicing rich women. He certainly modelled himself on Valentino when he went for, and eventually got, parts in 'legitimate' theatre. Although he was slightly shabby, the girls were crazy about him.

Archie met Jack Benny, Gracie Allen and George Burns, who was mindful of the scandal that could ensue from Archie's homosexuality. Archie also began seeing the sexually ambiguous Moss Hart and, through Reginald Hammerstein, nephew of Oscar, got a part in the musical *Golden Dawn* which featured a cast of semi-nude girls.

Although his voice was barely adequate, Archie got more singing roles, though often he had only to open and shut his mouth while a professional singer delivered the song from behind a curtain. This did not concern the girls in the cast who made themselves available to him. However, Archie was still surrounded by an almost exclusively homosexual coterie, though his affair with Orr-Kelly was cooling. Other young men were being entertained in the loft. They developed a system. If Orr-Kelly heard classical music playing through the door, he was not to come in. Soon Orr-Kelly had had enough of this and moved to Hollywood as a designer.

During the run of *The Street Singer*, Archie met Frank Horn, who would become his secretary in Hollywood; and he became deeply involved with composer Phil Charig.

The talkies had just come in and British actors were in demand. On-screen Americans sounded nasal, but Britishers, even ones with working-class accents like Archie, sounded polished and cultivated. Archie also had the looks that made women swoon. So with Phil Charig, he sold up and set off for the coast.

They found an apartment together in West Hollywood. From the beginning, Ben Schulberg at Paramount took a shine to Archie. He immediately cast him as a cuckold and a man about town in two separate movies being shot at either end of the lot. No one liked his name and he had to change it. Fay Wray came up with 'Cary'; Paramount's publicist provided the 'Grant'.

Grant was soon making good money, and he teamed up with young clothes designer Wright Neale and interior decorator Bob Lampe to open a boutique on Wilshire Boulevard. Grant was very much a sleeping partner and Neale's notes to him addressed him simply as 'Sister'. Meanwhile, he was posing with pretty girls in bathing trunks for Paramount publicity shots.

During a lunch break at the studio, Grant met contract player Randolph Scott who was filming *Sky Bride* on an adjacent sound stage. Howard Hughes had taken handsome young Randy under his wing and it was rumoured they were lovers.

Grant and Scott hit it off immediately. Phil Charig had returned to New York, so Scott moved into Grant's apartment. It was unusual for two handsome young actors to live together and soon rumours were flying, encouraged by the two of them brazenly turning up to movie premières together, without female escorts. The studio panicked. They put out the story that the two men were only sharing an apartment – which either one of them could easily have afforded – to save money; and they came up with two girls – Sari Maritza and Vivian Gaye – for the chaps to be seen out with, indulging in healthy pursuits like dancing, swimming and playing tennis.

Grant and Scott found a new home near the homosexual hang-out Griffith Park and moved in with interior decorator Mitchell Foster, business partner of the disgraced gay movie star William Haines.

Grant played opposite Marlene Dietrich in *Blonde Venus*. He was captivated by her. She did not indulge him because of his reputation as a homosexual, but Grant's sexual orientation was plainly on the swing.

One night, after attending the première of *Blonde Venus* with Scott, Grant was coming out of the Brown Derby restaurant on Wilshire when he bumped into a young homosexual actor who had with him, as a walker, Virginia Cherrill. Grant had seen her in *City Lights*, but her career had waned after she rejected Chaplin's advances. She had been greatly taken with Grant's performance in *Blonde Venus* and agreed to go out with him. They attended parties given by Sari Maritza and Vivian Gaye together.

Jack Orr-Kelly warned her that Cary was the lover of Randolph Scott and that she should think very seriously before getting involved. Virginia was too young and innocent to understand. When he took her out for candlelit dinners, Cary was the perfect gentleman. He never made a pass and she felt comfortable in his home. His roommates shared so many of her innocent, girlish interests.

Publicity shots for *Hot Saturday*, in which Grant and Scott appeared together, show the two chums in matching aprons, doing the washing-up.

'I wonder which one of those guys pays the bills,' said Carole Lombard.

Schulberg was all too aware of the dangers of the image Grant was acquiring so, to build him up as a hetero heart-throb, he cast him opposite Mae West in *She Done Him Wrong*.

Although Grant's relationship with Virginia Cherrill was still chaste, he grew moody and jealous over her. He turned up on the set of *The Nuisance* and glowered at her during her love scenes. She complained that he was spying on her, but she had fallen in love with him already.

When Virginia went off to Hawaii to film *White Heat*, Grant became pathologically jealous of producer William Fiske. This was doubly galling for Virginia as, each night after filming,

Fiske and the rest of the crew and cast would disappear to a nearby brothel, leaving her on her own. Nevertheless, when shooting was over, Grant bribed the operator at the Beverly Hills Hotel, where Fiske lived, to listen in to his calls to Virginia. They were entirely innocent. Grant had Virginia herself followed by private detectives. When she found out, there was a furious row.

Plans were afoot for Virginia, Grant and Scott to go to England. Then Virginia and Grant took off to Arizona on what was billed as an elopement, but was, in fact, a sight-seeing tour. There were more arguments. On the day they returned to Hollywood, Randolph Scott announced his engagement to Vivian Gaye. A catastrophic row ensued between Grant and Virginia. She took off to England as planned. Grant and Scott followed, sharing a state room on the SS *Paris*. After a week in the Savoy with Grant, Scott had had enough and returned to New York. Grant managed to paper over the cracks with Virginia and took her to meet his father in Bristol.

Grant suddenly became ill and had to undergo painful rectal surgery. Once he was up and about, he rushed Virginia to Caxton Hall where they were married. Then they jumped on the *Paris* and sailed back to America.

Virginia moved into the homosexual household near Griffith Park. After three weeks, they moved to an apartment in Havenhurst. Randy came too, taking the flat next door.

The rows continued. Grant became even more jealous and possessive. On the way back from the beach one afternoon, on Sunset Boulevard, a man in a car overtaking them waved at Virginia. She waved back and Grant popped her in the mouth. She bled all over her dress. Virginia ran off to stay with a girl-friend. Next day, Grant called her. He remembered nothing about the incident, he said, and begged her to come back.

There were other, similar incidents. She was getting ready to go out to a party with him one night when they had a minor row about her always being late. He pushed her violently to the floor. Her head struck the iron fender on the front of the fire. He left her to bleed on the floor and went to the party alone. When he returned, he asked her with what seemed to her to be genuine concern if she had had an accident.

This tormented behaviour continued throughout the summer of 1934. Grant was drinking heavily, disguising his habit at the studio by sipping booze from a coffee cup. When Virginia eventually fled home to her mother, Grant attempted suicide. He was found by their Filipino houseboy in his undershorts on the bed with an empty bottle of sleeping tablets beside him.

Grant was rushed to hospital and his stomach pumped, but Virginia suspected the suicide attempt was a fake and filed for divorce on the grounds of cruelty.

Judge Charles Haas gave her her freedom after just fifty minutes in his Los Angeles courtroom. That was not the end of it. Grant got wind that Virginia was on her way to England, via New York, to film there. Convinced she was, in fact, having an affair with another man, he flew to New York ahead of her, but could not find her in the city.

He took up with acclaimed beauty Sandra Rambeau, then dropped her for actress Betty Furness. They were seen everywhere together but Betty later claimed their relationship was chaste. Behind the scenes, Grant was having an affair with Randolph Scott's old flame Howard Hughes. They went on a romantic cruise together down the coast to Ensenada and remained close for the rest of their lives.

Grant was filming the crypto-homosexual film *Sylvia Scarlett* with the bisexual George Cukor. The young Katharine Hepburn spends much of the film disguised as a boy and Grant is shown fondling her. Hughes was a regular visitor to the set and often took Grant flying. Randolph Scott was still living next door.

Grant's next film, *The Amazing Quest of Ernest Bliss*, was shot in England. Grant spent some time with Virginia there. She had largely forgiven him. Back in the US, he took a great deal of interest in his leading lady, Texan beauty queen Mary Brian. When Grant's father died, Mary comforted him through the grief. Their affair was romantic, but platonic.

Back in Hollywood, Grant was on hand when Hughes was

charged with negligent homicide after a car accident – he was acquitted – and it was Grant Hughes turned to when his affair with Katharine Hepburn was on the rocks.

Grant asked Mary to marry him, but she did not think he really meant it. To put him to the test, she left for New York to see whether he would follow her. His interest quickly waned. For some time he had been seeing Frederick Brisson, the twenty-four-year-old son of friends.

Vivian Gaye had jilted Randolph Scott to marry Ernst Lubitsch. On the rebound, Scott had married the chemicals heiress Marion duPont. They stayed together only a few months, but she settled millions on him.

When Scott returned to Hollywood to make *The Last of the Mohicans*, he bought a beach-house in Santa Monica and Grant moved in. Scott was not the least bit jealous when, at the house-warming party, Grant got off with stunning blonde actress Phyllis Brooks.

The whole of Hollywood breathed a sigh of relief when they were seen out on the town. There were no more veiled references to Grant's ambiguous sexual proclivities in the gossip columns. Phyllis was convinced it was the real thing. Grant desperately hoped it was.

'If anything ever happens to us, I am done for,' he said. 'You are young enough to find love again, but I would be lost.'

Nevertheless, Grant continued to play openly with his chums. He gave a big bash at the Trocadero to celebrate his record-breaking, coast-to-coast flight, and he turned up to a fancy-dress party with Randolph Scott, dressed identically as acrobats. Hedda Hopper noted caustically that neither Phyllis Brooks nor Marion duPont was there.

When Marion did come to town, Grant discreetly rented the house next door. When she left, he moved back. The fan magazines snapped Grant and Scott coyly playing beach-ball, fooling around in the pool or doing the domestic chores together like two old maids. Grant was still seen out with Phyllis and, intermittently, with the curvaceous Jean Rogers. He was also having an affair with a pianist, a man.

Despite the disapproval of the studio bosses, Grant and Scott were still seen out and about together. One night they were even caught kissing and cuddling in the car park at the Mocambo. But Phyllis was in hot pursuit. She ignored the rumours of his homosexuality and was determined to marry Grant. Even William Randolph Hearst's warning, after considerable investigation in England, that she should think twice before marrying a Jew did not faze her.

However, Joan Fontaine was very much fazed by Phyllis' presence on the set of *Gunga Din* when she was trying to excite some romantic interest in him.

Shortly before the outbreak of war, Grant got engaged to Phyllis secretly in Paris. As his wedding neared, Grant had a pre-nuptial agreement drawn up. It stipulated that Phyllis' disruptive mother should never enter the marital home. When Phyllis' mother read it, she screamed for four days. The wedding, and the relationship, was off.

Grant's relationship with Scott was most definitely on. When they were filming *My Favourite Wife* together, they had to shoot a pool sequence at the Huntington Hotel in Pasadena. Grant and Scott turned up as a couple and to everyone's astonishment, instead of taking separate suites, they moved into the same room together. Everybody looked at everybody else. It hardly seemed believable.

For show, Grant was seen out with Louise Stanley and Rosalind Russell, who later married Frederick Brisson, Grant's one-time beau; Fay Wray co-hosted his Christmas party and he was also seen with Italian actress Elissa Landi and singer Constance Moore. Then Dorothy di Frasso introduced him to twice-divorced Woolworth heiress Barbara Hutton.

They began going out. Barbara knew of his relationship with Scott, but spurned the advances of Frank Sinatra and stayed on in Los Angeles to woo Grant. At one party they attended, Randolph Scott turned up with Phyllis Brooks as his date, which gave the gossip columnists something to cluck about. Actually, Phyllis found it painful to see Grant with Barbara Hutton and was relieved when a job on Broadway took her out of town. At the same time, Grant became infatuated with the bisexual writer Clifford Odets, who seemed to understand him like no other man ever had.

On 3 December 1941, Grant bought Hutton a large diamond engagement ring. She had to bribe the Nazi government in Denmark to obtain her divorce from her last husband, the Danish Count Kurt Reventlow. Four days later, the Japanese attacked Pearl Harbor.

Hutton grew impatient to marry and when Grant seemed reluctant to set a date she flew to New York and took to her bed. Randolph Scott was in a huff, too, over Grant's putative nuptials and flew home to Virginia.

Grant managed to reconcile with Hutton and they married on 8 July 1942 at the Lake Arrowhead home of Frank Vincent, Grant's agent and business partner. There was no honeymoon because Grant was filming *Once Upon a Honeymoon* and had to report for work the next morning. Columnist Sheila Graham claimed she overheard Grant saying that the wedding night was the best night of his life. Hutton's friends insist that the marriage was not consummated.

It certainly was not a very happy union. Cary was arrested in a public lavatory with a sailor but charges were quashed because of his secret intelligence work. Grant was keeping track of Nazis in Hollywood under the auspices of Noel Coward. This work kept him out of the British and then the American forces after he took US citizenship in 1941.

Grant also made propaganda films and entertained the troops. At a gala for the US Army and Air Force at the Masquer's Club in Hollywood, Grant was accompanied by Frank Vincent, dressed in a replica of Hutton's bridal outfit. She was not amused.

She was even more put out when she turned up for an Orson Welles Magic Show, to find Grant in drag. In fact, they were no longer seen out as a couple. Barbara was usually accompanied by Randolph Scott or Hutton's infamous cousin, Jimmy Donahue.

Barbara Hutton, who maintained a live-in female companion

at Grant's Los Angeles home, flew off to San Francisco with actress Gene Tierney. Grant begged her to return and Gene interceded. Barbara came back, but stayed only a few days before seeking sanctuary with Frederick Brisson and Rosalind Russell. Grant pursued his wife. He and Barbara wound up sleeping in Brisson's room, while he moved in with his wife. In the morning, Brisson returned to his room to get some socks and found Barbara alone in bed. Grant was asleep on the floor in the bathroom. Soon after, the Grants announced they were going to divorce. Grant told Louella Parsons that they could not make a go of their marriage because of the difference in social class. Her friends were the crowned heads of Europe, while he liked going to the fight with the boys.

At the time, he was playing Cole Porter in *Night and Day*. He was an odd choice for the part. As an Englishman, he was playing a quintessential American. Also all hint of Porter's homosexuality was excised from the script. Casting Cary might give the game away, but Porter himself insisted that no one else could play him.

During the filming of *Notorious,* Cary began dating twenty-two-year-old blonde Betty Hensel. She cancelled her forthcoming wedding at the last minute, telling her parents that she was in love with Cary Grant. Meanwhile, Barbara stirred things up by flaunting her affair with actor Philip Reed.

Grant's relationship with Hensel was full of rows and rec-onciliations. He stuck close to Randolph Scott and Howard Hughes, though he also spent time with Virginia Cherrill and he began dating actress Peggy Cummins.

In London, Grant saw young, leggy American actress Betsy Drake in the play *Deep Are the Roots*. She was also on board the *Queen Mary* when he sailed back to New York and he pursued her, although she eluded him. Eventually, he got Merle Oberon, who was also on board, to invite them both to lunch. The rapport was immediate. Even though observers say that their relationship was more that of brother and sister than lovers, he persuaded her to come to Hollywood with him where, as a favour to Grant, David Selznick put her under contract.

Hughes later bought into it.

Grant steered her away from Hollywood parties and kept her to himself, grooming her for stardom. She went with him when he returned to London to film *I Was a Male War Bride*, in which he got to play a scene in a WAC uniform. Macho director Howard Hawks cracked down on Cary's camp gestures and forced him to act like a man, even when he was in drag.

The critics savaged Betsy's acting and Grant found himself increasingly isolated once more with a woman with whom he had nothing in common. He was obsessively tidy, she was a mess. She was an avid reader, he never opened a book. However, her knowledge impressed him and, gradually, he started reading too.

Meanwhile, Grant met the young Stewart Granger, fresh in town after his success in *King Solomon's Mines*. He spotted the young actor in the MGM commissary and suggested they lunch together.

'I knew he was sexually attracted to me,' said Granger. 'He never laid a hand on me. But I knew.'

The lunch became a daily event, not in the commissary but in Grant's home. Nevertheless, at Christmas, Howard Hughes flew Grant and Betsy down to Phoenix Arizona where they married. Again there was no honeymoon.

The marriage was childless. Betsy longed to adopt. Grant took to heavy drinking.

Filming *The Pride and the Passion* in Spain, Grant had to put up with insults about his homosexuality from Frank Sinatra, who called him 'Mother Cary'. Even so, it was Grant who got close to Sophia Loren despite Sinatra having his eye on her and the fact that she was dating Carlo Ponti at the time.

Betsy had written the script for *Houseboat,* intending to play in it opposite Grant, but while he was in Spain, Grant offered Sophia Loren the part, ruthlessly elbowing his wife aside. Betsy flew to Spain to try to reclaim her film and her marriage, only to find Grant totally enamoured of Loren. She was the woman, he believed, who would finally make him a man.

On the set, he took absurd risks to impress her. In the

evenings, he ignored Betsy and went for romantic meals with Sophia. Eventually, he proposed. Sophia was dumbstruck; Betsy devastated. She headed back to the US on board the *Andrea Doria*. The ship collided with the *Stockholm* outside New York harbour and sank.

Betsy was rescued, but the emotional jolt the news of the sinking had delivered sent Sophia reeling back to Carlo Ponti. Grant announced that Betsy was back on *Houseboat*. However, the studio had already tied up the contracts, so in the end Betsy had to face the ordeal of watching her husband's true love playing the love scenes she had written for herself and Grant.

Sophia Loren was not best pleased that Grant had tried to bounce her from the film either. When he went to make his peace with her, his longing for her welled up again. Here was the woman who could save him from the morass of his confused sexuality. He went to visit Carlo Ponti and promised to make four films for him virtually for nothing, if he would give up Sophia. Ponti turned him down in disgust.

Grant could not believe that Sophia preferred the short and unattractive Ponti to him, the Hollywood idol millions of women drooled over. He hired a private detective in the belief that she was having an affair with the handsome actor Harry Guardino. The gumshoe reported that, in fact, Guardino was bedding someone else. Sophia Loren, he was sorry to report, was totally faithful to Carlo Ponti. In desperation, Cary Grant turned to LSD.

He confided a lot of his drug experience to acid-guru Timothy Leary, who was surprised to find that the object of so many women's fantasies had the same emotional and sexual hang-ups as the guy next door.

Acid did not help. When Loren married Ponti in Mexico, Grant was devastated. He began to try to prove his manhood by sleeping with other women. Ironically, he used his reputation as a homosexual as a cover. Believing Grant to be gay, men thought their wives and girlfriends would be safe with him.

Grant's relationship with Betsy broke down and they began divorce proceedings. When asked how he felt about Betsy dating other men, Grant said: 'Betsy would be incapable of being unfaithful. None of my wives have been unfaithful. Neither have I. This has never been the problem.'

But it was. After they separated, Grant's chauffeur cum minder starting seeing her. When Grant found out, he grew violently jealous and sacked him.

To allay any gossip about adultery, Betsy accompanied Grant to England when he went there to film *The Grass is Always Greener*. However, in London, Grant became openly infatuated with busty singer Alma Cogan and was also seen out with oriental beauty Jackie Chan, Anthony Armstrong-Jones' girlfriend before he married Princess Margaret.

Betsy returned to Hollywood. Grant stayed on in London to continue his affair with Alma Cogan. When he got back to Los Angeles, he took up with actress Ziva Rodann. He gave her a bracelet inscribed with the words: 'To Ziva, the only one who really knew. Love, Cary.'

Nevertheless, he continued living with Betsy. Somehow the relationship struggled on. She even accompanied him on another trip to London to see Alma Cogan.

Grant decided that he wanted a child; not just any child – a Jewish child. He started dating Susan Strasberg, daughter of Actors Studio founder Lee Strasberg, and promised her marriage and security if she would have a baby for him.

Then at home in Hollywood one night in 1961, Grant saw Dyan Cannon on the TV. He phoned around and discovered she was filming in Rome. He told her agent that he was considering her for a part in a forthcoming film. When she asked for the airfare to Los Angeles, Grant, notoriously mean, refused. Cannon stayed on in Rome until she had finished the picture.

Back in Hollywood, Grant gave her a cursory screen test, then started pestering her for a date. She was less than enthusiastic, turning down his invitations, then accepting them and standing him up. Eventually, when she was convinced that he really wanted her, she succumbed and he began to change everything about her – her hairstyle, her clothes, even her behaviour. He used hypnotherapy and LSD to make her over completely. It was as if he was creating the woman who was to be his next wife, and mother of his child.

Meanwhile, he was having a much publicized affair with former Miss Denmark Greta Thyssen. It was a light, superficial affair, much in keeping with his screen image.

'I might love you today,' he told her, 'but I can make no promises if I find someone as pretty as you tomorrow.'

He also told her: 'You have the sexiest-looking body I have ever seen.'

How much use he made of it is uncertain. At the time, he was living with Dyan Cannon and was still married to Betsy Drake, whom he saw frequently. He would often pursue young women for the sake of his image but on the quiet, he continued his old ways. In Paris, while shooting *Charade,* one of the crew spotted him in a gay bar with a handsome young man – 'Every eye in the room was on him and his companion. He didn't seem to care.'

While in Cannes, he became enamoured of Kim Novak. Nearer home, he was seen with Sheila Mosier, an exotic dancer who worked in Las Vegas under the name Yellow Bird. Then there was twenty-three-year-old Yugoslav basketball star Luba Otasevic, whom the press described as 'a girl almost embarrassed by her physical opulence'.

He often complained that the press got the wrong end of the stick when he was seen out with a different girl every night.

'Just think, it would be much worse if they said you were out with a different boy every night,' said his chauffeur.

In 1962, Betsy was granted a divorce on the grounds of mental cruelty.

'I still love him very much,' she told the judge, 'but Cary told me that he didn't want to be married.'

Grant's relationship with Dyan Cannon became abusive. He would beat her with his fists and laugh when she cringed in fear. His pathological jealousy came back. He objected to her wearing miniskirts and when she defied him, he knocked her to the ground.

When she toured with the play *How to Succeed in Business*

Without Really Trying, he paid for her to fly back to Los Angeles every Sunday from whichever city they were playing. By this time she was so enslaved to his will that she raised no objection.

When she became pregnant, he was delighted. At last he had proved to the world that he was a man. After the customary vacillation, he married her.

Two months after the wedding, Grant went to Tokyo without Dyan to film *Walk, Don't Run*. There he hooked up with his old friend Senator Ted Kennedy but he denied himself the pleasures of the geisha houses.

A month after he returned to California, Dyan gave birth to a healthy girl. They named her Jennifer. Grant became obsessive about the child. Dyan was prevented from leaving the house and could go nowhere without him. Eventually the tension became too much. She took the baby and escaped to the Esalen Institute on the Big Sur, where avant garde therapists experimented with personal freedom through nudity, free love and orgies. In 1967, she sued for divorce on the grounds of cruelty. While the divorce was going through, Dyan got herself cast in the movie about wife-swapping *Bob and Carol and Ted and Alice*.

Grant took the divorce stoically. He said: 'I was making the mistake of thinking that each of my wives was my mother.'

Like his old friend Howard Hughes, Grant became reclusive. The two men spoke on the phone frequently. Unlike Hughes, Grant occasionally ventured out in the dead of night. One night the police brought him in for questioning after a woman complained that he had picked up her under-aged son in his Rolls-Royce and made an indecent proposition to him.

He slapped a $10 million lawsuit on Chevy Chase for damaging his 'masculine image' when Chase called him a 'homo' on TV. Chase settled out of court, but the incident earned Grant *In Touch* magazine's coveted 'Heterosexual of the Month' award.

He dated the voluptuous Cynthia Bourbon, who had formerly attracted the attention of Jerry Lewis and Frank Sinatra, but the romance never got beyond the champagne and candlelight stage.

Shortly after Grant tired of her, she announced that she was pregnant and claimed the child was his. He denied it and demanded blood tests. Cynthia never turned up to give a sample. Two years later she was found hacked to death in her car in a Valley parking lot.

For succour, Grant spent time with his old friend Noel Coward in Jamaica. At this time, he was at his most vehement about women. Mothers mess up your mind as a child, Grant maintained. His had. Millions of women around the world slavered after him, but was it really him, Archibald Leach, they wanted or the screen creation, Cary Grant?

This did not stop him having an affair with the beautiful widow of a Hollywood producer. He ended it when he discovered that her feelings were much more intense than his. She tried to commit suicide. He did not even send flowers to the hospital where she was convalescing and his attitude was described as cold and cruel.

He continued seeing young women and even had a serious love affair with twenty-something British photographer Maureen Donaldson. He was in his late sixties and had mellowed some. He did not object to her tight T-shirts and hotpants. Behind her back, he continued his long-term affair with Princess Grace, whom he had met as plain Grace Kelly on *To Catch a Thief*.

'She was the most beautiful woman I'd ever known,' he said.

His affair with Maureen Donaldson lasted for five years. He nursed her through a bout of ill health and, she said, he exhibited none of the violence or jealousy that had surfaced in his other relationships, perhaps because he saw a string of other women behind her back. If he saw a woman he fancied he would send one of his aides to ask if she would like to have dinner with 'an ageing movie star'. Usually, they ended up back at his place and his houseboy would have to drive them home at dawn.

Grant still felt the need to prove he was a man. He picked up the fabulously attractive Vicki Morgan, mistress of the vicious sadist Alfred Bloomingdale, the department store owner and confidant of the Reagans. Bloomingdale had pulled her up outside a restaurant in West Hollywood one day by shoving a cheque for $8,000 in her hand. He took her back to his apartment where he whipped two naked prostitutes before spanking Vicki's own delicious behind. He was a wealthy and generous man, so Vicki stuck with it.

In her spare time, her hobby was straightening out gays. She would walk around Grant's house naked in an effort to excite him. She gave up when it became clear that he was not going to give her any money. Later, she was murdered by her gay flatmate.

Grant continued to see Randolph Scott, who was now happily married, Virginia Cherrill and Phyllis Brooks. Barbara Hutton phoned at all hours. He saw Dyan Cannon in the law courts, when he was fighting over visitation rights, and he wrangled with Sophia Loren about her account of their affair in her memoirs.

In London, he met PR lady Barbara Harris, who was in her twenties and whisked him around town in her Mini. She was dark and good-looking, and took him to see her parents. She returned with him to the US and moved in with him. He began devouring honey and walnuts when a friend told him that it would prolong his sexual prowess. On 15 April 1981, they were married.

On 29 November 1986, he died, after warning his wife that people would write awful things about him once he was in his grave.

'The victimized dead cannot defend themselves,' he wrote. 'Though the fabrications are refuted by others close to them, the damage has been done. I've always conditioned my wife and daughter to expect the biographical worst.'

They will not have been disappointed.

9

PILLOW TALK

Straight leading men are as scarce as hens' teeth, or so say Hollywood insiders. Few covered their tracks as well as all-American, clean-living Rock Hudson – until he got AIDS.

Elizabeth Taylor came on to Rock during the filming of *Giant,* but soon admitted defeat. No woman could ever 'light his fire', she conceded. No woman ever did. Rock was a predatory homosexual, more at home in the bathhouses of Castro Street than the chintzy kitchens of suburbia with Doris Day.

Rock Hudson was born Roy Sherer Junior on 17 November 1925 in Winnetka, Illinois. His father ran off leaving his mother, a tall, cheerful woman, to bring the child up alone. At the age of eight, after seeing a Jackie Cooper movie, he decided to become a movie star so he could buy a new bike.

That same year, his mother married again. It was a rocky marriage and she divorced but later remarried the same man. In the meantime, she worked as a housekeeper for a wealthy family and Roy, until the age of fifteen, slept in the same bed as his mother in the servants' quarters.

Despite his sexual inclinations, he dated girls at school, largely because he loved to jitterbug. He was handsome and popular with the girls. No one in Winnetka ever believed he was a homosexual.

At eighteen, when war broke out, Roy signed up as a sailor.

It was then that his true sexual awakening came, shut up in an aircraft carrier with a thousand other fit, good-looking young men. He tried to behave macho around his friends. On several occasions, he even ended up in bed with a woman just to show he was one of the boys. He wasn't a fighting man. He spent his war in the laundry, sweating over the officers' whites. In 1946, he sailed home from war, floating under the Golden Gate Bridge to the strains of Doris Day singing 'Sentimental Journey'.

Demobbed, he tracked down his father in Los Angeles – this was the place to be if he wanted to act. However, Roy did not get on with his father and soon moved out into a dingy boarding house. Los Angeles was a lonely place after the Midwest but he found company in a gay bar in Long Beach, where men sat around listening to a woman singing bawdy songs. The boys had parties on the beach and openly flaunted their sexual orientation. It was a freedom he had never known before.

Roy was twenty-one when met the immaculately coiffured Ken Hodge, the thirty-six-year-old producer of Lux Radio Theater. He was the first person Roy had met who had any connection with showbusiness. They became lovers.

It was at a party at Ken's penthouse apartment in the Chateau Marmont that Roy Sherer became Rock Hudson. Everyone decided that if he wanted to be an actor he would have to change his name as a sort of rebirth. Ken picked 'Rock' because it was a tough-sounding name. Hudson came from the Long Beach phone book.

Ken encouraged Rock to have some publicity photographs taken and they moved into a bungalow in the Hollywood Hills. Rock mailed out his publicity shots, while Ken worked on his showbiz contacts. He used his savings to put on parties for Rock. Henry Willson, agent turned talent scout for David Selznick, turned up to one. He took Rock aside and told him to call him at his office. Without telling Ken, Rock went to see Willson and signed.

Willson was a notorious homosexual and ugly with it. He did business with one hand under the table, usually on his young client's knee. He had an entourage of young men who would sit at his feet while he told them what big stars he would make them. They accompanied him to nightclubs and attended swimming parties at his house in Stone Canyon. Those who did not make it in the movies, he hired out to provide sexual services for influential producers or their wives. Pimping led to blackmail.

'He exuded evil,' said Rock's long-time friend George Nader.

Rock allowed himself to be seduced by the loathsome Willson for the sake of his career. Ken went back to Long Beach and went to pieces.

Willson may have been repulsive, but he knew talent when he saw it. Lana Turner, Natalie Wood, Tab Hunter, Troy Donahue and Rory Calhoun had all been clients. He poured money into Rock, paying for acting lessons, ballet lessons, tap-dancing lessons, special lessons to help him overcome his paralysing shyness and extra special elocution lessons to help him lower his voice. It did no good. Veteran director Raoul Walsh gave him one line in *Fighter Squadron* but it took thirty-six takes for him to get it right. Walsh took pity on Rock and employed him to paint his house.

Walsh also saw that Rock had a face the camera loved, so he put him under contract for a year and had his teeth capped. He sold the contract to Universal for $9,700, the exact amount that he and Willson had squandered on the boy.

Even though the studio now had Rock in hand, that did not mean that Willson had lost interest in him. He would visit him on set and insist that Rock spend his free time with him. But Willson had served his purpose and Rock wanted to hang out with friends his own age.

The studio fixed him up with a number of young actresses so that he could be seen gazing into their eyes in Ciro's and appear at swimming parties without fans getting the wrong – that is, the right – idea. Rock was marketed as all-American beefcake. The fan mags called him: 'A wholesome boy who does-n't perspire, has no pimples and has the appeal of cleanliness and respectability – this boy is pure.' That was pure something, too!

One of his dates was MGM dancer Vera Ellen. They turned up to the Hollywood press photographers ball as Mr and Mrs Oscar, in skimpy swimsuits with their bodies painted gold. It earned them a lot of press coverage and an interview with Louella Parsons, who was doing a live radio broadcast from the ball.

At the time, Rock was getting 150 proposals of marriage a week. Soon the fan magazines were asking: 'When will bachelor boy Rock choose a bride?'

Rock knew he had to be very careful. His career as a romantic lead would be over if the public got the merest hint that he was gay. He always had two phones installed in his home – one his boyfriends must never use. He also expunged all trace of feminine mannerisms.

'Rock's the straightest homosexual I ever met,' said one friend, Stockton Briggle.

He hung out with two closet homosexual friends, George Nader and Mark Miller. They would go out as a threesome, never four which would look too much like two gay couples. They would also avoid places where other homosexuals were seen. Instead they would stay at home and camp it up. On one memorable occasion, George put a duet between Marlene Dietrich and Rosemary Clooney on the record player. Rock and Mark burst out of the bedroom with neckties tied around them like bikini tops and bottoms and mimed to the record. Rock was Marlene and Mark was Rosemary.

On weekends they would drive up to Point Dume, a secluded beach near Malibu where they could sunbathe nude; or they would take trips to Lake Arrowhead where they could fool around with boys in relative safety. There was one problem though – Rock's prodigious sexual energy.

Rock did not like effeminate homosexuals. He preferred masculine types, preferably ones who also slept with women and 'had a story'. If he met a straight man who showed any sliver of interest, he would go to any lengths to seduce him. Meanwhile, Rock was being cast in 'T&S' movies: tits and sand.

These beach bunny movies gave the viewing public a lot of opportunity to see Rock in his swimming trunks. The fan magazines liked beefcake shots of him stripped to the waste doing masculine things like washing his red convertible. The captions positively dripped with saliva.

'Looking at him from any angle, the conclusion is: what a man!' said one.

Headlines asked: 'So you'd like to be Mrs Hudson?'

One proffered: 'Here's how to handle Hollywood's 'Big Rock'.'

Picture spreads show him at home with his roommate Bob Preble. One shot showed Rock – with his shirt off, naturally – lying in bed. Bob is standing over him with an alarm clock. The caption read: 'Rip Van Hudson invariably sleeps through the alarm which awakens Bob in the next room.'

The problem was that the house only had one bedroom. It had two single beds, but they were pushed together with a king-size coverlet over them.

Preble admitted that he and Rock did 'a little experimenting on a couple of occasions after we'd had a few drinks, but nothing you would call relations'.

He knew Rock was gay.

'I guess he hoped the barriers would come down,' said Preble. 'I was a little nervous, but I said to myself, just roll with the punches.'

So how far did you go, Bob?

'The situation did come close to spilling over to something that would have been foreign to my whole being, my whole behaviour,' he said.

In fact, Bob Preble was another actor hand-picked by Henry Willson for stardom. He lived with Rock for three years, then left to marry actress Yvonne Rivero and went on to build a career selling electric motors.

Rock got himself a new 'wife' – enter Jack Navaar, a twenty-two-year-old serviceman he met at a dinner party. Navaar became Rock's live-in lover and housekeeper. Like other Hollywood wives, he would phone the studio to see what time Rock would be home for dinner.

Jack said that Rock was a very romantic man. They would hold hands at the movies and Rock would call him 'baby'. They had a private code: '1-2-3' means 'I love you'. If they were in company, he would knock three times on a counter, or nudge Jack three times under the table. The affair started to fall apart when Jack began to get jealous. One night, he literally kicked Rock out of bed. Rock told Jack that he would give up the movie business and they would live quietly in the Midwest, but Jack did not want to live in Chicago with plain old Roy Sherer.

Confidential magazine was soon on the case. They offered Jack Navaar $10,000 for his story. Willson heard about it and the story was spiked. He had mob connections.

Even being seen out with beauties like Marilyn Maxwell and Lori Anderson was not enough to maintain a straight image. At a première, someone in the crowd yelled 'Faggot!' when Rock arrived. Something had to be done. Rock had to get married. Willson found a compliant candidate – his own secretary Phyllis Gates.

Phyllis was not aware that she was being manipulated, just as she was not quite sure what the failed young stars who Willson made his 'gofers' actually did. When her boss took her out to dinner with Rock then left them alone together, she just thought he was being a matchmaker.

Rock phoned her and made a date but did not show up. He stood her up on two more occasions. She even bumped into him with a handsome young surfer, Craig Hill, another of Willson's 'clients', but still she did not get the message.

After another dinner with Willson in tow, Rock made another date. This time he did turn up. He took her dancing and swept poor Phyllis off her feet. A kiss on the doorstep when he dropped her home left her with a sleepless night.

Then, just before Christmas, he kissed her for real.

'His lips were soft and pliant and thrilling,' she wrote in her autobiography. 'The kiss lasted a long time, and I didn't want it to end. His big hands were amazingly gentle as he began to explore, and I fell completely under his spell. He was masterful, yet tender, and he had a magnificent body.'

Then, God help us, Phyllis plunges on into more intimate details.

'The love act itself was sublimely passionate, though it ended sooner than I would have liked,' she wrote thirty-five years after the event. 'I figured that Rock was overly excited.' Poor baby. 'Soon he was sleeping like a baby – Rock Hudson naked in my bed. I contemplated that perfect face, that long but ideally proportioned body. How easy it would be to fall in love with him. Or had I already?'

Phyllis, sensible girl, wrote this off as a one-night stand, until Rock phoned and invited himself over for Christmas.

While Rock was in Europe filming *Captain Lightfoot,* Jack Navaar looked out for Phyllis. On Sundays, they would go to a gay bar in Santa Monica called the Tropical Village, and still she did not twig. Jack had his suspicions about Phyllis. One weekend he took her to Laguna. On the first night, in a bar called Camille's, Phyllis was chatted up by a woman and Jack did not see hide nor hair of her for the rest of the weekend.

At Willson's behest, they took a trip and, to save money, they booked into hotels as Mr and Mrs Navaar but they did not sleep together, Jack says. In Kansas, where Phyllis had been an airhostess before moving to LA, she took him to a gay party. When Rock found out, he went crazy.

When he returned to Los Angeles, Jack had fled. He went on to marry. Jack later suspected that the trip he took with Phyllis had been instigated by Willson to weaken the bond between him and Rock.

'Rock went into the closet and didn't start coming out for fourteen years,' Mark Miller said. The age of innocence was over. Hudson dared not be seen living with a man again until the late 1960s.

Back in Hollywood, Rock, Phyllis, George and Mark went out as a foursome. Then Phyllis moved in with Rock. If any other movie star lived with his girlfriend outside marriage the studio would have been terrified of a scandal. With Rock, they were hoping some scandal sheet would find out.

As cohabitees, Phyllis and Rock got on well. Rock told three of the men he lived with later that Phyllis was bisexual. Both Mark and Jack said they saw her in lesbian situations. She denied it.

On location in Texas for *Giant,* Liz Taylor admitted she was attracted to Rock but soon found she was up against, well, a rock. If anyone slept with Rock on *Giant,* it was James Dean, who shared a house with him. Dean was bisexual and said he would try anything, and anybody, once. When Dean died, Rock cried for hours.

Out of the blue, Rock suggested marriage. He had already given Phyllis a ring and Willson was at work on a 'secret' wedding in Santa Barbara before she had even said yes. The wedding was so secret that a Universal publicity department photographer would be there to record the happy moment. Although Phyllis was to tell no one, not even her mother, some-how Hedda Hopper and Louella Parsons found out about the forthcoming nuptials. Universal sent out the wedding pictures with a press release headed: 'Rock Hudson elopes with secret love'.

They honeymooned in Jamaica and Manhattan. Back in LA, the photographers and feature writers were queuing up to prove to the world that the Hudsons were the very picture of domestic bliss. They were, during the day; but at night, Phyllis found Rock a flop. For the sake of their marriage, she insisted that he seek psychiatric help. He refused but, for the sake of his career, he stuck it out for as long as he could.

Rock was at breaking point one day when he called Mark Miller.

'I have to have a boy,' he said. 'For a year, I've been faith-ful. I haven't had a boy and I'm going crazy. Can you fix me up with someone?'

Mark called a friend in Laguna who was interested and drove Rock down there after work one day. The friend said the encounter was incredible because Rock was so sex starved.

This eased the tension between Rock and Phyllis. It also opened the floodgates. At night, Rock would go out searching for rough trade, sometimes not returning until dawn.

Phyllis was planning to go with Rock to Italy where he was going to film *A Farewell to Arms,* but the day before he flew out, she was admitted to hospital with hepatitis, possibly contracted from one of Rock's nocturnal encounters.

There was comment in the press when Rock refused to fly back to visit her, despite her doctor's pleading. The studio put out a story saying that he was desperate to fly back, but his filming commitments made a visit impossible. In fact, he was having a torrid affair with a young Italian actor, plying him with expensive gifts and romantic trips. There was quite a scandal when the young Italian turned up later in Hollywood demanding Rock give him a hand-up as he had promised during their pillow talk in Italy.

A young Elaine Stritch was on the picture. Rock took her out but it was a month before he even kissed her goodnight.

'I'm a good Catholic girl. I grew up very slowly in the sex department ... but even I began to wonder,' she said. Rock told her that their fling could go no further because he was married. Eventually she figured it out for herself.

When he returned to Hollywood, Rock's marriage was at an end. He did the proper movie star thing, and moved out into the Beverly Hills Hotel. It was a sad time, but the marriage had lasted two years and had served its purpose. The rumours that Rock Hudson was gay had been quashed.

To further cement Rock's image as a hunky heterosexual, he was cast opposite Doris Day in *Pillow Talk.* The film cost $1 million and made $25 million profit. Rock Hudson was suddenly the world's number one romantic idol.

Hudson and Day soon became a Hollywood institution, following up *Pillow Talk* with *Lover Come Back,* with the inevitable beach scene. Behind the cover of his heterosexual screen image, however, he was on the hunt more vigorously than ever. His fame became a problem for him.

'I wish I could go to bed with a bag over my head,' he told a friend, Jon Epstein. 'When people get to bed with Rock Hudson, they're so nervous they can't do anything. It's a waste.

All they can think is: "I'm in bed with Rock Hudson."'

It became such a burden for him that when he went sailing on his new yacht he took two lesbians as his crew .

There was another woman in his life, a former Miss Black Cleveland called Joy. She was his housekeeper for fourteen years, living in the luxurious servants' quarters of his new home, the Castle. She actually fulfilled the role of Mrs Hudson. They would eat together, drink together, read scripts together. He bought her expensive clothes and jewellery. When they had parties he would proudly introduce her to all the celebrities. They were so close that, during the Watts riot in 1965, he risked his life to rescue her best friend from the burning ghetto. If the studio had known they would have flipped.

When he had men back to the house, he would make sure they left before she woke in the morning. She knew, of course, but they never talked about his love life. She said that only one woman stayed over, Marilyn Maxwell. He had known her since the early Fifties, but they only got together in 1961 when she broke up with her husband Jerry Davis. Rock played a father to her son. They even talked about marrying and having a baby. Rock said he would build a nursery over the garage. Marilyn thought about it, and thought better of it. She knew she was a jealous person and realized that Rock seeing men behind her back would make her miserable.

So Liz Taylor was wrong. One woman did light his fire. Although they never married, Rock and Marilyn were lovers on and off for some time.

In 1962, a young cowpoke named Lee Garlington moseyed into town as an extra on the TV series *The Virginian*. He knew all you had to do in Hollywood was be pretty, hang out and you would be discovered like Rock Hudson.

Lee heard all about Rock through the gay subculture and started hanging out outside Hudson's private quarters at the studios. He moved in with a young guy. When they broke up, he got a call from a friend saying that someone famous was interested in him. It was Rock Hudson.

Rock said he had wanted to make contact sooner but had

heard that Lee was involved. Now he was free, Rock would like to meet him.

'I was scared to death,' Lee said. 'We talked, and had a couple of drinks. Then we tried to play around, but I was so intimidated that nothing happened. Zero. I thought, oh well, he'll never want to see me again. But he was patient. He understood I was nervous and it wasn't a big deal to him that we couldn't have sex.'

They saw each other again. This time Lee got over his nerves. He used to go up to Rock's house regularly for midnight sex sessions. Rock even gave him the keys on a golden key ring. He had to be discreet, though, and not be around when Joy was up and about.

They went on a trip to New Orleans together. Lee gradually found himself subsumed by the relationship. To redress the balance, he began picking up younger, smaller men and one night, Rock called at Lee's apartment to find him with a young man.

'Rock was devastated,' Lee said.

However, the affair dragged on for nine years. Before he died, Rock told Mark Miller with tears in his eyes that Lee was one of the few people he had truly loved.

Around the time he met Lee, Rock dropped Henry Willson and found a new agent. The man who had made him, and his former lover, died a few years later, a penniless alcoholic in a home for distressed showbiz folk.

Rock picked Jack Coates up at a tennis party in Beverly Hills. Coates had been in love with Rock since seeing *Giant,* but at first he could not handle being with the man in the flesh. Rock invited him up to the Castle for a steam or swim and relaxed him by making lime daiquiris and chasing him around the garden.

'We just clicked,' said Jack.

But Jack felt Rock was not sincere and stopped seeing him. Then Rock's agent called up and told Jack that Rock was refusing to appear on the Bob Hope Special unless Jack agreed to see him that afternoon. Jack stopped by after class. They had mint juleps. Rock drove Jack down to his apartment, packed his things and moved him in. They 'honeymooned' together in the Holiday Inn in Monterey.

During the filming of *Darling Lili*, it was reported that Rock was involved in a *ménage à trois* with director Blake Edwards and his wife Julie Andrews, and that America's Mr Clean was hanging out in leather bars with Mary Poppins. Picture it.

Darling Lili was shooting in England and when Rock sent for Jack, he came over with a friend, a gay banker. Although Rock was in his mid-forties, he had to have sex every day and was always thinking about it. Jack claimed that he was a 'champion cuddler'. Eventually, Jack announced he was moving to Arizona. Rock could have stopped him going, but showed no emotion, so Jack left, but he came back for frequent visits and holidays.

By the early 1970s, the film offers were beginning to dry up. Rock bit the bullet and signed a contract for the long-running TV series *McMillan and Wife*. For a star of his stature, this was a big come down – worse than that, he had to do bed scenes with Susan St James. They even had a baby in the series! Rock could not stand it. He started drinking heavily which led to a dangerous flirtation with the burgeoning gay scene in San Francisco and LA Rock was seen at notorious gay discos, Trocadero Transfer and the I-Beam. In New York, he got involved in kinkier stuff. He moved in more or less exclusively homosexual circles and his image was almost destroyed when a rumour spread that he had 'married' actor Jim Nabors. Nabors had his own show on TV but, hearing the rumour, CBS cancelled it. The two men dare not be seen together. They never talked again. Rock was even afraid to go to Hawaii because he knew Nabors had a house there. In 1982, *Harvard Lampoon* announced their 'divorce'.

Rock was rescued by MGM publicist Tom Clark, whom he met at a bridge party. He began having dinner with Clark and his long-time companion Pete de Palma. Sometimes they were joined by other young men from the showbiz world. Rock went on a tour of the Far East with de Palma but it was Clark who moved into his home. Clark was near Rock's age. The two men would take a steam bath together around six and spend the evening relaxing in their bathrobes. Tom brought stability to Rock's life and kept him off the gay scene, temporarily. Rock sacked Joy, saying that he wanted an all-male household, so he could walk around naked if he wanted to. Tom tried to organize Rock's life, but Rock began to resent it. He was in no mood to temper his sexual wanderlust and searched with admirable diligence for the perfect one-night stand. Friends called him 'Trixie' because of the number of tricks he pulled. There were rows, but Tom was always there in times of trouble.

Mark organized swimming parties for Rock. On Rock's instructions, he would fill the pool with fifty tanned young men in swimming trunks.

'Who are they all?' asked a friend.

'The blonds are named Scott and the brunets are named Grant,' said Rock.

Rock liked multiple partners and anonymous trysts with airline stewards, carpenters and maître d's. He loved all-male parties – 'beauty parties' – he called them, where he did not know most of the beautiful young guests.

Jim Gagner met Rock at one of these boy parties and was immediately struck by the power of his libido.

'His sexual energy was so extreme, you could feel the heat,' he said. 'It made my ears burn. Rock's sexuality sucked people in like a black hole.'

With his career on the wane, Rock now concentrated all his energies on his sex life.

'If he could have you, he did,' said Jim. 'He could have sex once or twice a day with several different people.'

Jim watched as Rock turned the heat on man after man. His ego became inflated out of all proportion.

'I felt sorry for him,' Jim said. 'It was sad to see a fifty-three-year-old star so driven by lust.'

Rock took Jim to San Francisco to stay with Armistead Maupin, while Rock and Maupin went on a tour of the gay clubs. They went to Black Blue, a gay bikers' club, and visited the notorious backroom where a mass orgy was taking place.

Rock particularly enjoyed a place called Glory Holes, which reconstructed old public lavatory practices. There was a balcony, so you could view the action from above.

In 1980, Rock went to Malta to film *Martian Chronicles* for TV. There, he met talented young British actor John Cassady, who was co-starring. Cassady recalls that Rock took an inordinate interest in his bum.

'We were playing a scene on a beach,' said Cassady. 'Every time I sat down and my backside got sandy, Rock would brush it off for me.'

But it was someone else's buttock that interested him when he got back to LA In Brook's Baths, where Rock went for a sauna and massage, he met twenty-nine-year-old Marc Christian. Rock was fifty-seven. Marc was a perfect hunk, the ultimate Californian surfer, everything that Rock held up as male perfection. He was six-foot tall, blond, blue-eyed, moustached; he wore open-necked sports shirts, faded jeans and gleaming white tennis shoes; better still, he was bisexual. Since he was nineteen, he had been living with an older woman – even older than Rock – named Liberty Martin. They worked together on Gore Vidal's doomed Californian senatorial campaign. Despite her age, Liberty was an exotic beauty.

They met again at one of Vidal's campaign meetings. Rock shook his hand firmly. Christian was something of a recording buff. Rock asked him if he could transfer some old 78s to tape, cleaning up the sound in the process. He took Christian's phone number and said he would get in touch.

It began as a lunch-time affair. Rock wanted to keep it a secret from Tom Clark and the other boys at the Castle. After two months of these lunch-time assignations, Christian demanded to know why he had not been taken to Rock's house. Rock told him about Tom Clark. It was a situation Rock was about to resolve.

Rock and Tom were planning to spend the fall in New York. At the airport, Rock took Mark Miller aside and told him that he would be back in LA in a couple of days. When they landed in the Big Apple, Rock and Tom had a gay old time. They went to see *La Cage Aux Folles*. Claire Trevor gave them a huge 'Welcome to Civilization' party. Then Rock told Tom he was going home.

Tom protested that they had only just arrived. Rock was adamant. Tom could stay if he wanted to, but he was going home. Okay then, go, said Tom. Rock did. That was the end of their relationship.

Back in LA, Rock took Christian up to the Castle – Rock's crew there 'probably thought I was just some guy off the street'. Rock told friends that, with Christian, he had recaptured the passion and sexual ecstasy he had known when he was much younger.

'Rock was totally smitten with Marc,' said Stockton Briggle. 'He couldn't keep his hands off him.'

Christian tells another tale. He says he kept Rock waiting for six months before he finally gave him the keys to the inner chamber.

'We'd been out to dinner at the Black Forest [Rock's favourite German restaurant in the Valley] and he didn't want to go home,' Christian said. 'He asked me if I would stay with him. I said yes. We went to a motel.'

Rock was very nervous, according to Christian.

They took a trip to San Francisco and hung out on Castro Street. In Los Angeles, they went openly to the gay bars in Santa Monica and West Hollywood. Christian was nervous about Rock being seen in these places. Although he did not want to make a big to-do about coming out of the closet, he did not mind people knowing he was gay.

'If they know, they know,' he said. 'If they don't, they don't. Fuck 'em!'

While Rock was away in Israel, Christian was installed in the Castle in Tom Clark's place. Rock also put Christian on salary. He got his teeth fixed, enrolled him in a gym, signed him a personal fitness instructor, gave him a car, and organized tennis and acting lessons. He even had Christian's father's 1959 Chevy stationwagon fixed. The old man was dying of cancer, Rock explained, restoring his car would give his spirits a lift.

At first, 'it was wedded bliss' said Mark Miller.

They stayed in watching video tapes, including one Rock had made for Doris Day in which he appears as her, in blonde wig and drag, miming to one of her songs. Rock was introduced to Marc's parents. He paid for their fortieth anniversary party and Christian's sister's wedding reception was held at the Castle. They were all one big happy family.

Then they went through a phase where Marc would parade his conquest, Rock, all over town. After that, Christian would go out, not say where he was going, and not say when he was coming back. The whole thing became pitiful. George Nader recalled seeing Rock and Christian out together – 'a man whose cheeks are starting to fall in, who doesn't look good, sitting with a guy half his age who he doesn't like and who's using him.'

At first, Rock was pleased with his weight loss.

'I've lost another two pounds,' he would tell Mark Miller proudly. Mark thought this odd, as they had all be eating the same food.

In the spring of 1984, Marc moved out of Rock's room and into the guest room, which everyone called Tijuana. He didn't always come home at night.

Relations became strained even further when Christian admitted that he had taken money for sex and that he had deliberately hung out at Brook's Baths to hook Rock.

'The "accidental" meeting was planned,' Rock told Mark Miller. 'He kept flaunting himself until I finally noticed him. Jesus Christ, I still can't believe it. Yours truly, set up and seduced.'

Rock also told Mark Miller that he would be getting rid of Christian any day. Mark pointed out that Rock had said that about Tom Clark for five years.

'Are you going to wait another five years?' Miller asked. 'You don't have five more productive sexual years. You had better get out there in the field while you are still capable.'

Rock took off to Hawaii with another man. Then he got close to Ron Channell. He had met Ron in the gym. They worked out together and went shopping. Ron would come over for lunch then stay for dinner. Rock paid for acting lessons and did a screen test with Ron.

'There was something electric between them,' said John Dobbs.

They laughed together and Ron called Rock 'Speed'.

Ron was a new physical type for Rock. He had brown eyes and dark skin. He was straight and wanted to keep things on a buddy-buddy, locker-room basis. For Rock there was an element of flirtation and pursuit in their relationship.

Christian grew jealous of Ron and threatened to go to the *National Enquirer.*

While Rock's days were occupied working out with Ron, Dean Dittman organized his nights. Dean was a 'floweroholic' and Rock would smother him with roses from his garden. They would cook together and hang out together. One evening, in a gay bar in Long Beach, they met a blond boat builder in his twenties named Pierre. Pierre came up to the house and played the piano while Rock sat at his feet gazing up at him. They went to Mexico to meet Pierre's family. On the trip, Rock intended to consummate the affair.

'I looked at Rock and looked at my Dad,' said Pierre. 'They were the same age. I couldn't do it.'

While they were away, the gardener caught Marc in his bedroom with a blond boy.

At a reception at the White House, celebrity X-ray Nancy Reagan told Rock he should fatten up. He was down to 195 pounds. Pictures from the reception showed a large red sore on Rock's neck. It had been there for almost a year and eventually he went to a dermatologist who did a biopsy. The sore was Kaposi's sarcoma. Rock had AIDS. Everyone was shocked.

'I thought it was a disease that fairies on Santa Monica Boulevard got,' said Mark Miller.

They decided that Marc Christian should not be told. He would tell Liberty, then the whole world would know. Rock continued having sex with Marc Christian. With others he was more careful. He sent anonymous letters to a number of young men with whom he had had intimate contact, advising them to have AIDS tests. It is also said that he had a lot of anonymous sex with young men procured for him by an actor friend.

'Rock met a lot of boys at his place,' said an insider. 'There were a lot of nervous boys who had been to bed with Rock, riding up and down the elevators at that apartment building.'

On his doctor's advice, Rock bought condoms, but he could not figure out how to put them on gracefully.

'I've never worn a condom in my life,' Rock told Dean. 'Won't I give the show away if I suddenly start now?'

Rock continued losing weight and rumours spread that he had AIDS. He continued to deny it to Christian when he confronted him.

He went to Paris with Ron Channell to take a course of the anti-viral drug HPA-23 and, before he started on *Dynasty,* told everyone that he had licked the disease. He knew he had not. The doctors warned him that the job might shorten his life but he went right ahead, kissing Linda Evans full on the lips in one episode.

By the autumn of 1984, Rock had gone off sex completely. He no longer even watched pornography. If a sex scene came on the television, he turned it off. Even straight sex reminded him too painfully of his condition.

He grew closer to Ron Channell. They went to Hawaii together and Ron was Rock's constant companion when he returned to the Pasteur Institute in Paris.

Christian did not know that Rock had AIDS until the story broke in *Variety* on 23 July 1985. He, and the world, were aghast. He claimed that Rock had slept with him between the spring of 1983 and February 1985, knowing he risked passing on the disease. Christian went to see palimony attorney Marvin Michelson.

Celebrities rushed to Rock's bedside. On 2 October 1985, he died.

Christian sued. The estate countersued, claiming that Christian had extorted money from Rock by threatening to publish love letters that showed him to be homosexual. Marc Christian won $14,500,000 in damages.

10

REBEL WITHOUT HIS DRAWS

Since he died in a car crash on 30 September 1955, James
Dean's career has really taken off. He made only three movies.
If he had lived, it is unlikely that he would have made any more.
Everyone he worked with was heartily sick of him, partly
because he gave half the cast and crew of *Rebel Without a
Cause* the crabs. Humphrey Bogart said: 'Dean died at just the
right time. If he had lived, he would never have been able to
live up to his publicity.'

He left behind him a legend, largely manufactured by
Warner Bros. *East of Eden* had been a modest hit. *Rebel
Without a Cause* and *Giant* had yet to be released. *Rebel* had
been received well enough at a preview, but *Giant,* despite its
all-star cast, everyone knew was a turkey. A little hype around
the fallen hero, the youthful talent martyred, the fragile butterfly soul crushed beneath the wheels of the juggernaut of
Hollywood would do no harm, now would it? Dean became
Hamlet with a Porsche.

There are more books about his twenty-four-year life than
there are about stars with ten times the number of movies to
their credit. Andy Warhol called him 'the damaged but beautiful soul of our time'. His picture has decorated many teenagers'
bedroom walls, the perfect icon of tortured innocence.

But, of course, he was not innocent and he was only tortured because that was the way he got his kicks. His youthful talent only shone as a beacon to others because he slept his way to the top.

Born in Fairmont, Indiana, Dean grew up in Los Angeles until his mother died of cancer when he was nine. His father sent him back to Indiana to be raised by a kindly aunt and uncle.

At high school, he was called a sissy. He never had a girlfriend or a date. A lonely boy, he sought the companionship of the Reverend James A. DeWeerd, the local Wesleyan pastor who was then thirty. They read poetry together and listened to Tchaikovsky. A war hero, DeWeerd had a huge shrapnel wound in his stomach. Once, when they were out in the countryside, parked under some trees in DeWeerd's convertible, he asked Jimmy whether he would like to put his hand inside the wound. It was almost big enough to accommodate Jimmy's whole first. This act of intimacy frightened and excited him. Some say DeWeerd introduced Dean into the delights of gay sex.

'Jimmy was usually happiest stretched out on my library floor,' he said after Jimmy's death. 'Jimmy never mentioned our relationship, nor did I. It would not have helped either of us.'

To prove to himself that he was not a 'queer' or a 'fairy', Dean began dating the young physical education teacher Elizabeth McPherson, who said later: 'He fell in love with me.'

A friend, Larry Swindell, recalled: 'Jimmy said his main priority of that school term was to lose his virginity. He openly wanted to lose his virginity, as opposed to getting laid. He wanted to know what it was all about.'

DeWeerd encouraged Dean to become a thespian. One of his early leading roles at Fairmont High was in *Our Hearts Were Young and Gay* about the misadventures of two nineteen-year-old college girls in gay Paree.

One of his big lines was: 'Lady, come away from this nest of death, contagion and unnatural sleep.' The thing Dean liked most about acting was the make-up.

On his eighteenth birthday, 8 February 1948, Dean registered at his local draft board in Fairmont, but dodged the draft by telling them he was gay. When Hedda Hopper asked Dean how he had avoided service in Korea, he said: 'I kissed the medic.'

In 1949, Dean headed back to Los Angeles where he studied drama. At college, he was uneasy in the company of girls. On one occasion, at a co-ed literary evening, Dean read an explicit passage from Henry Miller's then banned classic *Tropic of Cancer*. He showed off sketches of bountifully endowed young men and produced a candle holder he had made shaped like a woman's vulva. Gleefully, he inserted a candle and lit it. When molten white wax started to drip down the shaft of the candle on to the labia, one embarrassed young girl fled from the room in tears.

There are allegations that, while trying to establish himself as an actor, Dean resorted to prostitution. He was certainly flirting with homosexuality at the time.

'He dabbled in everything,' a girlfriend said. 'He wanted to experiment with life.'

His friend Bill Bast was dating a young actress named Beverly Wills. He arranged a double date for Jimmy with Jeanetta Lewis, a brunette from UCLA's drama programme. Bill later discovered that Dean was wooing both Jeanetta and his girlfriend Beverly. Beverly broke the news one afternoon.

'Bill, there's something we have to tell you,' she said. 'We're in love.'

Bill was shocked.

'We tried not to let it happen,' said Beverly, 'but there was nothing we could do. These things just happen.'

Jeanetta was not best pleased either. The scene ended with Jimmy shaking Bill, slapping Jeanetta and bursting into tears.

Then Jimmy got lucky. He met TV director Rogers Brackett, a close friend of Rock Hudson's agent Henry Willson, and moved in with him.

'He said we could have twin beds,' the twenty-year-old Dean told his disbelieving agent, Isabelle Draesemer.

'I wasn't so easily fooled,' she said.

There was only one bed, which they shared.

'If it was a father–son relationship, it was also incestuous,' said Brackett. 'I loved him and he loved me.'

Within weeks, Dean had a string of introductions and jobs.

Thanks to Brackett, Jimmy took a trip to New York. The Reverend DeWeerd was sending him money too. Alone in New York, he studied the films of Marlon Brando and Montgomery Clift. He also met a singer–dancer named Elizabeth 'Dizzy' Sheridan and moved into her apartment on Central Park. She was two years older than him and the first woman he ever loved.

'We had a lot of fun,' she said.

But Jimmy had a problem – how to maintain a relationship with Dizzy while keeping hold of his sugar daddy? What he did was to tell Dizzy all about his affair with Brackett.

'He told me he was extremely unhappy about what he'd done, that he had succumbed to Rogers because he thought that he could help him,' she said.

Brackett was, by then, in New York, too, and Jimmy dragged her along to his apartment.

'He presented me as his girlfriend and he just hung on to me the whole time.'

This had the double bonus of making Brackett jealous, while convincing Dizzy that he was serious about finishing with Brackett. Of course, he was not. When Dizzy took a choreography assignment in New Jersey that summer, Jimmy moved back in with Brackett. They hung out together at some of the more notorious waterfront bars of the West Village. He may have loved Dizzy, but through Brackett he got TV work, usually walk-ons. This gave him a new chat-up line when he hung out late at night in bars.

'Hey, I was on television,' he would say. 'Did you see my show?'

He met aspiring young actress Christine White. Together they enrolled in the Actors Studio, where both Brando and Clift had trained.

Dizzy came back to town and moved in with Jimmy and Bill Bast, who had also made it to New York. Dizzy got a job as an usherette in the Paris movie theatre on 58th Street and Fifth Avenue. Jimmy called her there one day and asked her to marry him. When she stalled, he said: 'We must get married before we get caught up in all this' – by which he meant stardom.

Brackett introduced him to the homosexual set designer Lemuel Ayres. Jimmy went for a cruise on his yacht and Ayres used his influence to get him a part in N. Richard Nash's new play *See the Jaguar*. He got rave reviews.

'He sort of disappeared after that,' said Dizzy.

He had an erratic affair with actress Barbara Glenn.

'The sexual attraction was so powerful,' she recalled. 'There were a lot of people after Jimmy, men as well as women, but our physical relationship held.'

Barbara was leaving with a stock company for the summer. Friends gave her a going-away party. Jimmy sulked. At the end of the party, Barbara went to a bar with a girlfriend and, in tears, unburdened herself. Jimmy walked in, said nothing, took Barbara by the hand, led her out and back to his apartment and made love to her.

Dean started apartment-sitting for an English TWA steward. They lived together briefly, but Dean got sick of him.

'He considers me a victim,' he wrote. 'I refuse to be sucked into things of that nature.'

He began calling Montgomery Clift, trying to get to know him. Clift asked Elia Kazan of the Actors Studio about him.

'They say he likes racing cars and bikes, waitresses – and waiters,' said Kazan.

Brando was another idol Dean tried to befriend and, after the release of *The Wild One* in 1953, Jimmy took to wearing leathers.

Because of the persistent rumours of Clift's homosexuality and Brando's bisexuality, Dean was determined to experiment further with gay sex.

'He wanted to fool around, to do the forbidden thing,' said fellow actor Jonathan Gilmore. He tried it on with Gilmore.

'Frankly, it just didn't work,' said Gilmore, though Gilmore did turn up to a Greenwich Village party in drag as Dean's date one night.

'Jimmy was neither homosexual nor bisexual,' said Gilmore. 'I think he was multisexual. He once said that he didn't think there was any such thing as being bisexual. He felt that if someone really needed emotional support from a man he would probably be a homosexual, but if he needed emotional support from a woman he would be a heterosexual.'

Dean was playing the part of a homosexual Arab pimp and blackmailer in *The Immoralist*, when Warner Bros called him for an audition. Kazan gave him a screen test and signed him for *East of Eden*. Paul Newman was up for the part of Dean's brother and during his screen test, Dean asked him for a kiss. He pinched Jimmy's bottom.

Before he left for the Coast, Dean tried to seduce the assistant stage manager on *The Immoralist*, Vivian Matalon. On two occasions Jimmy suggested that Vivian sleep over at his one-bedroomed apartment. On the second occasion, he agreed. Jimmy dimmed the lights and put some seductive music on the gramophone. But when they crept into bed, Matalon said: 'If you think anything's going to happen, you're wrong. Now turn over and go to sleep.'

Later, Dean picked a fight with him.

Kazan wrote to Jack Warner asking him to impress on Dean when he arrived in California 'the great importance of living an outdoor life, sunshine, exercise, food and fucking, just all the healthy things'.

Dean grew restless back on the coast, even though Kazan introduced him to Tennessee Williams. He wrote to Barbara Glenn:

Honey!!! I'm still a Calif. virgin, remarkable, no? I'm saving it – H-bomb Dean. A new addition has been added to the Dean family. I got a red 53MG (milled head etc. hot engine). My sex pours itself into fast curves, broadsides and broodings, drags, etc. You have plenty of competition now. My motorcycle, my MG and my girl. I have been sleeping with my MG. We make it together. HONEY.

He wrote to her again a month later, again claiming that he had been to bed with no one and he was saving it for his return to New York City. However, he was hanging out in after-hours clubs, drinking beer and smoking marijuana. He bought a motorcycle to scare the hell out of anyone who rode with him. The beloved red MG was callously dropped for a Porsche Speedster.

Barbara wrote back to say that she was about to get married. Jimmy was crushed.

After that, he was not a California virgin for long. He hung out with actor Rusty Slocum and a crowd of what Slocum described as 'Jimmy's little girlfriends and boyfriends'. Women moved in and out of Dean's apartment in rapid succession. Friends soon lost count. He would pick them up casually in shops or drugstores. One girlfriend, Betsy Palmer, thought that Dean was uninterested in sex: 'As a matter of fact, my assumption about Jimmy was that he was almost asexual.'

Another girlfriend, Arlene Sachs, claimed 'the two of us really got it on together'. She was seventeen and said she was a virgin. He took her back to his apartment anyway.

'I guess he didn't realize I was telling the truth until I screamed, and suddenly there was blood all over,' she said. He mumbled an apology, and he got in trouble again with her mother when he took her home late.

One night, she invited him over to her new apartment for what she said would be an 'orgy'. It was a tame affair. The boys took off their shirts; the girls their blouses and they all got under a blanket together. Dean called their bluff.

'Okay, if you want to stage a so-called orgy, I'll show you orgy,' he said. And he got his penis out and began masturbating.

'That is not what I wanted to happen,' said Arlene.

She teased him about being 'queer'; he denied it. But she overheard a male movie star on the phone making suggestions to Jimmy. One day, he complained that his 'ass hurt'. When she asked why, he said: 'It was Rogers. I shouldn't have been with Rogers.'

Arlene closed her ears to all this. She thought he was taunting her and did not want to believe that he was having homosexual affairs while he was making love to her.

The affair ended when Arlene invited him over to dinner and he arrived with a hat-check girl called Barbara. Arlene went out to the grocery store to get some things and when she returned, it was clear that Jimmy had made love to Barbara.

'I went into the kitchen and thought I was going to faint and throw up at the same time,' she said.

During the shooting of *East of Eden*, the Sardinian beauty Pier Angeli was filming on the adjoining sound stage. The two young stars instantly fell in love. They shared a passion for fast living and fast cars. Everyone thought of them as Romeo and Juliet. He introduced her to a friend as 'my best friend, the only girl I ever loved'.

But as Dean was not a Catholic, Pier's mother insisted that he was unacceptable to her devout and virginal daughter. Dean cleaned up his act, appearing at the Angeli home in a suit and tie. He even considered becoming a Catholic so he could marry her. They discussed it seriously. His agent told him to wait until *East of Eden* was released: 'You'll be Mr Pier Angeli if you marry her now.'

She missed her period and Jimmy asked her to go to New York and get married. Pier refused, saying it would break her mother's heart if she eloped. He went alone to think things over.

'I wouldn't marry her unless I could take care of her properly,' he told a friend. 'And I don't think I am emotionally stable enough to do so right now.'

He talked to everyone about her, but a few days after he arrived in New York, he heard on the radio that she was going to marry Vic Damone, with whom she had had an affair before she met Dean. Jimmy was devastated. He could not even get Pier on the phone, though she went out on a date with him once when he returned to Los Angeles.

The night before the wedding, Jimmy saw Damone at Pier's favourite restaurant, the Villa Capri.

'You may be marrying Pier,' Dean said, 'but she isn't yours, never was, and never will be.'

Waiters had to pull them apart.

They met again at the Villa Capri the night Pier gave birth. Damone came over to Jimmy's table with a bottle of champagne and said: 'Come on, let's drink a toast to my son.'

Jimmy raised his glass.

'I'll drink a toast to my son any time,' Dean said.

Two days later, lunching with an old girlfriend, Damone confided: 'Pier's the mother all right, but I'm not so certain I'm the father.'

Although he later dismissed her as 'Miss Pizza', Jimmy carried a torch for her until his death and kept a lock of her hair in an enamel locket.

'It was all so innocent,' Pier recalled.

In later years, long after Dean was dead, she said that she loved him more than either of her husbands: 'I could only think of Jimmy when I was in bed with them. I could only wish it was Jimmy and not my husband who was next to me.'

After losing Pier, he began dating a new girl every night. He went out with Lori Nelson, Susan Strasberg, Terry Moore. Mamie Van Doren claimed that he took her for a spin on his motorbike, kissed her and cupped his hands over her breasts. Then he took her home and they never went out again. This seems like a typical encounter for Dean.

'He always had uncertain relations with girlfriends,' said Kazan. 'Jimmy was not a very effective lover with women.'

Jimmy, however, took himself extremely seriously.

'Showbusiness is in trouble,' he said. 'Barrymore is dead and I'm not feeling well.'

Dean got involved with 'Vampira' – a Hollywood eccentric named Maila Nurmi who introduced horror movies on TV. He became close to Eartha Kitt whom he would take for a spin on his bike. It seems that these relationships were platonic. At the time, Dean was intimately involved wtih actor Jack Simmons who doted on him.

'He gets Jimmy coffee or a sandwich or whatever Jimmy wants,' said a friend. Simmons was a regular fixture at Dean's apartment on Sunset Plaza Drive and it is certain that Jimmy was involved in homosexual activity at the time. When asked if he was gay, he replied: 'Well, I'm certainly not going through life with one hand tied behind my back.'

At night he would cruise the gay meat rack of Hollywood Boulevard. In the oral history of small leather and chains clubs there, it was said that he was 'an instant hit with the fist-fuck set' because he would do things that no one else would do.

One night in a bar on Sunset Strip, Dean was with Jonathan Gilmore when they met a girl who had lost a leg in a motorcycle accident. They took her back to Jimmy's place where they drank and smoked dope. Jimmy watched while Gilmore had sex with her.

Dean took up with nineteen-year-old Swedish actress Lili Kardell. They wore matching outfits and had their hair cut the same way. She recorded every intimate detail of their sex life in her diary, in Swedish, giving his performance a star rating, but she often complained that he flirted with other girls.

People who knew him thought that he was just playing the part of the star, being seen out with exotic people. Any emotion on their part frightened him and Lili was another girl doomed to disappointment.

Certainly press photographers followed him wherever he went. Back in Indiana he was photographed at a family grave. When he returned to Fairmont for his high school's Valentine's Day 'Sweethearts Ball', he went to Hunt's Funeral Home where he had his picture taken, lying in a coffin.

Rogers Brackett had lost his job and asked Jimmy to lend him some money to tide him over.

'Sorry Pops,' said Dean. 'I didn't know it was the whore who had to pay.'

During the filming of *Rebel Without a Cause*, Dean was involved with co-star Natalie Wood. They took a hairy trip up Mulholland Drive.

'We did the impossible,' he said. 'We made love in the Speedster.'

Everyone cracked up at the thought of them entangled in the tiny sports car.

However, Natalie seems to have been having simultaneous affairs with Nicholas Ray and Dennis Hopper. Perhaps because of the competition, Dean was more comfortable in the company of her stand-in, Faye Nuell Mayo. There were rumours that Dean, too, was having an erotic relationship with director Nicholas Ray. Ray certainly stayed with Dean in his tiny one-bedroomed flat in New York during a trip there.

Sal Mineo, who was also on the picture, admitted a strong homosexual attraction between them.

'We could have, like that,' he said with a snap of his fingers.

And Dean and Hopper were close. One night, the young nightclerk at the El Paisano Lodge recalled seeing the two of them rushing through the hotel brandishing women's clothes. Outside in a car, he found a waitress from El Paso.

'They talked me out of my clothes, then ran off,' she whimpered.

The nightclerk got a blanket which the naked girl wrapped around herself before disappearing into the night.

During the filming of *Giant,* Dean once more felt the need to be seen with an exotic-looking creature on his arm for publicity purposes. He two-timed Lili with another Swedish-born actress, Ursula Andress. Soon after they first met, she told Jimmy she had a date she could not break – but he could come along. The date was with Howard Hughes. The three of them were in Hughes' car, driving towards the beach. When they stopped at a traffic light on Santa Monica Boulevard, Hughes said he was out of cigarettes and asked Jimmy to go to the store and buy him some. When Jimmy got out of the car, Hughes drove off.

At that time Ursula was in love with John Derek, whose wife threatened to have her deported if she kept on seeing her husband. Nevertheless, Dean's involvement with Ursula became passionate and he soon started turning up late on the set in the mornings.

She said he was 'like a wild animal and smelt of everything I don't like. We fought like cats and dogs – no, like two monsters. But then we would make up and it was fun.'

Dean even said he was learning German so they could row in two languages.

His relationship with Andress got him into trouble with one boyfriend, who accused him of dating women for the sake of publicity. They were seen rowing at a gay party in Malibu the night before he died.

Then at six o'clock on the afternoon of 30 September 1955, James Dean ran his Porsche at full speed into the side of a black-and-white sedan which was crossing Route 466 near Cholame, California. His neck was broken. As Dean was lifted into the ambulance, his badly injured passenger, mechanic Rolf Wütherich, heard 'a soft cry escaping from Jimmy – the little whimpering cry of a boy wanting his mother or of a man facing God'. Dean was preparing to play Hamlet on Broadway when he died.

The coroner noted that Jimmy's torso was covered in scars. Towards the end of his life he had entered the twilight world of S&M. In an East Hollywood leather bar called The Club where he was known as the 'Human Ashtray', Dean would bear his chest and beg people to stub their cigarettes out on him.

11

IN BED WITH MADONNA

Warren Beatty said: 'If I tried even to keep up with what was said about me sexually, I would be, as Sinatra once said, "Speaking to you from a jar in the University of Chicago Medical Center."'

His former lover Joan Collins said: 'He was insatiable. Three, four, five times a day, every day, was not unusual for him, and he was also able to accept phonecalls at the same time.'

Orson Welles said: 'That's all he thinks of, day and night. Oh yes, he's a real satyrite ... calling different people all morning long to be sure that in the evening there's going to be somebody new. You know, that's the Casanova.'

It was Warren's good looks that made him a hit with the ladies. His sister Shirley MacLaine – she adopted her mother's maiden name when she became an actress – said: 'When I was three, I used to dandle Warren on my knee, and even then I knew he was prettier than me.'

Ironically, he first came to prominence playing the impotent gangster Clyde Barrow in *Bonnie and Clyde*. He gave the world the line 'What's new, Pussycat?' His agent, Charles Feldman, heard Beatty use it over and over as he fielded phonecalls from numerous women. In *Shampoo*, Beatty sought to demonstrate that the modern-day Don Juan was not a homosexual in denial.

251

Beatty has never talked openly about his sex life – 'Obviously, my sex life isn't mine alone to talk about' – but his list of known lovers include the sexiest women of the last few decades from Brigitte Bardot, through Julie Christie to Madonna.

There were, of course, humble beginnings. At high school, he flirted with the mothers of friends. One recalled: 'Warren would come to my house, sweep in and give me a big theatrical kiss. He gave the impression of being self-confident; actually, he was essentially a loner, never wanted to be committed and tied down.'

At college, he dated, particularly a girl named Ellie Wood. Although he had been a football star at school, he quit in college, finding himself too sensitive for the beer drinking and horseplay. Besides, he felt more at ease in the company of girls.

The young Warren dropped out and headed for New York, where he learnt the Method style of acting and got a few breaks in television. Doing the rounds of auditions allowed him to pick up young actresses. One of them was Diane Ladd, who found him attractive but overly ambitious. She recalled that, when he brought her home after a date, he would kiss her goodnight on the doorstep, then come in and kiss all her flatmates too.

When he went to Hollywood in 1959, he became a star practically overnight. He was screen tested with Jane Fonda for *Parrish*. Their embrace was so long and intense that the director had to shout 'Cut!' three times before they separated.

'We kissed until we had practically eaten each other's heads off,' Fonda recalled. The test was a success, but *Parrish* did not get made.

Afterwards, they had dinner at La Scala, where Beatty was spotted by Joan Collins. Joan, who was playing a stripper in *Seven Thieves*, ran across Beatty again at a pre-wedding party for Debbie Power, widow of Tyrone. They did not get a chance to talk, but he saw her looking at him. Next day when she got back from the beach, her message service informed her that there had been six calls from Beatty. She called back and fixed a date for dinner. That night, they began 'exploring each other's minds and bodies'.

'We could not bear to be apart,' said Joan.

While she prepared for her new movie, he called her hourly. In the mornings, she would turn up on the sound stage with bags under her eyes, barely able to stifle a yawn.

When Beatty went east to appear in the play *A Loss of Roses*, Collins followed. They shared his room in the Willard Hotel and visited his parents in Arlington together. Then they headed for the Blackstone Hotel in New York. Joan even turned down *Sons and Lovers* to stay with Warren. The studio put her on suspension, stopping her $2,000 a week salary.

Warren was cast with Natalie Wood in *Splendor in the Grass* and 'the inevitable happened, just like a bad novel', as Joan Collins put it.

She and Natalie's husband, Robert Wagner, had grandstand seats and were actually watching while 'the inevitable' happened. Director Elia Kazan gave them directors' chairs from which to watch Warren and Natalie shoot their love scenes. The Method, it seems, worked too well. They really got into their parts.

'All of a sudden they were lovers,' said Kazan. 'I wasn't sorry. My only regret was the pain it was causing Robert. His sexual humiliation was public.'

One day, Wagner turned up at the studio to find Beatty and Natalie in each other's arms 'rehearsing'.

'Keeping tabs on me, Bob?' said Beatty loudly.

Syndicated columnist Dorothy Kilgallen ran a piece saying that Beatty and Wood were 'staying up all night rehearsing their love scenes'. Wagner sent a lawyer's letter. Kilgallen refused to retract.

At the same time, Joan discovered she was pregnant.

'How did that happen?' asked Warren.

Joan found comfort in sarcasm and had an abortion. Then she headed off to film *Esther and the King* in Italy. Still she could not bear to be parted from Beatty for long and flew back for weekends. They agreed to marry. She would look for a wedding dress in Europe. Meanwhile, the tabloids announced she was dating Italian actor Gabriele Tinti.

Joan returned to Los Angeles with her wedding dress, which she hung in the wardrobe in the house she rented with Beatty on Sunset Plaza. They rowed, fought and made up constantly.

In London, Joan watched as Warren, playing an Italian gigolo, made love to Vivien Leigh in *Roman Spring*. Joan had to stay behind in England to look after her ailing mother when Beatty went on location to Rome.

There, he met Susan Strasberg. She asked if he could sit down in his tight gigolo pants. They went out to dinner and he moved into her apartment in Rome.

'I found him charming and intelligent,' she said, 'with a tremendous need to please women as well as conquer them.'

Susan took him to the salon of director Luchino Visconti, who surrounded himself with priceless antiques and beautiful men. Visconti perked up at the sight of Warren. Later, on his way to the bathroom, Beatty whispered to Susan to wait a few moments, then follow him. Inside the marble lavatory, Susan asked him what he wanted her to follow him for. Twenty minutes later, breathless, the two Americans strolled back into the salon. All eyes turned to Susan who had forgotten to button up her blouse.

'I wasn't quite sure how to act,' she said, 'but Warren beamed at one and all, an enchanting, ingenuous smile.'

When filming was over, Beatty flew back to London, picked up Joan and the two of them flew home to Los Angeles. They already knew the affair was over. The wedding dress remained unused. Beatty said that Joan was the best fiancée a man ever had.

Soon after, Beatty called Natalie Wood on the set of *West Side Story*. When she came to the phone, she was greeted with the now famous line: 'What's new, Pussycat?'

Natalie revealed that things were going badly for her on *West Side Story* and she needed a shoulder to cry on. Beatty obliged and he was soon seen hanging around the sound stage.

Wagner was having a party on the set of his new movie. Natalie promised to be co-host, but she turned up an hour late with Beatty on her arm. You could have cut the atmosphere with a knife. After Natalie had done the compulsory round of the guests, she disappeared with Beatty, only to reappear again an hour later. This time Beatty had Natalie on one arm, Joan on the other. He suggested the four of them go out for dinner. At the Villa Capri, Wagner and Collins had to look on as the two lovers flirted and giggled. The next day Wagner's press agent announced a trial separation. Louella Parsons said it was the biggest split since Douglas Fairbanks and Mary Pickford.

The Wagners' home was put up for sale. Natalie rented a house in Bel Air; Beatty moved in; Joan left for London; Wagner followed. They had a date, which prompted Fleet Street to speculate about a change of partners. The scorned couple went to see *Stop the World I Want to Get Off*. Backstage, they met the star of the show, Anthony Newley, who was to become Joan's husband.

Natalie filed for divorce. She and Beatty holidayed in the Bahamas, and got engaged. They were dubbed the poor man's Burton and Taylor.

Once the divorce was granted, Natalie and Warren headed for Europe. In Rome, they walked into a restaurant where Wagner was consoling himself with actress Marion Marshall. Wagner was delighted to see Natalie, less so to see Beatty. Nevertheless, he invited them over for a glass of champagne. He even danced with Natalie, though they barely touched.

Later that night, Wagner phoned her hotel, but could not get through because of Beatty's numerous calls to the womanhood of Hollywood. Wagner had wanted to suggest a reconciliation to Natalie. Already unhappy, she would have jumped at the chance but by the time she learnt that he had tried to call that night, he was already married to Marion Marshall.

Beatty was soon being compared to John F. Kennedy who had recently been installed in the White House. Both had good looks, intelligence, a command over women and lower back pain. Asked whether this hampered his sex life, Beatty replied: 'It doesn't hurt then.'

In Natalie's new home in Benedict Canyon, she and Beatty

entertained but there was a growing distance between them. He would roam. She had an affair with *Life* journalist Tommy Thompson who came to interview her. They shared a New York hotel suite when Natalie was in town for the première of *Gypsy*. Beatty turned up, blissfully unaware of the situation, and took them out to dinner.

Back in Los Angeles, Beatty walked out on her one night in Chasen's. When he turned up at Benedict Canyon a week later, Natalie refused to see him. The maid told him that Natalie had burned his clothes.

They met again at the Oscars. She was there with her new fiancé, Arthur Loew. Beatty walked in on the arm of Leslie Caron. They had met at a party in Beverly Hills in 1963.

'I was struck by his appearance and personality,' Caron said. 'He had star quality – very good looks, a great smile; he was tall and athletic. Seduction was his greatest asset.'

She was six years older than him and married to British theatre director Peter Hall. They had two children. Caron and Hall split amicably due to 'pressure of work'. She flew to Jamaica to film *Father Goose* with Trevor Howard and Cary Grant. Beatty turned up on the island.

'We practically did not leave each other for the next two years,' said Caron.

When she returned to London, Caron admitted to Peter Hall that, yes, she was in love with this young scallywag. Divorce followed. Beatty was named as co-respondent.

While the divorce proceedings were heard, Beatty and Caron were in Shepperton Studio filming *Promise Her Anything*. Friends were bemused. They were expected to believe that Beatty was ready to settle down with Leslie and be stepfather to her two children. What they saw was a panther on the prowl. But Caron was captivated.

'I want to live while I am alive,' she told the press. 'Life is great and I love Warren. Marriage? Not yet.'

Things were far from over for Beatty, too. While he was in London, he even tried it on with Susannah York during the filming of *Kaleidoscope*.

'As I was happily married,' she said, 'I found myself smacking his hand as he went to pinch my bum, saying "stop it, Warren".'

Leslie arranged a meeting for Warren with French director François Truffaut. Beatty wanted a role in *Fahrenheit 451*. Instead, Truffaut suggest *Bonnie and Clyde*, which was the first film Beatty produced. He selected for the role of Bonnie, not Leslie Caron, not even Natalie Wood who was down on her luck at the time, but unknown fashion model turned actress Faye Dunaway.

Faye was very protective of Warren.

'He has been hurt by those who persist in seeing him as some moronic super-stud,' she said. 'Women and sex are very important to Warren ... but he reserves himself for a chosen few.'

Asked if the idea of being irresistible to women appealed to him, Beatty said: 'If I thought it was true, it would appeal to me very much. It's a wonderful idea – would that it were true.'

Sadly, it wasn't. Around that time, the Los Angeles bureau chief of the *New York Times* had a very attractive assistant. Beatty pursued her relentlessly.

'He called her so often, he was driving her crazy,' the bureau chief said.

'Think of how many women would love to be in your position,' her boss told her.

'Think of how many have been,' she said.

The relationship with Leslie Caron cooled and Beatty began dating *Rowan and Martin's Laugh-In* star Judy Carne.

'He was one of the most beautiful men I have ever seen,' she said. 'His hair, his hands, everything about him.'

They met at a Hollywood party. Three weeks later Beatty called up and left a message. Judy called back and invited him over to her house. When he got there, he demanded to know what she wanted from him. She said she thought they might just spend a few pleasant evenings together. Soon she found it wearing.

'Sometimes I felt that there was nothing about women that

he liked except their bodies,' she said.

Returning to London, Beatty was said to have had a fling with Brigitte Bardot, who was still married to Roger Vadim at the time. Vadim recalled seeing Warren at a Malibu party in 1965 'surrounded by young actresses'.

'Warren explained that he had suddenly become impotent and would be leaving for India the next day,' Vadim said.

Of course, he was not. At a party around that time, Hollywood writer Sally Ogle Davis once watched Beatty make love. The party was at financier Bernie Cornfield's house. Bored by the conversation of stoned starlets and balding tycoons, Sally took herself down to the screening room to watch an undistinguished British thriller.

'About twenty minutes into the movie, Beatty walked in with a giggling young woman. Despite all the empty seats, they sat down on the seat in front of me and proceeded to make out. While Beatty was busily engaged in the activity for which he had become renowned, he kept winking at me over the young lady's shoulder as if to say, "How am I doing?" He appeared to be doing very well indeed. Such naked narcissism is rare even in Hollywood and so, not surprisingly, I have been fascinated with Warren Beatty ever since.'

In Paris, his name was linked with Madam Dewi Sukarno, the estranged wife of the philandering Indonesian president, who was seen exploding out of her dress at a chic party. Roman Polanski recalled meeting Beatty in Paris, ostensibly to discuss business, only to be confronted with a week-long orgy of parties, discos and girls.

Then there was Julie Christie. Their paths crossed several times on the international movie circuit. He phoned; she talked. They got together at the Oscars in 1967. She was filming *Petulia* in San Francisco and they spent a Californian summer together. The man in her life, artist Don Bessant, made a quiet exit.

Beatty made *The Only Game in Town* with Elizabeth Taylor. Burton turned up on the set during a bed scene in a truculent mood.

'I say, Elizabeth,' he yelled. 'Don't you think you should be a bit closer to your lover? And Warren, you look a touch bashful. Is my presence making you nervous?'

It did. Beatty fled back to Julie Christie.

In London, Beatty would hang out with Roman Polanski at the Bunny Club. When the news came that Polanski's wife, the heavily pregnant Sharon Tate, had been murdered by Charles Manson's Family, it was Beatty who escorted the heavily sedated Polanski back to LA.

The transatlantic affair with Christie continued. Asked whether they intended to get married, Julie replied: 'If we are, we are; if we're not, we're not.'

Meanwhile, there was Britt Ekland. Beatty had met her at a dinner party when he was with Leslie Caron and she was still married to Peter Sellers. Their affair developed while Julie was busy and, as Britt put it, 'foolishly absent'.

They would meet in dark corners of London nightspots. Then he would drive her back to her studio where they would make love until they fell asleep from sheer exhaustion.

She had to go to Los Angeles to appear on the *Dean Martin Show*. He found an excuse to follow. They spent days on end sprawling about his penthouse suite at the Beverly Wilshire. Britt said: 'Warren was the most divine lover of all. His libido was as lethal as high octane gas. I had never known such pleasure and passion in all my life. Warren could handle a woman as smoothly as operating an elevator. He knew exactly where to locate the top button. One flick' – yes, flick – 'and we were on the way.

'For a long spell, I lied to myself. I was convinced that Warren might abandon all his other women for me. Of course, he did not. There were always his whispered telephone calls to Julie. No man made me happier, and I fought hard to keep him, but he was always apprehensive about our affair in case Julie found out. I believed then that Warren was incapable of lasting love.'

The affair was doomed. After two months, Britt got a call from London and went back. Julie was now free of commitments and came over in her place.

During the two months that Christie and Beatty had been separated, she can hardly have expected him to be celibate. He expressed his views frankly in an interview in *Playboy* magazine: 'If you look at the real facts of life, you'll find that if you've not released your sexual energy you're in trouble. If you take a trip and you're away for three days and you don't relate to a chick then pretty soon that's all you think about; three days in a new town and you're thinking, "Why can't I find a beaver in a bar?" It's not that sex is the primary element of the universe, but when it's unfulfilled, it will affect you.'

I guess Julie understood – or perhaps she didn't. Julie Christie was fiercely monogamous.

'Infidelity destroys love,' she said. 'If you love someone and it's good, you've got to have the sense to stick with it. This doesn't mean you will never be attracted to another living soul. But if you give in to that attraction, then you risk losing the person you're in love with. You can't just go swanning off with everyone who attracts you. It's greedy and selfish. It sounds great to do whatever you want at a given time. But it never works out in real life – only in the movies.'

Their differing views were a recipe for disaster – especially as Warren was now running with 'Black Jack' Nicholson. Beatty got 'greedy and selfish' with Goldie Hawn on *Dollars,* while Christie consigned her relationship with Beatty to the dustbin of history with her graphic love scene with Donald Sutherland in Nicholas Roeg's *Don't Look Now.*

Soon Beatty was being 'greedy and selfish' all over the place, particularly with Swedish bombshell Liv Ullmann and Natalie Wood's sister Lana, who found Beatty 'a passionate and inventive lover'.

Beatty secured his reputation by appearing as the womanizing hairdresser George Roundy in *Shampoo,* which also stars Julie Christie and Goldie Hawn – art imitates life.

Meanwhile, Beatty and Nicholson were tearing up the town, combing the boulevards for pretty girls and having leggy models flown in from every point of the compass. They were called the

Odd Couple. While Jack drank and smoked dope, Warren's only vice was the telephone – 'his second most important appendage', as a friend put it. However, they were 'both utterly dedicated to the sexual act as the greatest form of pleasure'.

They had one other thing in common – Michelle Phillips.

A singer, she had been a member of the Mamas and the Papas and was the former wife of John Phillips. She had been married to Dennis Hopper for eight days. When her marriage broke up, she sought consolation with Jack Nicholson and moved in with him. Jack phoned Dennis to let him know. Hopper said: 'Good luck. I still love her, but it is all over.'

When Michelle and Jack split, she moved in with Beatty who had just bought a house that needed filling, while Angelica Huston moved in with Nicholson in Hollywood's age-old game of musical beds.

Michelle phoned Jack to see how he felt about her new domestic arrangements.

'I thought it was fabulous because I liked them both very much,' said Jack.

The new domestic arrangements did not slow Beatty down. In the mid-1970s, they went to a party at Marianne Hill's house. When Michelle vanished into the kitchen, Beatty surveyed the room and picked on a woman, not an especially beautiful woman, but sharply dressed. She had come with a man.

Beatty strode over and stood between them with his back to the man. Eventually, he took the hint and went away.

'Don't I know you?' said Beatty to the woman.

'No,' she said.

Then he began to act shy, looking at the floor, muttering. He bashfully kicked the floor with his toe. Then he offered the woman a cigarette.

'No, thanks, I don't smoke,' she said.

'Neither do I,' said Beatty.

'But you are smoking now.'

'That's only because I'm nervous.' Then he looked her in the eye and said: 'I'd really like to get to know you better.'

'But you came with someone,' she protested.

'Yeah, Michelle. Have you seen her?'

He scrambled off to find her, retrieved her from the kitchen and they moved on.

You can't win them all.

Although Warren and Michelle lived together as husband and wife, Beatty maintained his penthouse at the Beverly Wilshire where he carried on a distinctly bachelor lifestyle. On tour promoting *Shampoo,* he was seen with Russian actress Viktoria Fyodorova. In London, he made a very public display of his reconciliation with Julie Christie. They ate at the most prominent tables of the most fashionable restaurants and flew back to Los Angeles together.

Michelle moved out and went into therapy for the next two years.

'I don't think he felt that marriage was either a happy or productive way of life,' she said on reflection. 'He preferred not to be involved. What satisfied him more was a shallow, meaningless relationship which he believed was healthier.' Perhaps he meant they were the only kind he could have.

Beatty was called to account for himself before the Second International Festival of Women's Films in New York in 1976, as a panellist in a seminar entitled 'Where is Love?' While feminists everywhere would have had him lynched and castrated, Beatty simply turned on the charm. Having been tried and acquitted by the massed ranks of militant womanhood, Beatty felt completely justified in going back to his old ways and became a regular guest at Hugh Hefner's Playboy mansion in Bel Air.

He saw Diane Keaton in *Annie Hall* and began calling her, whispering endearments of charm and passion down the phone. She turned up to the 1979 Oscars on his arm. He was grooming her for the role of Louise Bryant, his on-screen lover in *Reds*. Beatty was also directing and Jack Nicholson played playwright Eugene O'Neill. The film was panned, except by Oona O'Neill. Her father never spoke to her again after she married Charlie Chaplin at the age of seventeen.

'After a lifetime of acquired indifference,' she said, 'thanks to you, dear Jack, I fell in love with my father again.'

After playing the womanizing John Reed in *Reds,* Beatty began work on a project about Howard Hughes and got involved politically with Democratic hopeful Gary Hart. Hart stayed at Beatty's Los Angeles home and later told the press: 'If people want to say there were orgies going on up there and I was chasing starlets, there was nothing I could do about it.'

Hart's presidential ambitions were snuffed out when he was caught getting into the jeans of model Donna Rice on board a yacht called *Monkey Business* in Bimini.

Keaton soon moved on. She was seen out with Jack Nicholson and Al Pacino. Beatty was playing the field again. Then the twenty-nine-year-old French actress Isabelle Adjani came to the front of the pack. Beatty had met her in Paris when she was playing opposite Roman Polanski in *The Tenant.* A French magazine thought it heard the sound of wedding bells. Instead, Beatty took her to America and on to Morocco to co-star with him and Dustin Hoffman in the ill-fated *Ishtar.* Beatty was knocked out by her beauty.

'She is the most gifted person for the screen I have ever known,' he said.

Beatty was reluctant to hire Madonna for the part of his girl-friend Breathless in *Dick Tracy* because he was a friend of Sean Penn's. But Madonna was desperate for the part. When she got it, Penn caused such a scene that he had to be led away in hand-cuffs by the police. Madonna had filed for divorce by the time they started shooting.

The outcome of their on-screen romance was inevitable, so they anticipated it. They became lovers before the cameras started rolling. He was twenty-two years her senior and Madonna said she would lie in bed thinking: 'This guy's been with the most glamorous women in the world.' But then she would think: 'What the hell, I'm better than all of them.'

On the set they were seen kissing and petting, and their frequent appearances in fashionable nightspots helped hype the movie; but when the shooting was over, she hightailed it back to New York.

At fifty, even Warren Beatty could not compete with the leather-clad young studs who peopled Madonna's sexually deviant stage shows. Of course, more hype was needed when *Dick Tracy* came out. They would dine at two fashionable restaurants a night – main course in one, dessert in another, always sitting at the most prominent table. For maximum exposure, Madonna also went in for maximum exposure, all miniskirts and sheer lace.

Beatty had to put up with the presence of Madonna's close friend and self-publicizing lesbian, Sandra Bernard. The two girls would disappear into the powder room and reappear dressed in each other's clothes. Fortunately, out nightclubbing, Beatty could rely on the support of Jack Nicholson who liked to get out while Rebecca Broussard, pregnant with his child, stayed at home.

Madonna built hyping *Dick Tracy* into her Blonde Ambition tour and stole the show. While she was out there saying, 'Dick? that's an interesting name', Beatty slunk into the shadows. On the Arsenio Hall show, she was frank about Beatty's attractions.

'What does Warren Beatty have that we don't have?' asked Arsenio.

'About a billion dollars.'

Smarting, Arsenio steered the conversation on to sex.

'Joan Collins said he was sexually insatiable,' he said.

'He was twenty at the time,' she pointed out. 'Aren't all twenty year olds insatiable?'

Figuring he had hit the spot, Arsenio came back with: 'Does the name Joan Collins make you jealous?'

'No,' said Madonna, in the ultimate put down. 'I mean, have you seen her lately?'

The best Beatty could come up with in an interview was: 'Madonna is more fun than a barrel of monkeys.'

The movie was out. The circus was over. Madonna moved on. She told him that she was seeing Tony Ward, a model who posed for pin-ups in gay magazines. When Beatty got angry, Madonna pointed out that he had been seeing other women and slammed the phone down. As one of Madonna's camp followers put it: 'She screwed his brains out and left.'

To add to his humiliation, taped phone conversations of him telling Madonna he loved her appeared in *In Bed With Madonna*. He insisted they be removed. As taping phone conversations without the permission of both parties is illegal in California, she had no choice. But she was sore.

'He just thought I was fucking around with some kind of a home movie,' she said.

Despite being thoroughly mangled by Madonna, Beatty was not ready to give up bedding his leading ladies. In *Bugsy*, thirty-three-year-old Annette Bening played Virginia Hill to Beatty's Bugsy Siegel. To get the best out of their erotic scenes on camera, Beatty began sleeping with Bening.

During the shooting, Annette conceived. So for the first time, Beatty got married. He became a doting father and a faithful husband. Even Jack Nicholson was shocked.

'It's the age thing,' he said dismissively. Jack, of course, never got the hang of the settling down thing. After Rebecca Broussard had a second child by him, he moved on, the unstoppable sex machine.

Annette Bening succeeded in doing what no other woman had done – she tied Hollywood's greatest stud down to a life of tranquil domesticity.

According to one of Beatty's biographers, John Park, Warren is 'the last great lover of Hollywood'. If he is, the world will be a poorer place. Surely, perched up there at the top of Mulholland Drive, being faithful to his wife, he is letting the side down just a little bit. For five years now he has been a good boy. Come on, Warren, it's boring – one more time now for the lads and lasses.

BIBLIOGRAPHY

The Barrymores, Hollis Alpert, W.H. Allen, London, 1965

Cary Grant: A Class Apart, Graham McCann, Fourth Estate, London, 1996

Cary Grant: A Touch of Elegance, Warren G. Harris, Sphere Books, London, 1988

Cary Grant: Haunted Idol, Geoffrey Wansell, Collins, London, 1983

Cary Grant: The Lonely Heart, Charles Higham and Roy Moseley, New English Library, London, 1989

Chaplin and American Culture – the Evolution of a Star Image, Charles J. Maland, Princeton Univesity Press, Princeton, New Jersey, 1989

Chaplin: Genesis of a Clown, Raoul Sobeland and David Francis, Quartet Books, London, 1977

Chaplin: His Life and Art, David Robinson, Collins, London, 1985

Charlie Chaplin, John McCabe, Robson Books, London, 1978

Clark Gable: Portrait of a Misfit, Jane Ellen Wayne, Robson Books, London, 1993

Confessions of an Actor, John Barrymore, Robert Holden & Co. Ltd, London, 1926

Cooper's Women, Jane Ellen Wayne, Robert Hale, London, 1988

Damned in Paradise: The Life of John Barrymore, John Kobler, Atheneum, New York, 1977

Douglas Fairbanks: The First Celebrity, Richard Schickel, Elm Tree Books, London, 1976

Errol Flynn, Charles Higham, Granada Publishing, London, 1980

Errol Flynn: A Memoir, Earl Conrad, Robert Hale, London, 1978

Errol Flynn in Northampton, Gerry Connelly, Domra, Corby, Northamptonshire, 1995

Gable and Lombard, Warren G. Harris, Corgi, London, 1974

Gable & Lombard & Powell & Harlow, Joe Morella and Edward Z. Epstein. W.H. Allen, London, 1976

Gable's Women, Jane Ellen Wayne, Simon & Schuster, London, 1987

Gary Cooper: An Intimate Biography, Hector Acre, William Morrow and Company, New York, 1979

The Girls, Errol Flynn and Me, Frank A. Casella, Anthony Press, Alhambra, California, 1981.

Goodnight Sweet Prince, Gene Fowler, Mayflower-Dell, London, 1966

The Intimate Life of Rudolph Valentino, Jack Scagnetti, Jonathan David Publishers Inc, New York, 1975

My Husband, Rock Hudson, Phyllis Gates and Bob Thomas, Angus & Robertson, London, 1987

Idol: Rock Hudson, Jerry Oppenheimer and Jack Vitek, John Curley & Associates, South Yarmouth, Ma., 1986

James Dean: The Biography, Val Holley, Robson Books, London, 1995

James Dean: A Short Life, Venable Herndon, Doubleday and Company, New York, 1974

James Dean: Boulevard of Broken Dreams, Paul Alexander, Little, Brown and Company, London, 1994

James Dean: Little Boy Lost, Joe Hyams and Jay Hyams, Random House (UK), London, 1992

James Dean: The Mutant King, David Dalton, Plexus, London, 1983

The James Dean Story, Ronald Martinetti, Michael O'Mara Books, London, 1975

The Last Hero: A Biography of Gary Cooper, Larry Swindell,

Robson Books, London, 1981

The Life and Crimes of Errol Flynn, Lionel Godfrey, St Martin's Press, New York, 1977

Madam Valentino: The Many Lives of Natasha Rambova, Michael Morris, Abbeville Press, New York, 1991

Mary Pickford and Douglas Fairbanks, Booton Herndon, W.H. Allen, London, 1978

My Early Years, Charlie Chaplin, The Bodley Head, London, 1964

My Wicked, Wicked Ways, Errol Flynn, William Heinemann, London, 1960

The Private Cary Grant, William Currie McIntosh and William Weaver, Sidgwick & Jackson, London, 1983

Rebel: The Life and Legend of James Dean, Donald Spoto, HarperCollins, London, 1996

Rock Hudson: His Story, Rock Hudson and Sara Davidson, Weidenfeld & Nicholson, London, 1986

Rudolph Valentino, Alexander Walker, Sphere, London, 1976

The Salad Days, Douglas Fairbanks Jnr, Collins, London, 1988

The Trial of Rock Hudson, John Parker, Sidgwick & Jackson, London, 1990

Valentino, Brad Steiger and Chaw Mank, Corgi Books, London, 1976

Valentino: The Love God, Noel Botham and Peter Donnelly, Everest Books,London, 1976

Warren Beatty, Suzanne Munshower, W.H. Allen, London, 1983

Warren Beatty: A Life and a Story, David Thomson, Secker & Warburg, London, 1987

Warren Beatty: Lovemaker Extraordinary, Suzanne L. Munshower, Everest Books. London, 1976

Warren Beatty: The Last Great Lover of Hollywood, John Parker, Headline, London, 1993

INDEX

Aadland, Beverly 142-3
Academy of Motion Pictures
Acker, Jean Mrs Rudolph
  Valentino 1st 35-8, 40, 41,
  42-3, 47, 49, 52
Acosta, Mercedes de 63, 64-5
Adjani, Isabelle 263
Alba, Maria 94
Albert, Katherine 108
Allan, Elizabeth 161
Anderson, Bronco Billy 7
Anderson, Gertrude 130-31
Andress, Ursula 249-50
Angeli, Pier 246-7
Arbuckle, Fatty (Roscoe
  Arbuckle) viii-ix, 42
Ashley, Lady (Sylvia
  Hawkes) Mrs Douglas
  Fairbanks Snr 3rd, Mrs Clark
  Gable 4th 95, 96, 109, 172-3,
  175
Astor, Mary 66-70
Ayres, Lemuel 243

Balfe, Rocky (Veronica
  Balfe) 188-91, 192, 193-5, 196-9
Bankhead, Tallulah 62-3, 105, 109, 177,
  186, 187
Banky, Vilma 50-51, 179
Bardot, Brigitte (Camille
  Javal) 252, 258
Barry, Joan 20-21, 22
Barrymore, Ethel 56, 60, 64
Barrymore, John 19, 55-88, 117, 131
  daughter, Diana 74, 87
  films
  American Citizen, An 60

Beau Brummel 70
Bill of Divorcement 72
Don Juan 70
Grand Hotel 72
Great Profile, The 87
Hamlet 72-3
Jest, The 61-2, 75
Living Corpse, The 61
Lost Bridegroom, The 60
Romeo and Juliet 80-81
Sea Beast, The (Moby Dick) 68-9
Sherlock Holmes 65
When a Man Loves 70
  plays
  Fortune Hunter, The 60
  Hamlet 65, 67
  My Dear Children 84-7
  Yellow Ticket, The 61
  radio, Twentieth Century 76
Barrymore, Lionel 60, 61-2, 64, 65, 88,
153
Barrymore, Maurice 55
Bast, Bill 241
Beatty, Warren (Henry Warren Beaty)
251-65
  films
  Bonnie and Clyde 251, 257
  Bugsy 265
  Dick Tracy 263-4
  Dollars 260
  Ishtar 263
  Kaleidoscope 256
  Only Game in Town, The 258
  Promise Her Anything 257
  Reds 262-3
  Roman Spring 254
  Shampoo 251, 262

Splendour in the Grass 253
play, *Loss of Roses, A* 253
wife *see* Bening, Annette
Beau Brummel, Barrymore 70
Benda, Marion 53
Bening, Annette 265
Bergman, Ingrid 192
Blondell, Joan 146
Blood and Sand, Valentino 42-4
Bonnie and Clyde, Beatty 251, 257
Bourbon, Cynthia 217-18
Bow, Clara 177, 179-82, 184-5, 189, 191
Brackett, Rogers 241, 248
Brady, William (William Aloysius Brady)
89
Brando, Marlon 243
Brent, Evelyn 181-2, 184
Briggle, Stockton 235
Brisson, Frederick 209, 210, 212
Brooks, Louise 19
Brooks, Phyllis 209-10, 219
Broussard, Rebecca 265
Bugsy, Beatty 265
Bundy Drive Boys 82-3, 84, 87, 88

Cannon, Dyan (Samille Diane
    Friesen) Mrs Cary Grant 4th 215-17,
    219
Captain Blood, Flynn 125
Carlo, Yvonne de 171
Carne, Judy 257-8
Caron, Leslie 256-7
Carroll, Madeleine 190
Chanel, Lorraine 197
Channell, Ron 236-8
Chaplin, Charlie (Sir Charles
    Spencer Chaplin) viii, 1, 3-10, 11-23,
    124
    films
    Champion, The 8
    Circus, The 18
    Gold Rush, The 15, 16
    Inferior Sex, The 11
    Intolerance 11
    Kid, The 15
    Modern Times 20
    Woman, A 8
    Woman of Paris, A 12

    sons
    Chaplin, Charlie Jnr 17, 20
    Chaplin, Sydney 17, 20
Chaplin, Sydney 1, 7, 10-11
Charig, Phil 204-5
Chase, Chevvy (Cornelius Crane
    Chase) 217
Cherrill, Virginia Mrs Cray
    Grant 1st 206-8, 212, 219
Chisholm, Betty 171, 175
Christian, Linda (Bianca Rosa Welter)
128-9
Christian, Marc 234-7, 238
Christie, Julie 252, 258-60, 262
Clark, Tom 232-5
Clift, Montgomery 243
Coates, Jack 231-2
Coco 26-7
Cogan, Alma 215
Colbert, Claudette (Claudette
    Lily Chauchoin) 160-61
Colby, Anita 170, 171
Collier, Constance 9
Collins, Joan (Joan Henrietta Collins)
251, 252-5, 264
Cooper, Gary (Frank James Cooper) 177-
99
    daughter, Maria 191, 197, 199
    films
    Arizona Bound 180
    Beau Sabreur 181
    Blowing Wild 197
    Bright Leaf 194
    Children of Divorce 180
    Cowboy and the Lady, The 191-2
    Darkened Rooms 184
    Desire 190
    Devil and the Deep, The 187
    Farewell to Arms, A 187
    Fountainhead, The 193
    Garden of Evil 197
    General Died at Dawn, The 190
    High Noon 195, 197
    I Take This Woman 185
    It 180
    Last Outlaw, The 180
    Morocco 184
    Northwest Mounted Police 190
    Return to Paradise 197

INDEX

Saratoga Trunk 192
Souls at Sea 191
Ten North Frederick 198
Today We Live 188
Virginian, The 183, 184
Wedding Night, The 190
Westerner, The 192
Wings 181
Winning of Barbara Worth, The 179
Wolf Song 182
Wreck of the Mary Deare, The 198-9
wife *see* Balfe, Rocky
Costello, Dolores Mrs John Barrymore 3rd 68-70, 72, 74, 76-7, 79-80, 100
Costello, Helene 100
Coward, Noel (Sir Noel Pierce Coward) 211, 218
Crawford, Joan (Lucille Le Sueur) Mrs Douglas Fairbanks Jnr 1st 93, 102-3, 105-10
  Clark Gable 145, 152, 155-6, 157-60, 161, 163, 169-70, 172, 175
  Gary Cooper 188
Cukor, George 146-7, 168, 208
Cummins, Constance 212

Dadolle, Suzanne 174-5
Damita, Lily Mrs Errol Flynn 1st 123-31, 135-6, 141
Damone, Vic (Vito Farinola) 246-7
Dana, Viola 37
Davis, Marion 51, 159
Davis, Nancy 171
Day, Doris (Doris Von Kappelhoff) 229
Dean, James (James Byron Dean) 228, 239-50
  films
  East of Eden 239, 244, 246
  Giant 239, 249
  Rebel Without a Cause 239, 248
  plays
  Immoralist 244
  Our Hearts Were Young and Gay 240
  See the Jaguar 243

di Frasso, Contessa (Dorothy Taylor) 185-7, 188-90, 194, 210
Dibbs sisters 119, 121
Dietrich, Marlene (Maria Magdelena von Losch) 111-12, 184, 190, 206
  film, *Knight without Armour* 111
Dillon, Josephine Mrs Clark Gable 1st 149-51, 152-3, 155, 157-8
Dixey, Phyllis 2-3
Donaldson, Maureen 218
Dorfler, Franz 148-50, 151-2, 155
Dove, Billie 104
Drake, Betsy Mrs Cary Grant 3rd 212-15
Dunaway, Faye 257

Eagle, The, Valentino 50
East of Eden, Dean 239, 244, 246
Eddington, Nora Mrs Errol Flynn 2nd 136-7, 139, 141
Eden, Sir Anthony and Lady 114
Ekberg, Anita 198
Ekland, Britt (Britt-Marie Eklund) 259-60
Ellen, Vera 224
Eltinge, Julian 9
Erban, Dr Hermann Frierich 120, 125

Fairbanks, Douglas Jnr 92, 96-115, 156, 160
  films
  Man of the Moment 110
  One Night at Susie's 104
  Outward Bound 104
  Prisoner of Zenda, The 115
  Romeo and Juliet 107
  Scarlet Dawn 105
  Woman of Affairs, A 102
  Young Woodley 101
  wives *see* Crawford, Joan; Hartington, Mary Lee
Fairbanks, Douglas Snr (Douglas Elton Ullman) 9, 89-96, 103, 203, 204
  films
  Private Life of Don Juan, The(Exit of Don Juan, The) 95
  Robinson Crusoe 94

wives *see* Ashley, Lady;
Pickford, Mary; Sully, Beth
Farewell to Arms, A, Cooper 187
Feldman, Charles 251
Flynn, Emmett 32-3
Flynn, Errol 72, 88, 112, 117-44, 171-2
book, *My Wicked, Wicked Ways* 144
films
Adventures of Don Juan, The 139
Big Boodle, The 142
Captain Blood 125
Crossed Swords 141
Cuban Rebel Girls 143
Dawn Patrol 129
Dodge City 129
Four's a Crowd 129
Gentleman Jim 135
In the Wake of the Bounty 120
Lilacs in Spring 142
Murder at Monte Cristo 123
Rocky Mountain 140
Sea Hawk, The 130
They Died With Their Boots On 135
Warriors, The 142
Fontaine, Joan (Joan de Beauvoir
de Havilland) 210
Four Horsemen of the Apocalypse, The,
Valentino 37, 38

Gable, Clark (William Clark
Gable) 109, 145-76, 197
films
Across the Wide Missouri 173
Betrayed 175
Call of the Wild 162
Chicago 153
China Sea 162
Copperhead, The 153
Dance, Fools, Dance 155-6
Dancing Lady 160
Free Soul, A 157-8
Gone With the Wind 146-7,
167-8, 174
Grand Hotel 159
Hold Your Man 160
Hucksters, The 170
Idiot's Delight 167
It Happened One Night 160-61, 166
It Started in Naples 176
Lone Star 173
Manhattan Melodrama 161
Men in White 161
Misfits, The 176
Mogambo 173-4
Never Let Me Go 174
No Man of Her Own 160
North Star 152
Pacemakers, The 152
Painted Desert, The 155
Plastic Age, The 152
Polly of the Circus 159
Possessed 158
Red Dust 159-60, 174
Saratoga 166
Soldier of Fortune 175
Somewhere I'll Find You 169
Tall Man, The 175
White Man 151
plays
Last Mile, The 154-5
Machinal 153, 154
Madame X 152
Romeo and Juliet 151
What Price Glory? 151
When Women Rule 148
wives *see* Dillon, Josephine;
Lombard, Carole
Garbo, Greta (Greta Lovisa
Gustafsson) 20, 72, 102, 157
Gardner, Ava (Lucy Johnson)
146, 170, 173-5
Gates, Phyllis 226-9
Giant
Dean 239, 249
Hudson 228
Gilmore, Jonathan 243-4, 248
Goddard, Paulette Mrs Charlie
Chaplin 3rd 20, 23, 124, 171,
190
Gold Rush, The, Chaplin 15,
16
Goldwyn, Sam (Schmuel
Gelbfisz) 179, 189, 190
Grant, Cary (Archibald Alec
Leach) 187, 201-19, 256
daughter, Jennifer 217
films
Amazing Quest of Ernest

Bliss, The 208
Blond Venus 206
Charade 216
Grass is Always Greener, The 215
Gunga Din 210
Hot Saturday 206
Houseboat 213-14
I Was a Male War Bride 213
My Favourite Wife 210
Night and Day 212
Notorious 212
Once Upon a Honeymoon 211
Pride and the Passion, The 213
She Done Him Wrong 206
Sylvia 208
To Catch a Thief 218
Walk, Don't Run 217
musicals
  Golden Dawn 204
  Street Singer, The 204
Great Profile, The, Barrymore 87

Haines, William (William Wister
  Haines) 146, 152, 157, 205-6
Hanson, Betty 132-4
Harlow, Jean (Harlean
  Carpentier) 106, 146,
  159-60, 162, 166
Harris, Barbara Mrs Cary Grant
  5th 219
Harris, Katherine Mrs John
  Barrymore 1st 59-61
Harris, Mildred Mrs Charlie
  Chaplin 1st 11-12, 15, 23
Hartington, Mary Lee Mrs
  Douglas Fairbanks 2nd 114-15
Havilland, Olivia de 125, 129-30
Hawks, Howard 177, 213
Hawn, Goldie 260
Hayward, Susan 175
Hepburn, Katherine (Katherine
  Houghton Hepburn) 107, 209
Hopper, Hedda (Elda Furry) 62, 130,
180, 196, 209, 228, 241
Howard, Leslie (Leslie Stainer) 104, 165
Howard, Trevor (Trevor Wallace
  Howard) 256
Hudson, Rock (Roy Sherer Jnr) 221-238
  films

Captian Lightfoot 227
Darling Lili 232
Fighter Squadron 223
Giant 228
Lover Come Back 229
Martian Chronicles 234
Pillow Talk 229
television
  Dynasty 238
  McMillan and Wife 232
  wife *see* Gates, Phyllis
Hughes, Howard 104, 129,
205, 208-9, 212, 213, 217, 249, 263
Huston, Angelica 261
Hutton, Barbara Mrs Cary Grant
  2nd 131, 210-11, 219
In the Wake of the Bounty, Flynn 120
It Happened One Night, Gable 160-61,
166

Jacobs, Elaine Mrs John
  Barrymore 3rd a.k.a.Elaine Barrie
  75-88
  book, *All My Sins Remembered* 77
  film, *How to Undress in
  Front of Your Husband* 83-4

Karno, Fred (Frederick Westcott) 1-3
Kazan, Elia 242, 243, 253
Keaton, Diane 262-3
Kelly, Grace (Grace Patricia
  Kelly) Princess Grace of
  Monaco 146, 174-5, 195, 218
Kelly, Hetty 3-5, 8, 23
Keystone Kops 7
Kid, The, Chaplin 15
Lamarr, Hedy (Hedwig Kiesler) 20
Landi, Elissa 111, 210
Landis, Carole 20
Langham, Ria Mrs Clark Gable
  2nd 154, 158, 167
Laurel, Stan (Arthur Stanley
  Jefferson) 1, 7, 23
Lawrence, Gertrude (Gertrude
  Alexandra Dagmar Lawrance
  Klasen) 101, 109-11
Leigh, Vivien (Vivien Mary
  Hartley) 167, 254

Lombard, Carole (Jane Alice
    Peters) Mrs Clark Gable 3rd]
    Clark Gable 145, 146, 160,
    161-2, 164-7, 168-9
    Cary Grant 206
    Gary Cooper 181, 185
Loren, Sophia (Sofia Scicolone) 213-14,
219

MacLaine, Shirley (Shirley Maclean
Beaty) 251
McMurray, Lillita (a.k.a. Lita
    Grey) Mrs Charlie Chaplin
    2nd 15-17, 23
Madonna (Madonna Louise
    Ciccone) 252, 263-5
    video, *In Bed With Madonna* 265
Maginn, Bonnie 59
Manners, Elsie 2
Marsh, Tara 132
Matalon, Vivian 244
Maxwell, Elsa 186, 186-7
Maxwell, Marilyn 230
Mayako 121
Mayer, Louis B (Louis Burt
    Mayer) 11, 108, 158-9, 160, 161,
    170
Mayo, Faye Nuell 249
Meyers, Carmel 34
MGM
    Barrymore contract 80-81
    Cooper contract 188
    Gable contract 155, 175
    The Cat House 163
Miller, Mark 224, 227-8, 231, 233, 234,
    236-7
Mineo, Sal 249
Minter, Mary Miles x
Misfits, The, Gable 176
Mogambo, Gable 173-4
Monroe, Marilyn (Norma Jean
    Mortenson or Baker) 146,
    176
Monsieur Beauclaire, Valentino 47
Murray, Mae 33-4, 48

Nader, George 223, 224, 227
Naldi, Nita 43-4, 49
Navarro, Ramon 33

Neal, Pat 193-4, 196, 198-9
Negri, Pola (Appolonia
    Chalupiec) 13-15, 51-3, 152
Nelson, Lori (Dixie Kay Nelson) 247
Nesbit, Evelyn 57-8, 86
Nicholson, Jack 260-61, 262, 263, 264, 265
Niven, David (James David
    Graham Nevins) 112, 129,
    165
Notorious, Grant 212

Oberon, Merle (Queenie
    O'Brian, a.k.a.Estelle Thompson)
    109, 165, 191-2, 212
Odets, Clifford 211
Olivier, Lawrence (Baron
    Lawrence Kerr Olivier) 105,106
O'Niell, Oona Mrs Charlie Chaplin 4th
    21-3, 262-3
Onstott, Eloise Ann 128
Orr-Kelly, Jack 203, 206
    Oscars
    best actor, Clark Gable 161
    best actress, Mary Pickford 93

Paget, Liz 109, 111
Parks, Madge 120
Parsons, Louella 94, 108, 174, 189, 212,
224, 228, 255
Peron, Eva (Maria Eva Duarte De Peron)
138-9
Phillips, Michelle 261-2
Pickford, Mary (Gladys Mary
    Smith) Mrs Douglas
    Fairbanks Snr 2nd x 9, 90-95, 161-2,
    203
Power, Tyrone (Frederick Tyrone
    Power) 129, 138, 171
Prisoner of Zenda, The,Fairbanks Jnr 115
Private Life of Don Juan, The
(Exit of Don Juan, The), Fairbanks Snr
95
Purvience, Edna 7-10, 23

Rambova, Natasha (Winifred
    Hodnut) Mrs Rudolph
    Valentino 2nd 38-45, 47-9, 51
Rappe, Virginia viii-ix
Ray, Nicholas 249

INDEX

Rebel Without a Cause,
   Dean 239, 248
Reds, Beatty 262-3
Reeves, May 20
Rodann, Ziva 215
Rogers, Millicent 171
Rooney, Mickey (Joe Yule) 139
Rubirosa, Porfirio 131
Russell, Rosalind 210, 212

St John, Adela Rogers 158, 169, 175
Satterlee, Peggy LaRue 132-5
Saulles, Jack de 29-31
Sawyer, Joan 30-31
Scott, Randolph 205, 207,
209-11, 212, 219
Sea Hawk, The, Flynn 130
Selznick, David O (David Oliver
   Selznick) 71
Selznick, Lewis 37
Sennett, Mack (Michael Sinnott) viii 7
Sex Lives of the Hollywood Goddesses,
Cawthorne book xi
Shearer, Norma 157, 167
Sheik, The, Valentino 41, 44
Sheridan, Elizabeth "Dizzy" 242-3
Sherman, Lowell 100
Shit Club 130, 135
Simmons, Jack 247-8
Slocum, Rusty 245
Splendour in the Grass, Beatty 253
Strasburg, Susan 215, 247, 254
Sully, Beth Mrs Douglas
   Fairbanks Snr 1st 90-92
Swanson, Gloria (Gloria May
   Josephine Svensson) vii 88
   film, *Sunset Boulevard* vii

Tashman, Lilyan 105
Taylor, Elizabeth 221, 228, 230, 258-9
Taylor, Robert (Spangler Arlington
Brugh) 171, 197
Thaw, Harry K 58
They Died With Their Boots On,
   Flynn 135
Thomas, Blanche (a.k.a.Michael
   Strange) Mrs John
   Barrymore 2nd 61, 63-4, 68,
   70-71

Tinti, Gabriele 254
To Catch a Thief, Grant 218
Tracy, Spencer 171
Tree, Sir Herbert Beerbohm 9
Truffaut, François 257
Turner, Lana (Julia Jean Mildred
   Turner) 169, 171, 175, 223

Ullmann, Liv 260
United Artists
   Fairbanks Snr 95, 97
   Valentino contract 48-9
Universal, Hudson contract 223, 228

Valentino, Rudolph (Rodolfo
   Alphonso Guglielmi di
   Valentina d'Antonguolla)
   25-53
   films
   Adventuress, The 37
   Alimony 32
   Beyond the Rocks 41
   Big Little Person, The 34
   Blood and Sand 42-4
   Camille 38
   Cheater, The 37
   Cobra 48
   Delicious Little Devil, The 34
   Eagle, The 50
   *Four Horsemen of the
   Apocalypse, The* 37, 38
   Married Virgin, A 33
   Monsieur Beaucaire 47
   Monsieur Verdoux 22
   Passion's Playground 37
   Sheik, The 41, 44
   Young Rajah, The 44
   musical comedy, *Masked
   Model, The* 31
   poems, *Day Dreams* 45
   wives *see* Acker, Jean;
   Rambova, Natasha
Velez, Lupe 'Mexican Spitfire' 101, 124-
5, 145
   Clark Gable 145
   Douglas Fairbanks Jnr 101
   Errol Flynn 124-5
   Gary Cooper 177, 182-3,
   185, 186, 188-90, 192-3

Virginian, The, Cooper 183, 184
Visconti, Luchino (Count Don
    Luchino Visconti di Morone)
    254

Wagner, Robert 253
Warner Bros
    Barrymore contract 66, 68
    Dean contract 239, 244
Warner, Jack (Jack Warden
    Lebzelter) 123, 125, 130, 155
Welles, Orson (Robert Orson Welles) 84-5,
251
West, Mae 206
White, Stanford 57-8
Williams, Kay Mrs Clark Gable
    5th 170, 171, 175-6, 197
Willson, Henry 222-3, 226-8, 231, 241
Winters, Shelley (Shirley
    Schrift) 171-2
Wood, Lana 260
Wood, Natalie (Natasha Gurdin) 248-9,
253, 254-6
Wray, Fay 182, 205, 210
Wymore, Patrice Mrs Errol
    Flynn 3rd 140-43

Y, Mme 112-14
Young, Loretta (Gretchen
    Young) 162
Young Rajah, The, Valentino 44

Zanuck, Darryl 10-11
Zorina, Vera 113